Rethinking Language Education

from a monolingual to a multilingual perspective

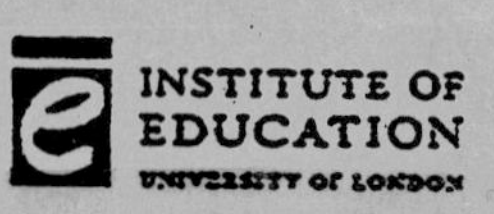

Rethinking Language Education

From a monolingual to a multilingual perspective

Edited by Arturo Tosi and Constant Leung

Acknowledgements

We would like to thank the Paul Hamlyn Foundation, the British Association for Applied Linguistics, Cambridge University Press and the Italian Department, Royal Holloway, University of London for their generous support for this project. We would also like to thank Roger Olsen for his invaluable editorial advice.

First published 1999.

ISBN 1 902031 06 7

A catalogue record for this book is available from the British Library.
Printed in Great Britain by Copyprint UK Ltd.

Published by the Centre for Information on Language Teaching and Research,
20 Bedfordbury, Covent Garden, London WC2N 4LB.
Typesetting by Karin Erskine, Croydon.

CILT publications are available from Grantham Book Services, Isaac Newton Way, Alma Park Industrial Estate, Grantham, Lincs NG31 8SD. Tel: 01476 541 080. Fax: 01476 541 061.
Book trade representation (UK and Ireland): Broadcast Book Services, 24 De Montfort Road, London SW16 1LZ. Tel: 0181 677 5129.

Contents

Contributors

Jean Brewster, Principal Lecturer in English Language Education in the Centre for Applied Linguistic Research at Thames Valley University, London, has extensive experience of teacher education for ELT practitioners from the UK and overseas. She has several publications on language and content integration in primary and secondary schools and gendered talk.

Professor **Chris Brumfit** is Dean of Education and Director of the Centre for Language in Education, at the University of Southampton. He has published over thirty books and many papers on language and literature teaching, and language policy in education. In recent years he has concentrated on work on the role of explicit knowledge in language teaching, on language rights, and on literature in education. Among recent books are: *Research in the language classroom* (with Rosamund Mitchell), *Teaching literature: a world perspective* (with Michael Benton), and *Language education in the national curriculum.*

Lynne Cameron is Senior Lecturer in TESOL and Co-ordinator of the Language Education Research Group in the School of Education, University of Leeds. Her interests include additional language development in the mainstream, metaphor in educational discourse, and the applications of complex/dynamics systems theory to applied linguistics.

Inge Cramer is a Senior Lecturer in the Department of Teacher Education at Bradford and Ilkley Community College. After a variety of teaching posts in schools, she worked with the National Oracy Project and as a primary advisory teacher for the LINC project. Her current research focuses on a connotative analysis of the oral story making, in English, of young children in a multi-lingual school.

John Edwards is a Senior Lecturer in the School of Education and Continuing Studies, Portsmouth University. He co-ordinates the PGCE programme for secondary English which involves working in partnership with schools in four local education authorities. His research interests relate to the effective mentoring of student teachers and curriculum innovation in language and literacy.

Viv Edwards is Professor of Language in Education at the University of Reading where she is also Director of the Reading and Language Information Centre. She is co-editor of the international journal *Language and education*, and has researched and published very widely in the area of multilingual classrooms.

Eve Gregory is a Reader in Educational Studies at Goldsmiths College, University of London. During the past five years, she has directed funded research projects into the home and school reading practices of families in London's East End. Her publications include *Making sense of a new world: learning to read in a second language* and *Many worlds: early learning in multiethnic communities.*

Roxy Harris is a Senior Lecturer in the Centre for Applied Linguistic Research in the School of English Language Education at Thames Valley University, London. He has extensive experience of working with teachers on questions of language and education and is particularly interested in the relationships between language, power, culture and ethnicity.

Moira Inghilleri is a Lecturer in Applied Linguistics at Goldsmiths College. She has been involved in sociolinguistic research in the United States and Britain for a number of years. Her research interests include philosophy of language, cross-cultural communication, discourse analysis and cultural and linguistic hybridity. She is currently working on a book examining the cultural and philosophical context of the paradigm shift in the teaching of school English in Britain in the 1960s and 1970s.

Roz Ivanič is a Senior Lecturer in the Department of Linguistics and Modern English Language at Lancaster University. Her interests include social approaches to literacy, educational linguistics, academic writing as a social practice, and alternative forms of knowledge and learning. Her publications include *Writing and identity* and, with Romy Clark, *The politics of writing.*

Lid King has extensive experience as a teacher, examiner and writer of publications at secondary and post-secondary levels. He joined CILT in 1988 as a Teacher Liaison Officer, becoming Director in 1992. Since then he has played a key role in developing a national network of resource and information centres in the UK, languages consultancy services to British business, and the establishment of European information networks.

Constant Leung is a Principal Lecturer in the Centre for Applied Linguistic Research at Thames Valley University, London. He has taught in schools and universities in Hong Kong and England. His research interests include language-content integration, second language policy, and bilingual education and language assessment. He is active in the field of teacher professional development and was the founding chair of the National Association for Language Development in the Curriculum (NALDIC).

Ben Rampton is a Reader at the Centre for Applied Linguistic Research at Thames Valley University. His current research focuses on language, discourse and ethnicity in urban education, and he is the author of *Crossing: language and ethnicity among adolescents,* as well as being a co-author of *Researching language: issues of power and method.*

Pauline Rea-Dickins is Senior Lecturer and runs the Language Testing and Evaluation Unit in the Centre for Language English Teacher Education, University of Warwick. She teaches, researches and publishes in areas of evaluation and assessment. Her most recent book is *Managing evaluation and innovation in language teaching: building bridges* (with Kevin Germaine).

Brian Street is Professor of Language in Education at King's College, London University and Visiting Professor of Education in the Graduate School of Education, University of Pennsylvania. He undertook anthropological fieldwork on literacy and education in Iran during the 1970s, and has since written and lectured extensively on literacy practices in a number of locations, including South Africa, Australia, Canada and the United States. His *Social literacies* was cited in his receipt of the 1995 David S Russell award for distinguished research by the National Council for Teaching of English in the United States. He has written six books and published over 60 scholarly articles. He is currently concerned to link ethnographic-style research on the cultural dimension of literacy with contemporary debates in education.

Arturo Tosi is Professor of Italian and head of the Italian Department at Royal Holloway, University of London. He is also visiting Professor of Sociolinguistics at the University of Siena. He has been actively involved in the field of language education since the mid-1970s when he co-ordinated the European Mother Tongue Project in Bedford. He has taught in universities in England, Canada and Australia. His research specialisms include bilingualism and bilingual education.

John Trim taught phonetics at UCL 1949–58, then established the Department of Linguistics in Cambridge. He was Director of CILT 1978–87 and directed successive Council of Europe modern languages projects 1971–97. A past Chairman of BAAL and Vice-President of AILA, he holds honorary doctorates from Dublin, Prague, Wolverhampton and Oulu. He has published extensively in phonetics, linguistics and language didactics.

David Wilkins joined the Department of Linguistic Science at the University of Reading in 1966 after beginning his career as a teacher of English as a foreign language in West and North Africa. He set up the Centre for Applied Language Studies in 1974 and was appointed to the Professorship of Applied Linguistics in 1986. His principal publications are *Linguistics in language teaching*, *Second language learning and teaching* and *Notional Syllabuses*.

Ann Williams is a research fellow at Goldsmiths College, London. Her research interests are in language and literacy, and she has carried out funded research projects on new town dialects, the role of children in language change, non-standard dialects and children's writing and the relationship between home and school literacy.

Rethinking Language Education
Royal Holloway, University of London
18–19 September 1997

» Jill Bourne   School of Education, University of Southampton

» Jean Brewster   Centre for Applied Linguistic Research, Thames Valley University

» Lynne Cameron   School of Education, University of Leeds

» Inge Cramer   Department of Teacher Education, Bradford and Ikley Community College

» John Edwards   School of Education and Continuing Studies, University of Portsmouth

» Viv Edwards   Reading and Language Information Centre, University of Reading

» Roxy Harris   Centre for Applied Linguistic Research, Thames Valley University

» Roger Hewitt   Centre for Community and Urban research, Goldsmiths College, University of London

» Roz Ivanič   Dept of Linguistics and Modern English Language, University of Lancaster

» Moira Inghilleri   Department of English, Goldsmiths College, University of London

» Lid King   Centre for Information on Language Teaching and Research, London

» Gunther Kress   Institute of Education, University of London

Constant Leung	Centre for Applied Linguistic Research, Thames Valley University
Ros Mitchell	School of Education, University of Southampton
Roger Olsen	Centre for Applied Linguistic Research, Thames Valley University
Euan Reid	Institute of Education, University of London
Pauline Rea-Dickens	Centre for English Language Teacher Education, University of Warwick
Alissa Shethar	Centre for Applied Linguistic Research, Thames Valley University
Paul Shrubshall	Centre for Applied Linguistic Research, Thames Valley University
Brian Street	School of Education, King's College, University of London
Alex Teasdale	Centre for Applied Linguistic Research, Thames Valley University
Arturo Tosi	Department of Italian, Royal Holloway, University of London
John Trim	Modern Languages Project, Council of Europe
Ben Rampton	Centre for Applied Linguistic Research, Thames Valley University
Mukul Saxena	Department of Linguistics and Modern Languages, University College of Ripon and York St. John
Mahendra Verma	Department of Language and Linguistic Science, University of York
David Wilkins	Department of Linguistic Science, University of Reading
Ann Williams	Goldsmiths College, University of London

Introduction

Constant Leung, Thames Valley University, and
Arturo Tosi, University of London

New communication needs

Since the mid-1980s the British education system has experienced some very major and rapid changes. The pace and magnitude of the changes, from the introduction of a National Curriculum for schools to the benchmarking of literacy and numeracy attainments (and lots of others in between) within ten years, have been truly breathtaking. The idea of inviting a group of people who have been actively involved in language education in this country as teachers, researchers, teacher educators and policy makers to a seminar to look at developments in the recent past and to identify issues of current interest therefore seemed eminently sensible. As applied linguists and language educators, we felt that we should create a forum to share ideas and exchange views in a friendly but critically constructive atmosphere. We wrote to a number of colleagues to sample support for the idea of a seminar and the responses were very positive. With the sponsorships from Royal Holloway, the Paul Hamlyn Foundation and BAAL/CUP we were able to run a two-day event in September 1997. We were very pleased that so many colleagues, all experts in their specialisms, were able to join us.

The two-day programme was divided into four sessions: language education: research and policy; literacy in school and society; languages, learners and curriculum; teacher education. There were nineteen 20-minute papers, each followed by a 10-minute discussion. John Trim opened the 'language education: research and policy' session with a paper calling for greater attention paid to the development of communicative abilities in young people, not just in English but also in other languages, so that they can participate in the 'information society' which does not have any place for inarticulate, unskilled labour. Arturo Tosi argued that aspects of current practice, e.g. the use of foreign language curriculum approaches focusing on practical transactions, prohibit the development of high-level bilingualism and biliteracy, particularly for some students from minority language communities with a measure of vernacular competence in the language of study. Moreover, he suggested that the realia, memorabilia and speech formulae commonly associated with foreign language teaching could be stereotypically demeaning and thereby trivialising the target language and culture. Ben Rampton offered a view on some of the problems in the research approaches of the 1980s. For instance, action research had failed to produce data to persuade the unsympathetic outsider of the multilingualism in society and theoretical development had yet to embrace the wider social developments such as globalisation of markets and cultures. Mahendra Verma discussed the concepts of language rights and the 'right' language with reference to linguistic minorities. After asking if English as an additional language (EAL) and bilingual support were the only possible educational response to the needs of bilingual pupils, he discussed findings from an LEA survey which indicated that, inter alia, all the 20 LEAs in the study gave support to bilingual pupils through English and 13 through a (non-English) mother tongue alongside English, and the lack of training for staff was identified as a major concern. Lid King summed up his discussion on the challenges for a multi-lingual Britain by asking why there was so much partial success: why did so many adults appear to be permanent beginners in evening classes and why were there so many youths (age 14–19), especially boys, for whom foreign language learning was an 'arduous mystery'.

In the 'literacy in school and society' session Brian Street raised concerns about policy makers' continuing insistence that literacy is a unitary phenomenon; he presented arguments for a more dialogic view of language and for more social approaches to literacy as an alternative. Gunther Kress took issue with the overemphasis on interpreting literacy as literacy in 'standard' language. He argued for a wider understanding of language and linguistic theory which took account of the rapid social and economic changes, global visual literacy and intertextuality. Ann Williams reported findings of a research project which studied the literacy practices experienced by Sylheti and English speaking children in school and at home. It was found that there were some differences in the way children engaged with, for instance, reading in the two settings. It was suggested that school reading practice could build on home experiences dynamically. Roz Ivanič discussed the influence of language in children's developing knowledge and understanding. She used some samples of written work by primary pupils (at Key Stage 2) to illustrate how children might see knowledge as unquestionable truth.

David Wilkins started the session on 'languages, learners and curriculum' with a discussion on the processes involved in foreign language speech production. He suggested that there was evidence that learners engaged in mental processes which had not been overtly acknowledged in many syllabi, e.g. using chunks or prefabricated sequences rather than building utterances 'bottom up' or monitoring an almost uttered speech with an interlanguage grammar. In other words, there might be a continuum of action between selecting on the one hand and constructing on the other. Pauline Rea-Dickens focused on the concept of evaluation with reference to a school-based EAL project. She pointed out the considerable complexity involved when trying to take into account both language and educational processes in schooling. Ros Mitchell offered an account of the conceptualisation of the Modern Foreign Languages National Curriculum and its impact on classroom teachers. She showed the progressive narrowing of aims, objectives and strategies. Viv Edwards highlighted the differences in teaching and learning styles in multi-ethnic classrooms. She pointed to the possible mismatches due to different cultural assumptions between pupils and teachers and among teachers of different ethnic and cultural backgrounds. Moira Inghilleri examined the intellectual context of developments within the English curriculum during the 1960s and 1970s and suggested that the notion of incommensurability might be explored in relation to understanding between minds and cultures. Roxy Harris drew attention to the tendency of socially positioning the 'bilingual' and 'ethnic minority' learner identity outside the 'mainstream' society in British education. He suggested that there was a much more complex relationship between language, culture and social identity which the binary insider-outsider model was ill-equipped to handle. In the final session on teacher education, Euan Reid raised educational and political issues surrounding the Standard English debate. The experience of the LINC project was used as a point of illustration. Jean Brewster examined the influence of gender. Her data suggested, inter alia, that speaker types and task types should be taken into account when trying to understand group discourse patterns. Lynne Cameron and Inge Cramer presented two linked papers. In the first part

Lynne Cameron reported the work of a teacher development project which focused on raising teachers' understanding of the collaborative nature of language use in the classroom and the use of enhanced understanding to effect pedagogic improvements. In the second half Inge Cramer analysed the role of oral storymaking in promoting cognitive and linguistic development and explored some of the classroom constraints which would inhibit this practice. John Edwards examined the current ITE curriculum and suggested that there was very little attention paid to the knowledge and skills required by a newly qualified teacher to operate in a multilingual classroom effectively. For instance, of 250 NQTs in his survey only 30% had covered EAL in their initial training and only 11% were confident about working with EAL pupils.

Two papers prepared by Chris Brumfit, on the need for a language charter, and by Constant Leung, on teachers' professional views on language development in multilingual and multiethnic contexts, have been included in this collection although, due to pressure of time and unavoidable last-minute programme changes, they were not presented at the seminar.

As this collection of papers testifies, the participants used this occasion to evaluate existing thinking and practice and to explore some of the key challenges before us: from theories of language and communication to multilingual policies within the European context; from language and ethnicity in Britain to literacies in the rapidly globalising communities. During the two-day discussion the participants repeatedly expressed the need to understand the educational potential of all language learners, and to find ways of motivating and encouraging young people of diverse social, cultural and linguistic backgrounds to realise their potentials. At the same time they voiced concern about easy policy solutions based on assumptions which have been built on simplistic compartmentalisation of different aspects of language in education, e.g. mother tongue versus foreign language. Such taken-for-granted approaches can no longer address the complexities of contemporary modes of communication.

We feel that the seminar succeeded in identifying some very important policy and practice questions in language education from a range of perspectives. At this time of rapid educational reform and policy development, we hope that the collection of papers presented in this volume will help to clarify and prioritise our focus of attention.

PART I
LANGUAGE EDUCATION POLICY

Language Education Policies
for the Twenty-First Century

JOHN TRIM
Modern Languages Project, Council of Europe

NEW COMMUNICATION NEEDS

The approach of a millennium inevitably leads us to attempt a fundamental reassessment of the values and beliefs on which our society rests, and the aims and objectives those values and beliefs cause us to set ourselves; as well as, secondarily, the methods we should use to achieve the objectives in the service of the aims. Millennialism, which looks forward to a thousand years of peace, righteousness and happiness (usually, adds the Random House Dictionary, in the indefinite future), can consider aims and objectives in a long-term perspective without limiting the imagination to what is feasible in the particular circumstances of the present moment. Utopian objectives have their place in the scheme of things. Indeed, it is always valuable to be able to steer a course through the flux of events, with a sense of long-term purpose based on stable values, and to give some time to taking stock and confirming – or not – their continuing validity.

Fundamental rethinking of this kind should, however, not take place too often. Without some stability in the framework of values and beliefs and of long-term aims within which to operate, surely individuals and societies are likely to lose their sense of direction and flounder in incoherence. Certainly, any major social innovation requires a large number of agents concerned with specific aspects of the social process to work in the same direction. In the educational field that means that the aims, objectives and methods underlying curricula, examinations and teaching materials should be methodologically coherent as well as appropriate and acceptable to teachers and learners. In the case of a particular curricular subject area, coherence is important not only internally, but also in the whole school and out-of-school context. Of course, once such coherence is achieved and a paradigm is established, it becomes very difficult to change, even if it ceases to correspond to the needs of learners and the society in which they live and work. If proposals for change are partial, incoherent and follow each other in rapid succession, the older paradigm continues to occupy the centre ground: 'the dogs bark and the caravan passes'.

There are situations, not necessarily at the approach of a millennium, which demand fundamental rethinking, more especially if there is some sense of disquiet, even malaise, or if there appear to be new opportunities and dangers arising from the events occurring, or about to occur in society which make a present disposition inappropriate and out-of-date. There are good reasons for thinking that our language education system is in such a situation at the present time.

It would take too long to trace in any detail the development of values, aims and methods in language education from the heyday of the classical paradigm, surviving in the term 'grammar schools', to our present situation, which is being transformed by the development of communication and information technologies. We have passed from a society based on agriculture, in which most people lived purely local lives in villages and market towns, with a relatively thin superstratum, through the early phases of urbanisation and industrialisation with their large concentrations of unskilled or semi-skilled manual labour in heavy industries and transport, and with a growing bureaucracy, and have arrived at the post-industrial society, with the physical decentralisation of industry and the rapid growth of high technology, especially in the information and communications industries. One aspect of these changes has been a change in the nature of labour. The demand for manual labour is diminishing, as gangs of unskilled labourers are replaced by sophisticated machinery, requiring skilled operation. Routine clerical work is increasingly carried out by computers, the control of which (not to mention dealing with their frequent malfunctioning) is intellectually demanding and decidedly non-routine. Indeed, it may be said that the effect of the electronic revolution has been (what Norbert Wiener has termed) 'the human use of human beings'. Communication skills and the ability to work independently are needed for work of all kinds at all levels.

These changes have partly necessitated, partly been stimulated and facilitated by, changes in education. There has been a steady widening of horizons, from the local to the national to the global, and a corresponding need to equip young people for communication on an ever wider scale. It is no longer sufficient to be satisfied with basic literacy and primitive numeracy as educational objectives. They are certainly necessary (though it is surely mere ludditery to ignore the existence of calculators and spelling checkers), but by no means sufficient. The central aim of language education must be effective language use in interpersonal communication (expressive and receptive) and the ability to process and supply information. I am sure that in the present company it is unnecessary to add that this aim in no way reduces the educational mission of the language components in the curriculum. Of course, communication can sometimes involve no more than routine exchanges to conduct the business of daily life. Even such encounters, which make up much of the essential fabric of social existence, can be impoverished or enriched by the quality of the exchanges. More demanding forms of communication, such as the exchange of ideas, values and beliefs, explaining, describing, narrating, negotiating meaning and deciding on courses of action in problematic situations, etc., call upon the ability to articulate the full range and depth of the participants' experience, knowledge and understanding, which it is the task of education to develop and raise into conscious awareness.

Such abilities can no longer be restricted to a socio-cultural elite or a managerial class. The behaviour which Bernstein attributed to 'restricted and elaborated codes' is unacceptable, not only as a mark of continuing and damaging class divisions, but as a major cause of societal retardation and uncompetitiveness. In the post-industrial world it is not enough for individuals simply to signal their solidarity on the issues before them. Participatory democracy in a well-functioning society can only be effective if individuals are skilled as well as confident in the exercise of independent thought, judgement, expression and action, and willing to accept with understanding the necessary disciplines of co-operation.

Those who are unwilling or unable to interact communicatively with others are likely to find themselves marginalised and deprived, victims of long-term unemployment – the inhuman disuse of human beings. The alienation which such marginalisation leads to is extremely dangerous for a society, especially if it affects a significant section of that society or even whole communities within it. There is abundant evidence that there is a danger of such margin-alisation and alienation resulting from linguistic and other forms of deprivation particularly in inner city areas across the world. It is strongly marked in the second generation of the waves of work migrants, some 16 million across Europe, and in an underclass of long-term unemployed among the indigenous population. It is beyond the scope of this paper and perhaps of this study to propose effective remedies for so deep-seated a social evil, but it is clearly an important part of the responsibility of the language-teaching profession to make its contribution to the reduction of communicative deprivation in our society.

NATIONAL LANGUAGES, FOREIGN LANGUAGES AND INTERNATIONAL LANGUAGES

It is particularly welcome that the title of this book recognises language education as a single entity. For most of the present century, the mainstream teaching of English and the teaching of foreign languages moved ever further apart, to such an extent that when George Perren attempted to bring them together, he called the record of proceedings *The space between,* so little had the parties to say to each other. Mainstream English teaching had little time for the study of the English language per se. Teachers' associations and examining boards (though not the lay public) followed academic linguists in rejecting the traditional, grammatical disciplines of parsing and analysis in that the grammatical categories employed had been taken over from the classical languages and were inappropriate to English. They also joined them in their ideological rejection of notions of 'good' and 'bad', 'correct' and 'incorrect' as applied to dialectal variation in relation to 'standard' usage. Under Leavisite influence, however, they considered the linguists' alternative proposals for grammatical description sterile and irrelevant to what they saw as their true mission: to develop children's moral and aesthetic sensibility through exposure to good writing and to awaken and foster their powers of creative self-expression. Teachers of modern languages, on the other hand, were still mainly concerned to give pupils mastery of the formal system of the language (generally French or German) and the ability to display that mastery in the error-free performance of formal exercises. There seemed to be no overlap between these concerns. If modern language teachers wanted anything from the English teachers it was a basic understanding of grammatical concepts and terminology – precisely what English teachers saw as backward-looking and unproductive. English teachers expected nothing from foreign language teachers, who appeared to be concerned only with a level of language they felt able to take for granted by the time pupils came into secondary education. The absence of foreign languages from the primary curriculum meant, of course, that it was only in secondary education that there could be any interaction.

During the late 1970s and the 1980s, two developments challenged the assumptions of both groups and brought them closer together. One was the arrival of considerable numbers of children whose home language was not English, first into primary education, then coming through into secondary education, together with others who, as a result of various kinds of deprivation, were not yet fully literate by age 11. Comprehensivisation meant that the problems of gross educational underachievement could no longer be ghettoised (though of course the problem was most severe in run-down inner city areas of high immigration and urban deprivation). Faced with such severe educational problems, it was not open to teachers of English to take for granted a basic command of English as a language for everyday communication, even on the most relativistic interpretation. At the same time, the unacceptably high rate of drop-out from French classes – generally some 60 per cent were abandoning the subject by 14 with nothing to show for it – had confronted teachers with the evident failure of the attempt to move foreign languages from a subject for the intellectual elite in grammar schools (and of the social elite in preparatory and public schools) to an obligatory subject in comprehensive schools with no change in methodology (aims, objectives and methods). There were calls for its reversion to an elite position, or even, in view of the increasing dominance of English in international communication, for its total removal from the secondary curriculum. Instead, however, an extraordinary bottom-up revolution took place: the 'graded objectives' movement. Stimulated by the 'defined syllabuses' of the Nuffield Foundation's Modern Languages Project housed at the University of York, and the closely related Council of Europe 'threshold level' specifications for language learning objectives, groups of teachers in many parts of the country began to define limited short-term objectives for early foreign language learning no longer in formal grammatical and lexical terms, but in terms of the language needed for the performance of practical tasks in everyday life, with communicative effectiveness rather than the avoidance of error as the criterion of success. In time, this grassroots movement, promoted from the start by the universities of Leeds and York, was supported by a number of departments of education and examining boards.

As Director of CILT from 1978 to 1987, I sought to promote a cluster of related developments within its remit: the teaching of English to migrants for communicative purposes, the maintenance and development of their languages of origin (a valuable but neglected personal and social resource); and the graded objectives movement in modern languages. The central concept of languages for communication linked them all together and, through CILT's links with the British Council, with the teaching of English as a foreign language, which had had a communicative orientation ever since the influence of Harold Palmer in the 1920s and 1930s. A growing cross-disciplinary interest in applied linguistics and in 'language awareness' also provided a common focus. The Department of Education in the University of Southampton combined English and modern languages in a single Chair. It became possible to begin to develop institutions which brought together the full range of interests in language and languages. The British Association for Applied Linguistics, founded in 1967 as part of the Council of Europe programme in preparation for the Congress of Applied Linguistics held in Cambridge in 1969, was the first and has proved the most vigorous and long-lasting. In the 1980s the National Conference on Languages in Education (NCLE) and the Languages Committee of the Royal Society of Arts accommodated a very fruitful interaction of all the language interests, but for different reasons neither survived to develop its full potential. Also, the joint British Council/CILT Language Teaching Library, which was split up when financial constraints forced the relocation of CILT.

In spite of these setbacks, and an increasing tendency in the 1990s for official thinking to look to a restoration of traditional, authoritarian patterns of learning and teaching to meet the crisis of mass educational under-achievement, the continuing, indeed accelerating computerisation and consequent internationalisation of an increasingly competitive global market-place make the development of communication skills a more and more important aspect of education.

The most recent developments in communication and information technology are no respecters of frontiers. The speed of travel by air and even by rail and motorway make it an everyday matter to cross several political and linguistic boundaries in a single day's journey. The effect of electronics is even more dramatic, since signals travel globally at the speed of light, so that information flow is effectively instantaneous and the 'virtual' mobility of individuals unlimited. Thus, television news coverage is global and immediate. Viewers all over the world are experiencing the same events at the same time. Financial markets, involving huge capital sums, operate globally and even the shortest delays in response can be disastrous. In trade and industry, economics of scale lead to the global organisation of the production and distribution of goods of all kinds. Employees in virtually any kind of enterprise may find themselves affected for better or worse by takeovers and mergers planned hundreds or thousands of miles away. Their day-to-day working may involve co-operation or negotiation and co-ordination with suppliers, colleagues and clients in many different countries. Thus international communication is an increasingly everyday experience for widening sectors of the population, not only when travelling abroad.

For native English speakers, the impact of these changes is softened and their effects masked by the emergence, as part of the process of globalisation, of English, for a complex of historical and functional reasons, as an international *lingua franca*. The Second World War facilitated a seamless transfer of hegemony along the lifelines of global communication from the British Empire to the equally anglophone United States, so that English became the universal medium of international travel. The Anglo-Saxon countries were the prime developers of communications and later information technology and also of mass entertainment. Political developments also played a part. Cultural and intellectual oppression in Germany hastened the transfer of international medical and scientific discourse from German to English. The combined effects of all these changes caused English to displace French from the position it had held as the leading language of rational modernity and of diplomacy. The education systems of almost all countries have responded by making English the first and, in some cases, the only foreign language on the secondary school curriculum and extending the length of study into primary education in one direction and into higher, further and adult education in the other. These educational measures have in turn made the use of English in international communication more effective and raised the level of demand, producing a self-reinforcing spiral towards second language status increasingly independent of the Anglo-Saxon countries themselves.

For the English-speaking countries themselves, the emergence of English as an international lingua franca is not an unmixed blessing. For Britain, especially, it masks the effects of the loss of imperial dominance, encourages complacency and perpetuates a sense of superiority as a result of a privileged position in unequal international communication based simply on linguistic advantage but no longer corresponding to the realities of political and economic relations. In international converse through the medium of English, native speakers tend to talk too much and listen too little, so that quite frequently an international free discussion turns into one among the native English-speaking participants, in which little account is taken of the demands made on the comprehension skills of the non-natives present. Monolinguals are tempted to confuse the skill with which an argument is formulated and the fluency with which it is expressed with the force and validity of the case itself, and are painfully surprised when, having had by far the best of the debate, they are outvoted or when they have contracts left unsigned because clients have felt unable to express fully their questions, doubts and hesitations, which therefore remain unresolved. Again, native English speakers frequently find themselves asked to act as chairpersons or *rapporteurs* in international meetings. This can place them in something of a quandary; if they act as impartial, neutral facilitators their own case may go by default. If they promote it, it seems a misuse of a privileged position.

There is little awareness among British or American people of the dangerous resentments which can be built up by unequal communication. As far as I can tell, nothing is done in mainstream English teaching to raise awareness of the implications of the international role of English for native English-speaking people, or to prepare them to use the language more effectively, both productively and receptively, in international communication. The issue of the responsibilities of the more experienced partner for the success of unequal communication plays no part, as surely it should, in discussions of the roles of home dialect and standard language, or of the need for clarity of diction or, more generally, of the need for a native speaker to adjust his or her use of language to the level of competence of the listener and to give sympathetic attention as a listener to the speech of a foreign learner struggling to express meaning with inadequate linguistic resources.

The experience of learning a foreign language, which should raise this awareness, does not necessarily do so. Pre-communicative approaches, whether following the classical grammar/translation method or the structuralist model (or even some avowedly 'communicative' approaches), were formalistic and presented learners only with artificial exercises which they could, and should, perform in an error-free way. It was considered illegitimate to place learners in a position in which they had to struggle as best they might with communicative tasks beyond what they had been taught. Two anecdotes may illustrate this. When specially designed examinations geared to the Nuffield German course *Vorwärts* were being developed, the proposal by the team to include a project component was vetoed because candidates might be tempted to try to go beyond the taught content of the course, using a combination of authentic native sources and bilingual dictionaries, thus encouraging plagiarism and error. Later, when the National Foundation for Educational Research was investigating the communicative abilities of pupils after two years of language study, they were not permitted to include tasks which related to past events, since the past tense had not yet been reached in the textbooks in use.

Concentration on the error-free performance of undemanding tasks naturally left learners reluctant to take risks or to launch themselves into communication situations which they had not been able to prepare carefully in advance, for fear of 'making fools of themselves' by committing errors. These fears were reinforced by a stereotype belief in a French intolerance and contempt for grammatical error. English speakers became notorious for their reluctance to use French, even though they might have learnt the language for five years or more. This reluctance is seen by many others not as humility or modesty but as a refusal to take part in unequal international communication except as the superior partner, which again increases resentment. To overcome this, the English must be seen to be willing to struggle and to take the languages of other people seriously both as media of communication and as the expression of a distinctive cultural identity. Fortunately, *Einsprachigkeit ist heilbar,* 'monolingualism is curable'. English children and adults learn foreign languages as well as anyone else once they recognise the need to do so in a multilingual and multicultural world.

THE EFFECTS OF INTERNATIONAL ORGANISATIONS

The European organisations, both the Council of Europe and the European Union, are agreed that plurilingualism, rather than the exclusive adoption of English as a universal medium of international communication, should be the aim of European language policy. The European Union has proclaimed the objective of 'mastery of three EU languages', whilst conceding that 'mastery' would need to be appropriately interpreted in each case. It is far from certain that the learner's interests are best served by pursuing the same objectives in two foreign languages of which neither can in any case be expected to reach the same level as their mother tongue by the end of secondary education.

The approach of the Council of Europe has been more flexible. European communication (which is a sector of a wider global communication) can be seen as a large multilingual and multicultural space, into which individuals expand throughout life according to their changing circumstances. Some experience multilingual situations and develop plurilingualism from their earliest years. Many learn first in a monolingual home environment and expand their communicative experience and competence successively into the public, educational and occupational domains in local, national and international contexts. The mission of the educational system in this respect is to facilitate the growth of communicative competence by: ensuring oracy and literacy in the national language and in the home language of pupils where this is different; raising awareness of and promoting favourable attitudes towards linguistic and cultural diversity; by providing access to and experience of forms of communication which might not otherwise fall within the individual's compass; by developing competence and confidence in the use of a suitable foreign language for purposes of reception, production and interaction; by providing opportunities for developing partial (especially receptive) competences in further languages; developing heuristic skills for making sense of texts in languages not otherwise formally studied; by the incidental, but planned and monitored, development of the ability to learn and use languages independently in later life.

These principles are applicable in the United Kingdom as elsewhere, with the necessary adjustment to its national and various regional and local circumstances. For instance, ways of developing, valorising and exploiting the national resource represented by the multifarious mother tongues spoken by varying numbers of immigrants in different parts of the country deserve careful policy planning. In addition, the balance between advanced multi-skill competence in a major language of international currency and partial competence in a range of languages may be different for an English-speaking country than for non-English speaking ones.

To encourage and promote European plurilingualism, the Council of Europe has developed three main tools. The first, now almost 25 years old, is the *Threshold Level* concept, which specifies the language needed for independent participation in the daily life of a country where the language is spoken, not only transacting the business of living, but also exchanging information, ideas and opinions with other language users. Originally applied to English, versions are now available for 21 European languages, with more in preparation. The *Threshold Level* attempts to define the minimum level at which an adequate independence can be achieved. *Waystage* defines the bare essentials of communication across the field, whilst the recently developed

Vantage Level describes a qualitatively higher level of competence given the same communicative aims.

The second tool, of more general application, is the *Common European Framework of Reference* for language learning, teaching and assessment. The Framework attempts to survey comprehensively (a) the domains, situations, conditions and constraints which constitute the context of language use, (b) the purposes, tasks, themes, activities and psycholinguistic processes involved in language use, (c) the competences, both general and language-specific, which underlie language use, and (d) the strategies by which competences are activated in language use. The Framework then provides descriptors for six levels of proficiency, both global and in the various parameters of competence and use. It is hoped that the Framework will be of use to the language teaching profession (primarily but not exclusively concerned with foreign languages) for reflection on present practice, planning of provision (including the specification of partial competences) and communication among providers and between them and their clientele. The Framework is now in its second draft and is in the process of being field-trialled by users in different fields. A series of user guides, one general and ten for various specialist users, is available and being trialled also.

The third tool is a proposed *European Language Portfolio* now under development. The Portfolio is conceived as a document in which an individual can enter experiences and achievements in respect of as many European (and other) languages as possible, even if they do not reach a level suitable for certification as qualifications. It will provide a basis for learner self-assessment, closely related to the levels and descriptors of the Framework.

These tools are all non-directive instruments, designed to facilitate independent decision-making and planning by those responsible for language policy, from national curriculum planners and examination boards, through textbook and course planners, teacher trainers, language inspectors and advisors to classroom teachers and, where possible, to learners themselves as a means to autonomy. Although they have been designed to promote the development of plurilingualism, the Framework and the Portfolio are capable of wider use. The Portfolio can be used by children from minority languages to chart their mother-tongue development and to assess their proficiency in its use, if these are not built into the mainstream educational apparatus of teaching, assessment and qualification. The Framework provides a comprehensive analysis of language use as well as the underlying competences of a language user and the strategies for activating competences for use in the situations which arise in the various domains of social existence. As such, it is completely general and can be used for reflection, planning and information in mainstream mother-tongue education as well as in the education of the speech and hearing impaired. In fact, it can well function as a central reference document for a unified approach to the development of overall communicative ability, and for interdisciplinary co-operation in furthering that development as part of the growth of the individual's understanding of the physical and social environment and ability to function effectively in the local, national and international environment.

Of course, the conception and implementation of a holistic policy, with its parts clearly articulated but well interrelated within a common approach to the curriculum, can only be brought about if they are understood and accepted by all who are called upon to operate it. That means clear and enlightened leadership, with determination on all sides to surmount the obstacle which must inevitably be encountered, as well as commitment, goodwill and a sense of common purpose. There is no way forward for an educational establishment or institution divided into separate empires, each jealously guarding its own territory. Perhaps the place to start is in teacher education and training, where a school or department can establish an overall ethos and communicate its values and attitudes to future teachers at a formative stage in their development. They may then be prepared for willing and competent co-operation in a whole-school context, having themselves experienced its challenges and benefits. Perhaps, after all, a new millennium is the time for seeing the value and practicality of such an educational paradigm.

In summary, interrelated technological and social changes make the time ripe for a major rethinking of language policy as part of the nation's effort to improve its internal and external communication. A clear-sighted appraisal of national foreign language needs and requirements is called for. Some consequences appear to be:

1 The development of communicative abilities, being of universal relevance, must regain a central position in education, from which it has been displaced over the past century.

2 The development of a young person's communicative abilities is to be seen as a continuous, unified, though complex and differentiated, process, interrelating home language (or dialect), the standard state language and other languages in the environment, as well as those of European neighbours and other world languages. It involves attitude formation,

language and cultural awareness, and oracy and literacy as appropriate in those languages required for communication.

3 Education for communication is not simply a matter of training surface skills of reception and production, but of developing positive intercultural attitudes and building up knowledge of the world as well as the underlying linguistic and socio-cultural competences which those skills bring into action.

4 Many disciplines are involved in education for communication. Cross-curricular education policies are required at national level, to be implemented in whole-school strategic and tactical planning.

5 Applied linguistic theory and empirical research should provide a unifying foundation for the interdisciplinary co-operation which is indispensable to the proper understanding of the deep and complex issues involved in the formulation and implementation of valid and feasible objectives across this central area of human concern.

6 A common Resource Centre for Languages in Education could provide a focus for the interdisciplinary co-operation envisaged here. This might most economically be provided by an expansion of the responsibilities of CILT and the national network of Comenius centres.

Challenges to Multilingualism

**Lid King, Centre for Information on
Language Teaching and Research, London**

The context of what I have to say is provided by renewed demands for greater coherence in language provision in the UK, and specifically (for that is CILT's major concern) for the development of some kind of strategic view of foreign languages. Such indeed is very much the theme of the papers by John Trim and Christopher Brumfit and it is a central issue for this book. During the recent past we have also witnessed other initiatives seeking to establish such coherence, involving professional language bodies such as the University Council for Modern Languages, the National Association of Language Advisers and the Association for Language Learning, as well as generalist organisations like NATFHE and the Society of Education Officers. It seems likely that a concerted effort will be made over the coming year or so to articulate such a coherent view of languages in the UK (e.g. through the recently announced Nuffield Inquiry).

It might be said that there is nothing new about this. After all it was in 1641 that the educational reformer and linguist, Comenius was asked to develop plans for a Universal College ('a living laboratory for schools, lending them sap, vitality and strength'). More recently we might recall the influential but never fully implemented Leathes Report of 1918, as well as the various commissions and reports on languages dating from the 1960s and 1970s.[1]

Such historical precedents are not entirely encouraging. Following Mao's dictum that even an absence of policy is a policy, it is possible to construct a kind of 'policy for languages' in the UK in 1998. It would combine a number

---

1 Comenius J A, The Great Didactic referred to by Hawkins E H (1996) in *Thirty Years of Language Teaching,* CILT, p1; Leathes S (1918) *Modern Studies: Report to Prime Minister,* HMSO; and other reports by Annan (62); Robbins (63); Newsom (63); Plowden (67); Bullock (75); Swann (85); Kingman (88); Cox (89); Harris (90).

of official orders, most obviously the National Curriculum, with various initiatives, both governmental and voluntary (Languages Lead Body, Department of Trade and Industry languages support, primary languages initiatives in local education authorities, even HEFCE inspections ...) but the resulting 'policy' would be both inconsistent and incomplete, particularly in relation to young and older learners and in the key interface between foreign language and mother tongue learning. It may be our hope that the conditions of society in the late twentieth century.– and in particular the tendencies towards globalisation and democratic access to information identified by John Trim (this volume) – may provide the basis for more productive discussion on a strategy for languages in the future.

My purpose, however, is not to set out what I think such a policy or strategy might look like. It would certainly derive from many of the principles outlined elsewhere in this study. It may also find some resonance in the imaginary blueprint for languages in the year 2026 which we developed as part of CILT's own 30-year celebrations and which addressed such issues as the contribution of modern foreign languages to personal language development, the content of the foreign language curriculum; the often false dichotomy between education and training and issues relating to equal opportunities.[2]

In many ways such an articulation of a coherent vision is the easier part of the problem. In the rest of this paper I therefore choose to wear my practical hat and to pose the question of whether and how we might actually be able to develop such coherence. Much of what follows relates to languages in the compulsory school sector, since this is in many ways the key to other developments, but it should also have some resonance for language policies throughout UK society.

There is of course no simple answer to this apparently simple question and if answers are to be found they are most likely to be in our responses to the major challenges which face us. These can of course be described in many ways and with a variety of subsets, but for the purpose of our current discussion I have identified just four:

- the challenge of English
- the challenge of democracy
- the challenge of systems
- the challenge of technology.

---

2   Hawkins E H (1996) p333ff, a chapter on which the present article is based.

Of one thing we can be certain. The future will not develop either smoothly or as we expect. The common image of progress as a road – or in technological terms a superhighway – while appealing is also fundamentally misleading. Things develop not in smooth straight lines but through conflict and paradox (even chaos). We may as teachers and examiners be attracted by the idea of a regular progression of levels. As educators and as linguists we also know that in reality learners advance in contradictory, often surprising and rarely linear ways. It seems that life is not dissimilar and thus it is the way in which we identify and respond to current and approaching challenges (rather than the perfection of our planning) which will largely determine the shape of our future.

THE CHALLENGE OF ENGLISH: WHY SHOULD ENGLISH SPEAKERS LEARN LANGUAGES?

The first challenge is the simplest and perhaps the most intractable. Do we need linguists at all?

The question is put so bluntly because it often seems that it has been definitively resolved, only for it to be raised again. It is argued that the 'triumph' of English on a world scale makes redundant our efforts to inculcate the rudiments of French/German/Spanish/Japanese in recalcitrant pupils or university students. Better by far to teach them 'correct' English or 'real' content. A current variant of this theme is a view which is being whispered – among some teachers, in LEAs and even in 'official' circles – that perhaps languages for all pupils in Keystage 4 (14–16) are not necessary or in some cases desirable. Such opinions are also reflected, often in more subtle mode, in key parts of the academic world and also (perhaps even more so) in business. Their persistence suggests that despite the advances made in recent decades, of which the implementation of the National Curriculum, for all its faults, was undoubtedly one, the argument for foreign language learning even in schools has still not been won.[3]

This may be seen as a slightly controversial point in the context of this book which is concerned with language education in general. I certainly hope that it will not be regarded as a sign of a limited perspective, and indeed I am greatly encouraged by the insistence of many involved in this debate that foreign

---

3   See, for example, *The Times,* 28.7.1994; *Education,* 24.9.1995.

language learning must be part of a wider concept of literacy .There is also, of course, some truth in the premise that English – or at least a form of what we might call 'project English' – is for many purposes an international language, and this tendency is probably increasing. Anyone who has worked in international contexts will know this from direct experience. Quite recently I was astonished to discover that a French multinational company has adopted English as its official language for internal communication.[4]

To face up to this challenge then dreams and fine words will not be enough. Why indeed should we learn languages?

In the UK itself our recent experience of the role of languages in business has underlined the 'bottom line' significance of language competence – not least on the switchboards of our major companies. Most interestingly of all we are seeing a convergence between such sternly instrumental views of language learning and the more humanist traditions of linguists. Perhaps in line with the 'softer' approaches of modern business management theory the importance of human *communication* is increasingly stressed. Language – including foreign language – is seen as key to such communication and real interchange.[5]

Such identifiable concerns of the business world may lead to a broader understanding of the purposes of language competence which is not so very different from the kind of perspectives developed by John Trim and based on the seminal work of the Council of Europe and the real demands of globalisation and mobility. One, as yet not fully articulated, aspect to this – the humanistic bottom line – is the development of employee (i.e. people's) interest in language learning. Perhaps indeed this will be the key to the future expansion of languages in the world of work: employees rather than employers may be the driving force of increased language use and competence as 'learning companies' provide the possibilities for their workforce to develop their linguistic skills for both professional and personal purposes. In this sense 'business' becomes just one (important) aspect of human inter-action. Language – communication with other humans – is perhaps even more fundamental a need.[6]

---

4   Discussion with a research manager from Cap Gemini Telecom, September 1997.

5   Handy, C, *The Empty Overcoat* (Hutchinson, 1993); Peters, T, *The Pursuit of WOW!* (Vintage Books, 1994).

6   Council of Europe, *Modern Languages: Learning, Teaching, Assessment. A Common European Framework of Reference* (Draft 2) Strasbourg, 1996, *Teaching and Learning – Towards the Learning Society*, European Commission, 1996. Discussions with training officers at large firms such as Volkswagen and Unilever.

It is certainly this need which underpins the 'educational' arguments for foreign language learning. We must undoubtedly transcend the strictly instrumental arguments about language learning for they are limiting and incomplete. Not least they can not be justified for all of our people. Some will not need languages for economic purposes. And yet some of the most moving and relevant examples of language learning in practice have been the attempts of the very young, and the striving of those with learning difficulties, to communicate in foreign tongues. Through it they have learned – about themselves, about the world, about their own language. It is here that the arguments about MFL must, in my view, be brought into the mainstream arguments about language development and literacy in general.

For this to happen there must be increased dialogue (and where necessary debate and disagreement) between those involved in mother tongue teaching (not only English) and foreign language teachers and researchers. Necessary as this is, we should not underestimate the potential difficulties. In 1973 a distinguished predecessor of mine – George Perren who sadly died last summer – was the main force behind a conference of English and foreign language teachers organised in order to discuss *The Space Between.* The outcomes were fascinating, yet a quarter of a century later there is still a chasm between the perceptions and even the discourse of these two key groups (Perren G E (ed) *The Space Between* (CILT, 1974); Pomphrey C, 'The language awareness of PGCE modern languages and English students', in *Links* no 17 (CILT, 1997)).

Would it not be a marvellous tribute to the memory of George Perren if we were again to face up to the challenge of the space between?

THE CHALLENGE OF DEMOCRACY: THE UNEVEN PLAYING FIELD

The transformation in foreign language learning from a subject for the elite to a subject for all – what we might call the democratisation or normalisation of language learning – is only partially complete. The past 30 years have shown both the desirability and the possibility of making foreign language learning a meaningful experience for all. Yet there remain many pupils in schools who resist language learning and who significantly underachieve. Proportionately more of these are in the 14–19 age group, in particular working-class children and above all working-class boys. In our universities foreign language competence is still not universally accepted as a prerequisite of professional life. Despite the growing and documented enthusiasm among adults for languages there remain many for whom language learning is an arcane mystery.

In this area we can show only partial progress. There is more than a suspicion that our subject, as it is currently taught and resourced, favours the more privileged sectors of society. The paradox here, which has been pointed out by Eric Hawkins, is the way in which the (desirable) introduction of communicative approaches to language learning and teaching has also meant a shift in what Eric calls the 'laboratory' for language learners: from the library which is accessible to all to the target country itself. The move to greater 'relevance' has thus brought with it obstacles relating to access and equal opportunities which the educational system has only partly been able to resolve. Since experience of gîtes on the Loire and nights at the opera are advantages for young students of languages, foreign languages learning has retained an element of elitism (Hawkins E W (1996) 'An uneven language playing field', in Hawkins E W (ed) *Thirty Years of Language Teaching* 121–132 (includes references)).

That this is not inevitable can be seen from a number of remarkable successes. CILT itself has played a part in supporting successful language learning by all pupils, including those with special educational needs. Significant steps have been made in making language learning 'real' through links and exchanges, including electronic links.[7] In many ways the conditions are now far more propitious than they have ever been for making a significant shift in British attitudes and expectations. The very existence of the National Curriculum provides a powerful institutional context for normalisation in language learning. Other influences – the European Union's insistence on multi-competence in languages, the work of the Council of Europe, the concerns of exporters and their promoters in the DTI, the significant expansion of languages in higher education, the pressures from adults for language competence as a need in the multinational workplace – all provide strong support for the dream of multilingualism.

And yet the challenge remains.

---

7   See, for a discussion, *Modern Foreign Languages and Special Educational Needs: A new commitment,* NCC, 1993; McLagan P, (1994) *Steps to Learning; Modern languages for pupils with special educational needs,* CILT; Jones B (1996) 'Contacts with the foreign country', in Hawkins E W, *Thirty Years of Language Teaching,* CILT, pp238–244. 1998 is also the 50th anniversary of the establishment of the Central Bureau for Educational Visits and Exchanges which has done so much to promote the international dimension in education.

The underlying causes and solutions are varied. They are partly to do with resources and in particular the continuing supply of well-trained teachers (a possible 5th 'challenge' which has emerged in recent years). But they are also to do with other rather more fundamental issues – relating to the historical development of institutionalised language learning in the UK.

If we are really to cut the monolingual loop, it seems to me that we need not so much a breaking with as a building on the recent past. The significant expansion of language learning in our schools during the 1970s (coincident with the promotion and introduction of communicative methodology), provides a rich seam of experience which should help us in our current endeavours. Much was learned and it is perhaps the synthesis of this learning which we need more than the construction of new and perfect systems. To take one example – the Graded Objectives in Modern Languages movement (GOML) – it is unlikely that such a national structure could or should be resurrected, but that does not mean that the collective wisdom of those teachers, the 'corporate memory' should be forgotten. One essential characteristic of those efforts was that they involved teachers working together, taking ownership of the curriculum; another was that they also sought meaningful content for learners who might not always wait patiently for the deferred reward of an examination grade. It is our task to incorporate such elements of our corporate memory into our plans for the future (Page B and Hewett D, *Languages Step by Step: Graded objectives in the UK* (CILT, 1987).

There is no *potion magique* in any branch of learning – far less in languages – but the search for relevance, for contact with the target culture will continue. In this respect it is fascinating to note the recent recrudescence of interest in two aspects of language learning – the learning of serious subject matter 'through the medium' and the study of language 'for itself'.

If we are to progress it seems likely that these two approaches, or indeed a combination of the two, will be at the centre of our thinking in the coming period. Quite simply, unless our learners see the 'point' of language learning, both/either because language study is of relevance in its own right, and/or because it provides access to knowledge and understanding of value to the learner, then 'languages for all' will remain an aspiration rather than a reality.

We know, from partial experience, that it can be so. To achieve it will require continued discussion, debate, training and curricular development, above all (to revisit the GOML analogy) involvement of and 'ownership' by the teachers. The spiral will continue.

THE CHALLENGE OF SYSTEMS: HOW ARE LANGUAGES LEARNED?

Although the search for 'perfect systems' is a delusion, it does not mean that systems have only marginal effects on the learning process. In fact it is all too easy to accept what exists as natural without really questioning its effectiveness. It was only recently when listening to two headteachers outlining the organisational constraints which they experienced in supporting language learning that I even thought of the need to re-examine the systems.

As well as debate on the content of learning, the future will also require change in the mechanics of the curriculum. If language learning (perhaps any learning?) is to be really 'for all' then the systems which we have inherited from the 1950s will inevitably need to change.

Let us consider just one example – the timetable. The division of learning into short chunks of time – the drip-feed method – which teachers have often demanded may actually be preventing effective language learning. How long is it since Eric Hawkins first provided us with the image of the language teacher as a gardener in the gale of English? And what have we sought to do about it? What progress has been made in integrating intensive learning and study visits into the curriculum?

As the number of pupils, students, learners increase and the complexity of their demands and needs expands the present set-up will come under greater and greater tension. A radical rethink of the learning day, the nature of learning activities, the role of the teacher and of technology will be inevitable. Better that it should be sooner – and with the participation of teachers and learners – than later and imposed by necessity or government.

We are also, perhaps uniquely in the developed world, bedevilled by continuing debate about the ways we divide up our pupils (selection by attainment, income, geography). Whatever the rationale for the differing views and whatever their outcomes, the existence of such debate is a continuing threat to the democratisation of language learning.

What after all could be easier than to justify the restriction of language learning opportunities to the highest attainers, which in turn brings us back to our first challenge? Why learn languages at all?

Beyond this discussion on purpose and principle we also need further debate about the ways in which we organise language learning. This must be more than a discussion about teaching organisation. It implies continued reflection about how different learners learn – the role of the group, individual learning, whole class teaching. It implies reassessing the way we make use of resources and attacking the fundamental question of how we deliver better and more learning with the same or sometimes even less. It involves examining the possibilities for self-tuition of various kinds (learning how to learn). It involves some radical thinking about boys and girls and mixed groups and single sex groups and appropriate styles of teaching and learning.

The agenda is a long and rich one. The answers will not necessarily come quickly and those who seek them will often be overwhelmed by systems they did not choose and confronted by learners they did not ask for, but unless we can break through at some point in the organisation of learning then 'languages for all' will remain a dream (or worse a pretence).

THE CHALLENGE OF TECHNOLOGY: HOW TO MAKE LANGUAGE LEARNING EFFECTIVE AND EFFICIENT?

The fourth challenge can be and is seen as both a threat and an opportunity.

Quite accidentally (and unusually) it happened that in the autumn of 1996 I attended two international conferences in the same week. One was mainly about technological 'solutions' to international communication needs; the other was mainly about the challenges of multilingualism in the information society. Unsurprisingly there was a gulf between the problem-free confidence of the technologists and the complex concerns of the educators and linguists. This struck me as a metaphor for the uneasy relationship between education and new technology

On the one hand the talk is all of 'solutions', on the other we have not yet defined the problem.

Certainly in the recent past we may have been deluded by what have been called the 'glittering streams' offered by technology: whatever the proposed medium – tape recorder, video machine, computer – the potential seems never to have been matched in reality. As we now enter the information age, some would say that nothing has really changed. Technology is still no more than an adjunct, the provider of tools which may or may not be of use in simple tasks; the Internet is less important than the printing press.

For others there is a qualitative change – the 'knowledge society' is at hand. The new information technology will hold the key to the problem of numbers and needs. It will provide solutions to the constraints of time and space and resource. The speed with which information can be accessed, the possibilities for distant communication will provide endless new possibilities and needs for language learning.

The truth probably lives in the rather messy place in between these two visions. Language learning, after all, is not simply the processing of information, and speed of access may be quite irrelevant. On the other hand there is at least a convincing argument that certain characteristics of the new communications technology mean that it will be more than just another tool. What is exciting to some about the new technologies is the potential which they seem to hold for making language learning more relevant and rewarding for greater numbers of people. Whether it be through the interactive potential of electronic communications or the learner centredness of recent CD developments there seems to be something about current technological developments which is qualitatively different from what has gone before. If this is the case, and not simply the amazement of simple folk in front of the camera obscura, it is because the new information technology can be about choice, about content, about interaction. It can, in a word, be communicative.[8]

This in itself will present us – language educators – with new challenges. What is the relationship between teacher and resource? What is the effect of virtual (as opposed to real communication? How do learners access information? Will English dominate the Internet (and what kind of English will it be)? Which brings us back full circle to our first fundamental challenge. And so the spiral continues.

CONCLUSION

By its nature such a discussion should have no conclusion. I have chosen to touch on four large areas which subsume others, which could indeed have been described using other patterns and which also have an interrelation. For example I have suggested how the challenge of technology relates to the challenge of English and how systems relate to content. I am also conscious that I have largely ignored some major issues of resource, not least that of teacher supply (although even here there is a relationship to the discussion about content and the possibilities of technology).

---

8   See, for example, Hawkins (1996) 209–237; CILT Conference 'Education in the communication age', January 1998 (report to be on WWW); Esch E (ed) (1994) *Self Access and the Adult Language Learner,* CILT.

To find solutions to such challenges will not be easy. It will involve dialogue, it will require vision and an understanding of our past. Many individuals and institutions will play their part and of course there will never be a solution – rather the imperfect resolution of some paradoxes and the creation of new ones. The process will be chaotic rather than perfect, and all the more valuable for that.

This book has been a part of that process and I am delighted to have had the opportunity to contribute. It is perhaps worth remembering that the developments which we are considering are fundamental ones for which we should not expect simple answers. In the words of H H Stern (Hoy P H (ed) *The Early Teaching of Modern Languages* (Nuffield, 1977):

The introduction of a foreign language into this limited monoglot world has far reaching consequences. We are in fact breaking with the nineteenth century tradition of literacy in terms of a national language if we propose to introduce into the concept of fundamental literacy the mastery of another language. It has repercussions which are not confined to the primary (and the secondary) stage, … Just as we take it for granted that the ordinary man and woman in all westernised countries is literate and numerate in terms of his own society, in about fifty or a hundred years' time it might perhaps be regarded as a matter of course that he has the command of at least one other language.

A Policy for Language in British Education

CHRISTOPHER BRUMFIT, University of Southampton

The establishment of the National Curriculum has established a de facto language policy in British education. But as it was created by accident, in the course of laying down guidelines for the teaching of all subjects, it is not as coherent and consistent as it might be. The purpose of these remarks is to establish the basic principles for achieving a just provision of language in schools.

Any coherent language policy must start with the central fact of the British situation – that English is the main language and other language provision must respond to the implications of that fact. Although language policies frequently concentrate on the needs of bilingual learners or of foreign languages, for the UK this is inappropriate, because direct access to the major language of international communication places other languages in a uniquely difficult position in relation to the (largely unexpressed) attitudes of the majority of first language English speakers. Any language policy which is to command widespread acceptance by the monolingual majority and simultaneously be responsive to the complexities of the British linguistic context for bilingual learners must start from this fact. Any policy must set out to be just to all learners, and at the same time to accept the needs of typical learners. Thus deeply entrenched English-speaking monolingualism has to be accepted as a starting point for the foreseeable future.

Yet the whole purpose of a language policy is to erode deeply entrenched monolingualism. Neither internally nor externally can Britain afford to be monolingual. All major industrial countries are becoming increasingly multilingual, as labour mobility indigenises more and more previously foreign languages, and as a resurgence of support for older mother tongues creates subcultures associated with the languages marginalised by the monolingual policies tacitly espoused by nineteenth century nationalism.

CONCERNS OF A LANGUAGE POLICY FOR LANGUAGE IN SCHOOLS

The language repertoire needed by learners has a number of dimensions, and each of these has different implications for the curriculum in educational institutions. Broadly, language can be said to perform three main roles. It has a pragmatic function as a means of getting things done in the world. It has a learning and conceptualising function, as a means of understanding the world, of making sense of ideas and evidence. And it has an archive function, as a means of storing understandings from the past. Each of these implies a different aspect of the curriculum. The pragmatic function relates to a skill orientation, for which learners need to be able to perform effectively in the future, after they have left school. The conceptualising function is concerned more with the personal development of the individual and has immediate pay-off in contributing to educational understanding. The archive function has implications for what previous understanding is necessary to locate ourselves in the contemporary world. But these orientations are not tidy, for all three of them can realise themselves through the skills of performance, all three of them require appropriate knowledge, and all three have an affective and personal dimension too.

Nonetheless, using such categories reminds us that we cannot separate the school experience from a requirement to consider individuals acting in the world after leaving school, personal developmental needs, and needs relating to heritage from the past. And different languages will provide bases for different kinds of experience. Some (and particularly the major languages of national and international communication, including English) will provide a basis for action in the world, as well as for personal growth. Some (and particularly mother tongues in the early years) will be crucial at particular stages in personal growth. Some (particularly classical languages and those with strong literary traditions) will have a major role to play in reinforcing understanding of heritage. But, again, these categories are untidy, and the interplay of heritage, growth and pragmatic/communicative competence will be a feature of provision in any language.

Finally, we need to stress three central features of language: its capacities in speech and argument; its potentialities in written form; its interconnectedness with visual and other media. In all the aspects referred to, literacy is as important as oracy, and neither of these is independent of our abilities to interpret through technology, through pictures and diagrams, through the whole semiology of our culture.

Because of the structure of the national curriculum, language work will in practice operate through school subjects. Any policy will on the one hand need to permeate the school, and on the other need to show itself through concentrated and dedicated provision within its own subject slot.

AN EQUALITY OF PROVISION

Equal provision is never achievable in detail, but it is necessary to state expectations as a goal so that the agenda remains consistent. Because there are so many language groups, and because provision has major resource implications, we can only provide (i) as far as resources permit, and (ii) subject to local demand and needs – even in the best of conditions.

But the charter outlined below (page 33) may help. It attempts to state what, subject to the two restrictions mentioned above, we should be offering all learners in Britain as an entitlement.

Language charter [8]
(original version)

It is the policy of
(insert name of institution or authority)

to enable all learners, to the maximum extent possible within available legislation and resources

(i) to develop their own mother tongue or dialect to maximum confident and effective use;

(ii) to develop competence in a range of styles of English for educational, work-based, social and public-life purposes;

(iii) to develop their knowledge of how language operates in a multilingual society, including basic experience of languages other than their own that are significant either in education or the local community;

(iv) to develop as extensive as possible a practical competence in at least one foreign language.

It is our belief that the development of these four strands in combination will contribute to an effective language curriculum for Britain in the twenty-first century more than emphasis on any one of them separately at the expense of the others.

Signed:

Date:

---

8 Sources: Brumfit, C J, (1996) 'Towards a language policy for multilingual secondary schools', in J Geach (ed) *Coherence in Diversity,* CILT (originally a lecture given in 1986). Developed at book length in Brumfit, C J (ed) (1995) *Language Education in the National Curriculum,* Blackwell.

MORE RADICAL PROPOSALS FOR BILINGUAL LEARNERS [9]

Further to the charter, it would be possible to push towards more detailed specification for particular groups of learners. For bilingual learners in the UK this could consist of the following goals.

Full equality of opportunity for bilingual learners would consist of:

1 Development of full proficiency in spoken and written English, with command of a variety of styles appropriate to the needs of public, vocational and private life.

2 Development of parallel proficiency in the mother tongue (and where appropriate in a related written language variety), in the range of styles necessary for fullest participation in the life of the relevant speech community.

3 The opportunity to learn at least one further, foreign language to an advanced level.

4 The opportunity to enter relevant public examinations in English, heritage language(s) and foreign language(s).

5 Full access to all non-language strands of the school curriculum.

6 The right and opportunity to use both the national standard language and the mother tongue/heritage language as media for learning across the curriculum wherever practicable.

7 Multilingual home-school communication, as needed to facilitate contact with families, etc.

8 A 'Knowledge about language' curriculum strand for all learners, incorporating understanding of language variation and multilingualism, information about English as an international, national and local language, as well as understanding about other local heritage languages and speech communities, and their roles, national, international and local, inside and outside the UK .

---

9 For a discussion see Mitchell R and Brumfit C J (1997) 'The national curriculum experience of bilingual pupils', in *Educational Review*, 49, 2, pp159–180.

IMPLICATIONS OF THE LANGUAGE CHARTER FOR THE CURRICULUM

Language is a vehicle for a wide range of activities and is closely bound up with personal development, concept formation and identity. Simultaneously, it is tied in to public and private communication processes. The language curriculum must therefore reflect a range of activities with different purposes.

These can broadly be defined as:

developmental, helping learners to become confident users for purposes of their own choosing, to become creative and imaginative, to be willing to think about and reflect on their own language practices;

understanding heritage, making sense of past achievement and traditions with language;

functional, enabling learners to operate with the conventions demanded by society.

Most language work should incorporate aspects of all three of these.

Furthermore, enabling this to happen requires the curriculum to draw upon literature, drama, and media understanding, so that implementation of the language charter requires integration of all these activities, though the ways in which this will happen will vary at different levels of education, and with different language groupings.

The charter proposal is based on views of social justice. It is entirely compatible with National Curriculum orders, but it provides a coherence and a focus on learners' entitlement which is more specific than offered there.

It could also be translated into any level of education, for it can be adapted to pre-school, community, further, and higher education as well as mainstream schooling and provides a rationale for language teacher education.

PART II
EVALUATION OF RESEARCH AND THEORY

Multilingualism in England:
A Review of Research

BEN RAMPTON, ROXY HARRIS and CONSTANT LEUNG
Thames Valley University

A great deal has happened in the study and understanding of multilingualism in England over the last ten years or so (cf Reid, 1985; Taylor and Hegarty, 1985), and this review concentrates on the dynamic and contested relationships between (a) educational policy, (b) academic discourse, and (c) everyday sociolinguistic practice. Our account is limited to England and to its newer heritage languages, and it is necessarily empty of any detailed discussion of particular languages. For fuller sociolinguistic discussion of 31 of these, we refer the reader to Alladina and Edwards (eds, 1991), a major step forwards in the documentation of linguistic diversity in the British Isles which provides an idea of the wide but uneven spread of multilingualism across a range of institutional sites (including, for example, press and broadcasting[1] as well as education).

The review begins with an sketch of recent responses to multilingualism in the national education system, and then points to growing tension between education policy and research. After that, it suggests three weakness in

---

1   In London and to a lesser extent in other English cities, there is a substantial amount of illegal radio broadcasting (sometimes called 'pirate' radio), and in 1995 there were 645 official raids to suppress 166 illegal radio stations. There is no significant research on these stations and certainly nothing on their language use (the national agency responsible explicitly disavows any interest in their nature, and claims to be interested simply in the fact of their illegality). However, one major source of illegal radio is the black, Caribbean-descended population, and it therefore provides an important publicly visible/audible space for the maintenance of Caribbean, principally Jamaican speech, observable in the talk of DJs, phone-in participants and characters in advertisements. On multilingualism in the ethnic minority press, see Peak and Fisher, 1996.

research in the 1980s, outlines major research developments in the 1990s and offers some evaluative comments on these in the final section.

LANGUAGE EDUCATION IN A MULTILINGUAL SOCIETY

Traditionally in England, a number of different interest groups have played a significant role in the language education policy and provision – central government, local government, schools, community organisations, examination boards, professional bodies – but since the late 1980s, a torrent of central government legislation has radically changed the balance of power between them. The influence and resources of local government have been very substantially reduced, and for the first time, (Conservative) central government formulated a national curriculum for school pupils aged 5–16. Although never considering any strong forms of education through two languages (cf Baker, 1993, p153), in the 1980s local education authorities were starting to address themselves to the possibilities for teaching community languages (Bourne, 1989, ch6), and in some regions, local government commitment to multilingualism remains quite strong (cf the special edition of *Language Issues,* 8.1.1996, 'Sheffield the Multilingual City'). But there is now very little encouragement for this from central government, which has instead stressed that with 'the ethnic diversity of the school population and society at large, ... the cardinal point [is] that English should be the first language and medium of instruction for all pupils in England' (DES, 1989, para 10.1; DES, 1985, para 3.16). In the new National Curriculum, language is mainly addressed under two headings – 'English' and 'Modern Foreign Languages' (MFL) – and while many have welcomed the emphasis on 11–16 (but not 5–10) year olds learning a modern foreign language, it is by no means clear that this will to lead to any significant growth in the teaching of minority languages.[2]

Space prohibits a full description of how schools have responded to linguistic diversity in recent times, and of how they have adjusted to new

---

2   Among other things (see below), the provision for minority community languages at secondary level is likely to be inhibited by curriculum specifications that assume a monolingual English starting point (DFE, 1995, pp6–9), the absence of support for the development of pedagogies capable of responding to groups of pupils with mixed levels of proficiency, and the realities of local and national resourcing. See Brumfit (ed) 1995, ch8 and Stubbs, 1991, 1994, pp200–203, which capture much of this quite subtle accumulation of pressures.

constraints (cf Bourne, 1989; Stubbs, 1991, 1994; Edwards and Redfern, 1992; OFSTED, 1994; Bangs, 1994). Broadly speaking, in England, educational provision for children from bi- and multilingual homes can be characterised as 'submersion' for some (i.e. no effective in-class support and in some cases no English as an Additional Language (EAL)/support teacher at all), and content-based 'partial shelter' for others (EAL support in class), with a limited amount of transitional bilingual support available to some children in their early years. Conservative government policy was here driven by an explicit concern for social cohesion (DES, 1985, pp406–407; Tate, 1996), and ideological commitment to a nationalistic equation of land with language (and culture) explains the sharp contrast between England and Wales, where the same government gives extensive support for Welsh-English bilingual education – 'English in England, Welsh in Wales' (Cameron and Bourne, 1988, pp153–154; Stubbs, 1991, 1994, p204).

Promoting these strikingly different educational approaches, national policy documents have argued that they are responding appropriately to quite different sociolinguistic phenomena in the two countries (DES, 1985, p404; DES, 1989, para 10.9), and their discussion of bilingualism slips with unreflective ease from an assimilationist idiom in England to an idiom in which cognitive benefits and cultural enrichment are taken for granted in Wales (e.g. DES, 1989, chs 10 & 13; cf Bourne, 1989, pp166–167). There is however no warrant in the research literature for this sharp dichotomisation (Baker, 1988, ch 3; Garrett et al, 1992), and prior to the official recognition of Welsh in 1967, there were (and still are) a number of ways in which the position of bilinguals in Wales resembled the contemporary position of bilinguals in England (Bourne, 1989, p192; Stubbs, 1991, 1994, pp205–206).

This disregard for research underpinning government language education policy (Brumfit, ed, 1995) requires further elaboration.

NATIONAL CURRICULUM DEVELOPMENT:
GOVERNMENT POLICY VS ACADEMIC RESEARCH

The long process of national curriculum formulation and redrafting has seen the relationship between government and the academic community become progressively worse. The first formulation of a National Curriculum for English – the 'Cox Report' (DES, 1989) – was a generally well-argued attempt to bring central ideas and findings from contemporary educational, functional and sociolinguistics to bear on language education. It was in competition, however, with a call from the conservative Right for a return to traditional standards, values and methods in the teaching of English, and over time, this has become increasingly influential (see Cameron, 1995, ch 3; Cox, 1992, pp242–268 and 1995 for some participant retrospection).

The final version of the National Curriculum for English (DFE, 1995a) represents an uneasy mixture of influences: it combines notions of discourse structure, register, contextual appropriateness and oral/aural as well as written performance with the shibboleths of prescriptive grammar, while language awareness, welcomed by Stubbs in 1991 as one of the 'bright spots' in the new curriculum (1991; 1994, p193), is now refashioned into the category 'Standard English and Language Study (DFE, 1995a, p2).[3] Set within a wider context of increasingly restrictive government research contracts (Pettigrew, 1992; also Reid, 1985, p217), in 1991 government refused to allow the publication of INSET materials developed by a £21 million language curriculum development project (the Language In the National Curriculum (LINC) Project), objecting, among other things, to a chapter on multilingualism (Abrams, 1991) and asking, in the words of the minister of state:

> *Why ... so much prominence [is] given to exceptions rather than the norm – to dialects rather than standard English, for example ... Of course language is a living force, but our central concern must be the business of teaching children how to use their language **correctly**.* (Eggar 1991)

These restrictions have been followed by initiatives designed to draw teacher education away from universities and colleges (Rampton, 1995c, pp251–252), culminating most recently in the idea of a national curriculum for teacher education.

Up to a point, growing academic disaffection with serving the central state in an advisory capacity can be explained in terms of the then Conservative government's ideological character. (At the time of revising this paper, the newly elected Labour Government has just come into office.) Even so, government still has to provide some public justification for its actions, and this raises the question of why applied linguists have not been more effective

---

3   The latest version of the modern languages curriculum now carries *no* reference to the fact that there are pupils with multilingual backgrounds, and it is backed by a stipulation that schools can only teach non-European languages if they also offer at least one of the eight working languages of the European Community.

in winning popular support? Have there been inadequacies in the case made by academics and language professionals (Carter, 1992, p19)?

WEAKNESSES IN THE ARGUMENTS OF ACADEMICS IN THE 1980s

This is an issue addressed at length in Cameron (1995), and interpreting the back-to-basics call for grammar as a moral panic with deep symbolic resonances in people's anxieties about moral and social order, she argues that the ineffectuality of linguists has stemmed from their exclusive commitment to facts and reason and from their failure to argue about values. An alternative view would be, however, that the late 1980s and 1990s have seen applied linguists drawing much closer to the indigenous English tradition of language in education, where political commitments have been much more explicit, and that academic views have been dismissed partly because they have actually been *too* ideological, not managing to maintain *enough* of a clear distinction between facts and values (Carter, 1990, pp18–19; Rampton, 1995c, pp236–237, 240–241, 250–251).

Adequately diagnosing the source of the difficulties between academy and government is obviously a highly complex task well beyond the scope of this review, as is a discussion of the relationship between fact and value in public debate (though cf Cameron, 1995, pp223–228; Rampton, 1995c, pp249–250). But looking back with the benefit of hindsight at research on multilingualism in the 1980s, there were at least three general characteristics which weakened the persuasive power of those opposing the back-to-monolingual-basics lobby.

First, for a number of reasons, including the lack of central support and a longstanding lack of both standardisation and face validity in English as a Second Languate (ESL) assessment (CRE, 1986; OFSTED, 1994; Leung, 1995), there was (and still is) a major scarcity of any research in England on the effectiveness of different language pedagogies that was capable of convincing the sceptical outsider[4] (cf Rampton, 1988). Classroom processes were certainly investigated in a number of local and national language curriculum development projects in the 1980s (e.g. Norman, ed, 1992), and these often entailed teacher action research with a strong interest in multilingualism (Levine, ed, 1990; Bourne, 1989, p113). Through first-hand

---

4　There was important research on bilingual education in England in the late 1970s but this was never followed up. See Fitzpatrick, 1987.

experience, they enabled participants to assess the value of different kinds of language pedagogy; they were the form of educational innovation most likely to have an immediate impact on pupils; they moved towards an ideal of flexible multilingual pedagogy hospitable to the diversity of pupils' language backgrounds and proficiencies (Bourne, 1989, pp63–64); and the reports they provided could be persuasive for colleagues. But, as with a great deal of action research, they did not produce claims supported by a body of evidence – a body of publicly recognisable 'facts' – that was capable of withstanding the scrutiny of unsympathetic outsiders,[5] and beyond their articulation within the broad tenets of 'good practice', loosely drawing in ideas from first language acquisition, process writing, communicative methodology and collaborative teaching (CRE, 1986, Appendix 7; Bourne, 1989, pp63–64), they were not elaborated into a theoretical framework capable of systematic comparative examination (Brumfit, 1985, p52; 1995, p39). Measures of educational attainment have shown that contrary to what has often been assumed, certain minority ethnic groups were actually doing better than whites in education (Jones, 1993; Gillborn and Gipps, 1996), but there has been hardly any research capable of indicating whether or not this was the result of special curriculum provision, and it would be just as possible to claim most of the success for a policy of unstructured assimilation (see, however, Gillborn and Gipps, 1996, pp25–28).

A second difficulty lay in the fact that during this period, the major inquiries into multilingualism were overwhelmingly oriented to the data of self-report rather than to empirical evidence of multilingual practice in or out of school. There were major surveys over this period that played a key role in establishing the fact and degree of England's multilingualism, and apart from its practical convenience in survey research, the principle of self-report recognised the importance of creating space for the perspectives of minority language users themselves (Rosen and Burgess, 1980, p43; LMP, 1985; Alladina and Edwards, 1991, p11). But describing one's own multilingualism

---

5 More generally, this is quite often a problem with generalisation in ethnography. Ethnography has held quite an exalted position in the action research tradition, but its persuasive power (and hence its strategic potential in e.g. debates about policy and practice) relies on interested and sympathetic readers who are willing and able to connect imaginatively and translate the ethnographic description into contexts they are themselves familiar with (cf Nunan, 1992, pp69–70). Where readers start out truculent or suspicious, the claims made in ethnography may prove much less compelling than the claims presented in e.g. survey research, where the reader's imaginative engagement is less important and where generalisations are much more extensively produced by the researchers on their own.

is not necessarily easy: spontaneous interaction can often involve subtle mixings and renegotiations of identity that can be hard to reflect on explicitly, that one may want not to admit to, and that short descriptive labels inevitably reify and treat simplistically (cf Roberts, Davies and Jupp, 1992; Hewitt, 1986, pp7–8). Although it provides no guarantee against it, research on the data of spoken interaction can be crucial in moderating these oversimplifications, and its scarcity and its absence from public discussion permitted the development of a vision of multilingualism in which languages, cultures and communities were clearly bounded, relatively homogeneous, and principally preoccupied either with maintaining or losing their ethnic distinctiveness (cf Harris, 1997).

Committee reports formed another major strand of inquiry during this period (DES, 1981; 1985; 1989), but since they are in principle much more geared to a fair and conciliatory representation of lay, professional and expert opinion than to the commissioning of new research, they did little to challenge this vision, and in the end, the prevailing ideas about ethnicity were ill-equipped to question the cultural essentialism that legitimated the policy of Welsh being promoted by the Welsh state, English by the English state, and minority languages being largely left to the minority communities.[6]

Admittedly, there was one strand of research which did draw attention to the minority language forms emerging in urban vernacular English and to new mixed cultures that challenged the very basis of official ethnic classification. But the impact of this work was inhibited by a third characteristic of research in the 1980s. This third characteristic was quite a marked tendency to address issues relating to Caribbean language separately from other minority languages. From the outset, research on Creoles in England was as much committed to the analysis of actual language data as to the data of self-report, outside school as well as in, and in attempting to demonstrate the systematicity and cultural authenticity of the speech of pupils of Caribbean descent, discussions of Creole were linked with attempts to establish a more tolerant approach to white non-standard dialects (Trudgill, 1975; Edwards, 1979). Youngsters of African Caribbean descent were situated in a wider context of English vernacular youth culture, and pedagogically, the central concern was (a) with providing recognition in the mainstream English curriculum for the symbolic and expressive values associated with Creole, and (b) with

---

6   In fact, government itself now admits that, for administrative purposes, there are serious weaknesses in its ethnic categories (DFE, 1995c; Harris (forthcoming)), though this admission involves no concessions in its approach to education through two languages.

developing in pupils a bidialectal capacity to use standard English as and when appropriate (DES, 1981; Sutcliffe, 1982).

This contrasted with the approach to pupils whose home languages were more obviously different from English. Here the debate was framed much more in terms of the supposedly competing demands of school, home and adult community, and it was assumed that the minority language was the important vehicle for cultural identity (in line with the ethnic essentialism identified above), that English was just an instrumental tool of learning, and that the principal task was a structured induction into the patterns of standard English grammar and discourse (e.g. DES, 1989, ch 10). The result of this was that when research started to demonstrate that *white* youngsters were making use of Creole forms, that inherited ethnicities were being destabilised and that new mixed ethnolinguistic identities were emerging (Hewitt, 1986; 1989; 1992; Gilroy, 1987; Gilroy and Lawrence, 1988), the impact on official discourse about non-Caribbean minorities was limited. The discursive differentiation of African Caribbean from other minority pupils obscured the new alignments developing in the complex interaction of locality, class, generation, gender and ethnicity in English cities, and in the official view, other minorities continued to be viewed as politely treated but rather peripheral strangers until the time that they assimilated.[7]

So far then, we have referred to current educational policy on multilingualism, to strained relations between government and academics, and to some significant weaknesses in research in the 1980s. How have these influenced research in the 1990s? What new approaches and themes have developed? What gaps and weaknesses remain?

RESEARCH ON MULTILINGUALISM IN THE 1990s

For several reasons, the 1990s have seen a clear methodological shift towards ethnography and case-study research. In part, this has been motivated by a sense of the explanatory limits of the survey research that dominated the 1980s (Nicholas, 1994; Martin-Jones, 1991; McGregor and Li Wei, 1991), and by a

---

7 Official discourse continued saying that minority languages at school could 'only be of relevance to mother tongue speakers of languages other than English' (DES, 1985, pp406–407), and that the principal task of school was to overcome the 'negative perceptions of the "strangeness" of ethnic minority groups, which lie at the roots of racism' (DES, 1985, pp406–407), and to instil ' "civilised respect" for other languages' (DES, 1989, para 10.12).

desire to find out what actually happens inside multilingual settings (Martin-Jones, 1995, p90). This has been supported by the growth of interest in dialogic interaction and in social constructionism across the social sciences (e.g. Donald and Rattansi, eds, 1992; Rampton, 1997), to the extent that after 'deficit', 'difference' and 'domination' (cf Reid, 1990), 'discourse' is now emerging as a fourth orientation to linguistic and cultural diversity in education (see Table 1). And the shift can also be seen as a move away from the increasingly constrained and ill-funded arena of government-sponsored policy research towards a more congenial involvement with local, regional and professional groups and organisations where an active commitment to multilingualism remains (see, for example, contributions to the professional journals *English in Education, Language Matters, Language Issues, The English and Media Magazine* and *NALDIC News*).

Continuing important precedents set in the 1980s (and enhanced by the ethnographic turn), there is also a growing interest in collaborative research, sometimes leading to academics co-publishing with the practitioners and others acting as informants (e.g. Roberts, Davies and Jupp, 1992; Hamilton, Barton and Ivanič, eds, 1994; Verma, Corrigan and Firth, eds, 1995; Kenner, Wells and Williams, 1996; Clegg, ed, 1996; Cameron, Moon and Bygate, 1996; for methodological discussion, cf Cameron et al, 1992; Nicholas, 1994).

Substantively, the 1990s have seen a major increase in the description of everyday interaction. Much more attention is now being given to the linguistic and cultural knowledge and practices operating in multilingual social networks, and this is often linked to a concern with the ideological character of the dominant institutional theories, policies or practices that multilinguals regularly engage with. In fact, it is possible to bring a great deal of the recent research together under the following five broad thematic headings.

Though still small in comparison with work in North America, a significant body of research focuses on *interaction styles* – on the different pragmatic, interactional and social expectations and practices involved in trying to manage and make sense of encounters between people with different ethnolinguistic backgrounds. Some of this focuses on the discourse strategies used in trying to achieve understanding between minority and majority adults in work and bureaucratic settings (Roberts, Davies and Jupp, 1992; Bremer et al, 1996; Roberts and Sarangi; 1995); some focuses on pupil-teacher interaction, addressing issues of teacher effectiveness and stereotyping (Roberts et al, 1992, 1995; Biggs and Edwards, 1991; Ogilvy et al, 1992; Thompson, 1994); while some presents an important challenge to dominant

Table 1 Four orientations to cultural diversity in education

Interpretation of linguistic diversity	Diversity as deficit	Diversity as difference	Not diversity, domination	Domination & diversity as discourse
View of culture	Culture as elite canon/standard	Cultures as sets of values, beliefs & behaviours	Culture as reflection of socio-economic relations	Culture as processes of dialogical, negotiated sense-making
Approach to language	Prescriptivism: norms and standards to be followed	Descriptivism: system & authenticity of non-standard forms	Determinism: language either subordinate to, or a distraction from, structures of political & economic domination	Social constructivism: reality extensively constructed through institutional discourse and discursive interaction
View of research	Neutral, objective, informative	Neutral, objective, advocate	Part of apparatus of hegemony; scientific imperialism	Either regime of truth/ discipline, or empowering, giving voice to subjugated knowledges
Descriptive concerns/ focus	The canon. The Other lacks culture & knowledge. 'Them' at fault	The Other's autonomy & integrity. Cultures incommensurable: 'we' can't say 'them' at fault	Self & Other in larger system. Capitalist oppression. Resistance through the unity of oppressed groups	Global & national discourses, diaspora & multi-local sites. 'Them' resists, or sees things differently
Philosophical emphasis	Superiority of own (ethnocentricity)	Relativism	Power	Power, difference & contingency
Assumption about the world	Universals & grand narratives: development/modernisation/ global markets	Grand narratives maybe, but celebration of the sub-plots	Universals and grand narratives: imperialism/ dependency	Universals and grand narratives disclaimed
Intervention strategy	Assimilation	Multiculturalism	Anti-racism/anti-imperialism	Anti-essentialism
Typical politics	Conservatism	Liberal pluralism	Marxism	Post-modernism

educational conceptions of literacy acquisition by examining the different conceptions of reading and learning involved pupil-teacher interaction in the early years at school (Gregory 1990, 1993a, 1993b, 1994).

This last body of work overlaps to some extent with newly emerging and hitherto broadly ethnographic work on *multilingual literacies,* which seeks to document diversity, conflict, change and the sociocultural embedding of traditions of literacy lying outside the monolingual standard English model dominant at school (Saxena, 1994; Bhatt et al, 1994; Hamilton et al, eds, 1994; Kushari Dyson, 1994; Morris and Nwenmely, 1994; Schwab, 1994; Nwenmely, 1995; Baynham, 1995 (which also includes some interaction analysis)).

Codeswitching constitutes a third major topic, addressed in infant school settings (Moffat, 1991; Moffat and Milroy, 1992; Martin-Jones, 1995; Martin-Jones and Saxena, 1995, 1996), in family settings (Li Wei, 1994, 1995; Li Wei and Milroy, 1995; Milroy and Li Wei, 1995; Huang and Milroy, 1995; Sebba, 1993, ch 6) and in informal adolescent recreation (Sebba, 1993).

This work leads towards a view of ethnic identity as a motile and situated interactional production, and the challenge to ethnic essentialism is taken further in research on *language crossing,* which describes the ways in which adolescents in multiracial peergroups make use of each other's minority languages (Hewitt, 1986, 1992; Rampton, 1991b, 1995a, 1995b, 1996a, 1996b; Back, 1995, 1996).

In crossing, the relationship between ethnicity and language becomes the focus of heightened attention and, as such, it represents an informal vernacular manifestation of *language awareness,* another topic receiving a significant degree of attention. As a curriculum objective, language awareness (or 'knowledge about language') has been advocated as having special value in multiracial settings for a number of years (Hawkins, 1992) and it is encouraged in part by researchers' growing commitment to working collaboratively with informants (Cameron et al, 1992, chs 2 and 5). In line with Cox's recognition that in some respects pupils know more about language than their teachers (DES, 1989, para 6.11), work in this area blurs the distinction between research and pedagogy (Harris et al, 1990; Clarke and Smith, 1992; Sayers, 1992; Pardoe, 1994), and there has also been critical discussion of ideological trajectory of language awareness work in multilingual contexts (Bhatt and Martin-Jones, 1992; Parke, 1993; Rampton, 1995a, ch 13.5).

What can be said of the strengths and weakness of this research effort?

RESEARCH ON MULTILINGUALISM IN THE 1990s: SOME EVALUATIVE COMMENTS

Although there is little evidence of research on multilingualism having a much wider impact on the understanding of ethnic relations outside education (in, for example, sociology or cultural studies (cf Harris, 1996)), some coherence and scope for productive discussion across these projects derives from quite a high level of methodological consensus – in different combinations across and within the institutional sites conducting this research, there is a quite widely shared orientation to the ethnography of communication, interactional socio-linguistics, conversation analysis and/or critical discourse analysis, and a number of locally based research groups are also being consolidated.

In view of the diverse audiences and therefore different standards addressed – professionals, policy-makers, students, informants, academics in education, applied or sociolinguistics – it is hard to make general statements about the quality of recent research. Where the discourse analysis in some amounts at best to a few 'insightful observations', in others it is comprehensive, robust and innovative. Similarly, while the educational critique may be topical, profound and incisive in some, in others it can be tokenistic or banal. What can perhaps be said is that as yet, research seldom achieves high quality in both areas (a relatively rare example being Martin-Jones and Saxena's 1996 work on the way in which bilingual support policies are realised in classroom interaction).

Alladina and Edwards' impressive two-volume collection on multi-lingualism in the British Isles makes clear the massive amount of research that still remains to be done (1991, p11), but within the narrower educational brief set within this review, there are a number of areas in fairly urgent need of further research.

There is as yet comparatively little research on multilingualism in the later years of compulsory education (ages 11–16), when the tension between the values and priorities of formal education and vernacular culture is sharpest (a great deal of work focuses on 4–10 year olds and a significant amount looks at education post-16). Urban youth culture is a crucial site in the formation of new mixed ethnic identities (Gilroy, 1987), but as already suggested above, research has either neglected their influence in educational settings, or concentrated too exclusively on their development among youngsters of African Caribbean descent (cf Rampton, 1995a; Harris, 1996). As well as in language crossing, these processes are reflected in the very widespread emergence of a relatively unconscious 'multiracial urban vernacular', but so far, apart from some theoretical and educational commentary from Hewitt (1986, 1989, 1992) and Harris (1995, 1997), the systematic empirical analysis of these speech varieties has yet to be undertaken by variationist sociolinguists interested in urban dialects and language change (though Sebba, 1993, gives an important lead).

The absence of reliable educational assessment of the performance and abilities of pupils learning English as an additional language remains as before (SCAA, 1996, pp30–31); there was no language question in the 1991 census; and there continue to be restrictions on the publication of the limited policy research that government has funded (e.g. Leung, 1995). There is growing interest in genre and functional grammar, but research in England has as yet done little to provide detailed and systematic analyses of the linguistic and discursive demands of the curriculum. Britain is still only in the early stages of debate about the contribution that linguistic analysis might make to the 'good practice' approach to teaching English as an additional language that dominated the 1980s, with its emphasis on classroom organisation and on rather general communicative processes (Barrs, 1991/92; Leung and Franson, 1991; Leung, 1993a, 1993b, 1996a, 1996b, 1997; Cameron, Moon and Bygate, 1996).

Nearly all of the ethnolinguistic research in England focuses on processes of change and contact with the dominant language and cultures, and there is hardly any direct empirical research which stresses the reproduction of minority language tradition (cf Edwards and Katbamna, 1988; Li Wei, 1993; for critical remarks on 'hybridity talk' in cultural studies, see also Sharma, 1996, pp20–21, 29). There is relatively little empirical research on how minority languages are preserved or respected in the National Curriculum (apart from Martin-Jones and Saxena, 1995, 1996; and Verma, Corrigan and Firth, 1995); there is a major dearth of research on minority language teaching in community classes outside the state sector; and it is very difficult to find any direct observational research on early language socialisation of minority children at home.

At the same time, research on multilingualism has yet to engage properly with the debates about globalisation and contemporary culture. The people it studies are often at the front line of these experiences, operating everyday at the intersection of neighbourhood and nation state, diaspora and global markets. Applied linguistic research certainly describes many of the practices that this entails, and it has developed a set of descriptive terms that are potentially very useful (Hannerz, 1989; Hewitt, 1995). But it has yet to bring its resources to bear on the wider theorisation of late modernity.

ACKNOWLEDGEMENTS

An earlier version of this review has appeared in the *Annual Review of Applied Linguistics* 17 (1997), pp224–241. We would like to thank Marilyn Martin-Jones for some very useful references.

REFERENCES

Abrams F (1991) 'Accents and dialects still unmentionable subjects', *Times Educational Supplement,* 14 June

Alladina S and Edwards V (1991) *Multilingualism in the British Isles,* Vols 1 & 2, London: Longman

Back L (1995) ' "X amount of Sat Siri Akal!"': Apache Indian, Reggae music, and intermezzo culture', in A Aalund and R Granqvist (eds) *Negotiating Identities,* Amsterdam: Rodopi

Back L (1996) *New Ethnicities and Urban Culture,* London: UCL Press

Baker C (1993) *Key Issues in Bilingualism and Bilingual Education,* Clevedon: Multilingual Matters

Baker C (1993) *Foundations of Bilingual Education and Bilingualism,* Clevedon: Multilingual Matters

Bangs J (1994) 'Funding for race equality in education: Looking to the future', *Multicultural Teaching,* 13, 1, pp7–13

Barrs M (1991/92) 'Genre theory: What's it all about?', *Language Matters,* 1, pp9–16. (Also in B Stierer and J Maybin (eds) (1994) *Language, Literacy and Learning in Educational Practice,* Clevedon: Multilingual Matters, pp248–257)

Baynham M (1995) *Literacy Practices,* London: Longman

Bhatt A, Barton D and Martin-Jones M (1994) *Gujarati Literacies in East Africa and Leicester: Changes in Social Identities and Multilingual Practices,* Centre for Language in Social Life Working Papers Series 56, University of Lancaster

Bhatt A and Martin-Jones M (1992) 'Whose resource? Minority languages, bilingual learners and language awareness', in N Fairclough (ed) *Critical Language Awareness,* London: Longman, pp285–302

Biggs N and Edwards V (1991) ' "I treat them all the same": Teacher-pupil talk in multiethnic classrooms', *Language and Education,* 5, 3, pp103–115. (Also in D Graddol, J Maybin and B Stierer (eds) *Researching Language and Literacy in Social Context,* Clevedon: Multilingual Matters, pp82–99)

Bourne J (1989) *Moving into the Mainstream,* Windsor: NFER/Nelson

Bremer K, Roberts C, Vasseur M-T, Simonot M and Broeder P (1996) *Achieving Understanding: Discourse in Intercultural Encounters,* London: Longman

Brumfit C (1985) *Language and Literature Teaching: From Practice to Principle,* Oxford: Pergamon

Brumfit C (1995) 'Teacher professionalism and research', in G Cook and B Seidlhofer (eds) *Principle and Practice in Applied Linguistics,* Oxford: Oxford University Press, pp27–42

Brumfit C (ed) (1995) *Language Education in the National Curriculum,* Oxford: Blackwell

Cameron D (1995) *Verbal Hygiene,* London: Routledge

Cameron D and Bourne J (1988) 'No common ground: Kingman, grammar and the nation', *Language and Education,* 2,3, pp147–160

Cameron D, Frazer E, Harvey P, Rampton B and Richardson K (1992) *Researching Language: Issues of Power and Method,* London: Routledge

Cameron L, Moon J and Bygate M (1996) 'Language development of bilingual pupils in the mainstream: How do pupils and teachers use language?', *Language and Education,* 10, 4, pp221–236

Carter R (ed) (1990) *Knowledge about Language,* London: Hodder & Stoughton

Carter R (1992) 'LINC: The final chapter?', *BAAL Newsletter,* 35, pp10–16

Clarke P and Smith N (1992) 'Initial steps towards critical practice in primary schools', in N Fairclough (ed) *Critical Language Awareness,* London: Longman, pp238–255

Clegg J (ed) (1996) *Mainstreaming ESL: Case Studies in Integrating ESL Students into the Mainstream Curriculum,* Clevedon: Multilingual Matters

Commission for Racial Equality (CRE) (1986) *Teaching English as a Second Language. Report of a Formal Investigation in Calderdale Local Education Authority,* London: CRE

Cox B (1992) *The Great Betrayal,* London: Chapmans

Cox B (1995) *Cox on the Battle for the English Curriculum,* London: Hodder & Stoughton

Department of Education and Science (DES) (1981) *West Indian Children in our Schools. Interim Report of the Committee of Inquiry into the Education of Children from Ethnic Minority Groups,* London: HMSO

Department of Education and Science (DES) (1985) *Education for All. The Report of the Committee of Inquiry into the Education of Children from Ethnic Minority Groups,* London: HMSO

Department of Education and Science (DES) (1989) *English for Ages 5 to 16,* London: HMSO. (Also in B Cox (1991) *Cox on Cox: An English Curriculum for the 1990s,* London: Hodder & Stoughton)

Department for Education (DFE) (1995a) *English in the National Curriculum,* London: HMSO

Department for Education (DFE) (1995b) *Modern Foreign Languages in the National Curriculum,* London: HMSO

Department for Education (DFE) (1995c) *Ethnic Monitoring of School Pupils: A Consultation Paper,* London: DFE

Donald J and Rattansi A (eds) (1992) *'Race', Culture and Difference,* London: Sage

Edwards V (1979) *The West Indian Language Issue in British Schools,* London: RKP

Edwards V and Katbamna S (1988) 'The wedding songs of British Gujarati women', in J Coates and D Cameron (eds) *Women in their Speech Communities,* London: Longman, pp158–174

Edwards V and Redfern A (1992) *The World in a Classroom,* Clevedon: Multilingual Matters

Edwards V and Troyna B (1993) *The Educational Needs of a Multiracial Society.* CRER/ESRC Occasional Paper 9, University of Warwick

Eggar T (1991) 'Correct use of English is essential', *Times Educational Supplement,* 28 June

Fitzpatrick B (1987) *The Open Door,* Clevedon: Multilingual Matters

Garrett P, Griffiths Y, James C and Schofield P (1992) 'Differences and similarities between and within bilingual settings', *Language, Culture and Curriculum,* 5, pp99–115

Gillborn D and Gipps C (1996) *Recent Research on the Achievement of Ethnic Minority Pupils,* London: HMSO

Gilroy P (1987) *There Ain't No Black in the Union Jack,* London: Hutchinson

Gilroy P and Lawrence E (1988) 'Two-tone Britain: White and black youth and the politics of anti-racism', in P Cohen and H Bains (eds) *Multiracist Britain,* Basingstoke: Macmillan, pp121–155

Gregory E (1990) 'Negotiation as a criterial factor in learning to read in a second language', *Language and Education,* 4, 2, pp103115. (Also in D Graddol, J Maybin and B Stierer (eds) *Researching Language and Literacy in Social Context,* Clevedon: Multilingual Matters, pp49–61)

Gregory E (1993a) 'Sweet and sour: Learning to read in a British and Chinese school', *English in Education,* 27, 3, pp53–59

Gregory E (1993b) 'What counts as reading in the infant classroom?' *British Journal of Educational Psychology,* June

Gregory E (1994) 'Cultural assumptions and early years' pedagogy: The effect of the home culture on minority children's interpretations of reading in school', *Language, Culture and Curriculum,* 7, 2, pp111–124

Hamilton M, Barton D and Ivanič R (eds) (1994) *Worlds of Literacy,* Clevedon: Multilingual Matters

Hannerz U (1989) 'Culture between center and periphery: Towards a macro-anthropology', *Ethnos,* 54, 3&4, pp200–216

Harris R (1995) 'Disappearing language: Fragments and fractures between speech and writing', in J Mace (ed) *Literacy, Language and Community Publishing,* Clevedon: Multilingual Matters

Harris R (1996) 'Openings, absences and omissions: Aspects of the treatment of 'race', culture and ethnicity within British cultural studies', *Cultural Studies,* 10

Harris R (forthcoming) 'Romantic bilingualism: Time for a change?' in C Cable and C Leung (eds) *English as an Additional Language: Changing Perspectives,* Watford: National Association for Teachers of English (NATE)/ National Association for Language Development in the Curriculum (NALDIC)

Harris R, Schwab I, Whitman L et al (1990) *Language and Power,* London: HBJ/Harper Collins

Hawkins E (1992) 'Awareness of language/knowledge about language in the curriculum in England and Wales: An historical note on twenty years of curricular debate', *Language Awareness,* 1, 1, pp5–17

Hewitt R (1986) *White Talk, Black Talk,* Cambridge: Cambridge University Press

Hewitt R (1989) 'Creole in the classroom: Political grammars and educational vocabularies', in R Grillo (ed) *Social Anthropology and the Politics of Language,* Sociological Monograph 36, London: Routledge, pp126–144

Hewitt R (1992) 'Language, youth and the destabilisation of ethnicity', in C Palmgren, K Lövgren and G Bolin (eds) *Ethnicity in Youth Culture,* Stockholm: Youth Culture at Stockholm University, pp27–41

Hewitt R (1995) 'The umbrella and the sewing machine: Transculturalism and the definition of Surrealism', in A Aalund, and R Granqvist (eds) *Negotiating Identities,* Amsterdam: Rodopi, pp91–104

Huang G W and Milroy L (1995) 'Language preference and structures of codeswitching', in D Graddol and S Thomas (eds) *Language in a Changing Europe,* Clevedon: BAAL/ Multilingual Matters, pp35–46

Jones T (1993) *Britain's Ethnic Minorities,* London: Policy Studies Institute

Kenner C, Wells K and Williams H (1996) 'Assessing a bilingual child's talk in different classroom contexts', in N Hall (ed) *Listening to Children Talking,* London: Hodder, pp196–218

Kushari Dyson K (1994) 'Forging a bilingual identity: A writer's testimony', in P Burton, K K Dyson and S Ardener (eds) *Bilingual Women: Anthropological Approaches to Second Language Use,* Oxford: Berg. pp170–185

Leung C (1993a) 'The coming crisis of ESL in the National Curriculum', *British Association for Applied Linguistics Newsletter,* 45, pp27–32

Leung C (1993b) 'National Curriculum ESL in primary education in England: A classroom study', *Language and Education,* 7, .3, pp163–180

Leung C (1995) *English as an Additional/Second Language (EAL/ESL) Stages/Levels.* Consultant Report to Schools Curriculum and Assessment Authority, London

Leung C (1996a) 'Content, context and language', in T Cline and N Frederickson (eds) *Curriculum Related Assessment, Cummins and Bilingual Children,* Clevedon: Multilingual Matters, pp26–40

Leung C (1996b) 'Second-language learning and first-language pedagogical norms: A need for development in the National Curriculum', in F W Spliethoff (ed) *Second Language Acquisition in Europe: Proceedings of the International Conference on Second Language Acquisition in Secondary Education,* 'S-Hertogenboscho: KPC, pp153–162

Leung C (1997) 'Language content and learning process in curiculum tasks', in C Cable and C Leung (eds) *English as an Additional Language: Changing Perspectives,* Watford: National Association for Language Development in the Curriculum (NALDIC)

Leung C and Franson C (1991) 'English as a second language in the National Curriculum', in P Meara and A Ryan (eds) *Language and Nation,* Clevedon: British Association for Applied Linguistics/Multilingual Matters, pp117–125

Levine J (ed) (1990) *Bilingual Learners and the Mainstream Curriculum,* Lewes: Falmer Press

Linguistic Minorities Project (LMP) (1985) *The Other Languages of England,* London: RKP

Li Wei (1993) 'Mother-tongue maintenance in a Chinese community school in Newcastle: Developing a social network perspective', *Language and Education,* 7, 3, pp119–215

Li Wei (1994) *Three Generations, Two Languages, One Family: Language Choice and Language Shift in a Chinese Community in Britain,* Clevedon: Multilingual Matters

Li Wei (1995) 'Codeswitching, preference marking and politeness in bilingual cross-generational talk', *Journal of Multilingual and Multicultural Development,* 16, 3, pp197–214

Li Wei and Milroy L (1995) 'Conversational code-switching in a Chinese community in Britain: A sequential analysis', *Journal of Pragmatics,* 23, pp281–299

Li Wei, Milroy L and Pong S (1992) 'A two-step sociolinguistic analysis of code-switching and language choice', *International Journal of Applied Linguistics,* 1, pp63–86

Martin-Jones M (1991) 'Sociolinguistic surveys as a source of evidence in the study of bilingualism: A critical assessment of survey work conducted among linguistic minorities in three British cities', *International Journal of the Sociology of Language,* 90, pp37–55

Martin-Jones M (1995) 'Codeswitching in the classroom: Two decades of research', in L Milroy and P Muysken (eds) *One Speaker, Two Languages,* Cambridge: Cambridge University Press, pp90–111

Martin-Jones M and Saxena M (1995) 'Supporting or containing bilingualism? Policies, power asymetries, and pedagogic practices in mainstream primary classrooms', in J Tollefson (ed) Power and Inequality in Language Education, Cambridge: Cambridge University Press, pp73–90

Martin-Jones M. and Saxena M (1996) 'Turn-taking, power asymmetries, and the positioning of bilingual participants in classroom discourse', *Linguistics and Education*, 8, pp105–123

McGregor G and Li Wei (1991) 'Chinese or English? Language choice among Chinese students in Newcastle upon Tyne', *Journal of Multilingual and Multicultural Development*, 12, 6, pp493–510

Milroy L and Li Wei (1995) 'A social network approach to code-switching: The example of a bilingual community in Britain', in L Milroy and P Muysken (eds) *One Speaker, Two Languages: Cross-Disciplinary Perspectives on Code-Switching*, Cambridge: Cambridge University Press, pp136–157

Milroy L, Li Wei and Moffat S (1991) 'Discourse patterns and fieldwork strategies in urban settings', *Journal of Multilingual and Multicultural Development*, 12, 4, pp287–300

Moffat S (1991) 'Becoming bilingual in the classroom: Code-choice in school', *Language and Education*, 5, 1, pp55–71

Moffat S and Milroy L (1992) 'Panjabi/English language alternation in the early school years', *Multilingua*, 11, 4, pp355–385

Morris C and Nwenmely H (1994) 'The Kweyol Language and Literacy Project', in Hamilton et al (eds) *Worlds of Literacy*, Clevedon: Multilingual Matters, pp81–94

Nicholas J (1994) *Language Diversity Surveys as Agents of Change*, Clevedon: Multilingual Matters

Norman K (1992) *Thinking Voices: The Work of the National Oracy Project*, London: Hodder & Stoughton

Nunan D (1992) *Research Methods in Language Learning*, Cambridge: Cambridge University Press

Nwenmely H (1995) *Language Reclamation: French-Creole Language Teaching in the UK and the Caribbean*, Clevedon: Multilingual Matters

Ogilvy C, Boath E, Cheyne W, Jahoda G and Schaffer H (1992) 'Staff-child interaction styles in multi-ethnic nursery schools', *British Journal of Development Psychology*, 10, pp85–97

OFSTED (Office for Standards in Education) (1994) *Educational Support for Minority Ethnic Communities*, London: OFSTED (Reference: 130/94/NS)

Pardoe S (1994) 'Writing in another culture: The value of students' KAP in writing pedagogy', in D Graddol and J Swann (eds) *Evaluating Language*, Clevedon: British Association for Applied Linguistics/Multilingual Matters, pp37–51

Parke T (1993) 'Bilingualism and language awareness in young children', *Language Awareness*, 2, 2, pp77–83

Peak S and Fisher P (1996) *The Media Guide*, London: Fourth Estate

Pettigrew M (1992) 'Government regulation of applied research: Contracts and conditions', *BAAL Newsletter*, 42, pp4–7

Rampton B (1988) 'A non-educational view of ESL in Britain', *Journal of Multilingual and Multicultural Development*, 9, 6, pp503–529

Rampton B (1991a) 'Language education in policy and peer group', *Language and Education*, 5, 3, pp189–207

Rampton B (1991b) 'Interracial Panjabi in a multiracial British peergroup', *Language in Society*, 20, pp391–422

Rampton B (1995a) *Crossing: Language and Ethnicity among Adolescents*, London Longman

Rampton B (1995b) 'Language crossing and the problematisation of ethnicity and socialisation', *Pragmatics*, 5, 4, pp485–513

Rampton B (1995c) 'Politics and change in research in applied linguistics', *Applied Linguistics*, 16, 2, pp233–256

Rampton B (1996a) 'Youth, race and resistance: A sociolinguistic perspective', *Linguistics and Education*, 8, pp159–173

Rampton B (1996b) 'Language crossing, new ethnicities and school,. *English in Education*, 30, 2, pp14–26

Rampton B (1997) 'Retuning in Applied Linguistics', Special issue of International *Journal of Applied Linguistics* (entitled 'Retuning in Applied Linguistics?') 7, 1

Reid E (1985) 'Bilingual communities: England/National profiles and verbal repertoires', *Annual Review of Applied Linguistics*, 6, pp205–219

Reid E (1990) 'Culture and language: Teaching ESL in England', in B Harrison (ed) *Culture and the Language Classroom*, London: Modern English Publication and the British Council, pp66–75

Roberts C, Davies E and Jupp T (1992) *Language and Discrimination*, London: Longman

Roberts C, Garnett C, Kapoor S and Sarangi S (1992) *Quality in Teaching and Learning*, London: Department of Employment

Roberts C, Garnett C, Kapoor S and Sarangi S. (1995) ' "Tuning in" in Further Education multicultural classrooms', *Language Issues*, 6, 2, pp15–19

Roberts C and Sarangi S (1995) ' "But are they one of us?": Managing and evaluating identities in work-related contexts', *Multilingua*, 14, 4, pp363–390

Rosen H and Burgess T (1980) *The Languages and Dialects of London Schoolchildren*, London: Ward Lock

Saxena M (1994) 'Literacy among the Panjabis in Southall (Britain)', in Hamilton et al (eds) pp195–214. (Also in J Maybin (ed) *Language and Literacy in Social Practice*, Clevedon: Multilingual Matters, pp96–116)

Sayers P (1992) 'Making it work – communication skills training at a black housing association', in N Fairclough (ed) *Critical Language Awareness*, London: Longman, pp93–116

SCAA (School Curriculum and Assessment Authority) (1996) *Teaching and Learning English as an Additional Language: New Perspectives*. SCAA Discussions Papers No. 5,. London: SCAA

Schwab I (1994) 'Literacy, language variety and identity', in Hamilton et al (eds) pp134–142

Sebba M (1993) *London Jamaican,* London: Longman

Sharma A (1996) 'Sounds Oriental: The (im)possibility of theorising Asian musical cultures', in S Sharma, J Hutnyk and A Sharma (eds) *Dis-Orienting Rhythms: The Politics of the New Asian Dance Music,* London: Zed Books, pp15–31

Stubbs M (1991) 'Educational language planning in England and Wales: Multicultural rhetoric and assimilationist assumptions', in F Coulmas (ed) *Language Policy for the European Community: Prospects and Quandaries,* Berlin: Mouton de Gruyter. (Also in J Maybin (ed) (1994) *Language and Literacy in Social Practice,* Clevedon: Multilingual Matters, pp193–214)

Sutcliffe D (1982) *British Black English,* Oxford: Blackwell

Tate N (1996) 'Curriculum, culture and society'. Conference speech, 7 February. (Available from SCAA Publications, PO Box 235, Hayes, Middlesex UB3 1HF, England)

Taylor M and Hegarty S (1985) *The Best of Both Worlds? A Review of Research into the Education of Pupils of South Asian Origin,* Windsor: NFER-Nelson

Thompson L (1994) 'The Cleveland Project: A study of bilingual children in a nursery school, *Journal of Multilingual and Multicultural Development,* 15, 2&3, pp253–268

Trudgill P (1975) *Accent, Dialect and the School,* London: Edward Arnold.

Verma M, Corrigan K and Firth S (1995) 'Death by education: The plight of community languages in Britain, *Language Issues,* 7, 1, pp5–12

Verma M, Corrigan K and Firth S (eds) (1995) *Working with Bilingual Children,* Clevedon: Multilingual Matters

Cultural and Linguistic Diversity Revisited

MOIRA INGHILLERI, University of London

THE INCOMMENSURABILITY ARGUMENT

This paper examines several key philosophical issues relevant to educational debates concerned with the relationship between culture and language. It will make reference to the familiar, even overfamiliar, developments within the English curriculum during the period of the 1960s and 1970s, returning to them yet again to excavate some of the intellectual knots and philosophical issues from that period which continue to revisit us in many aspects of debates around multiculturalism, contemporary fragmentation and language.

In recent years, concepts of culture have undergone a radical upheaval especially derived from the critique of essentialism that has been widely articulated and has been particularly telling with respect to essentialist notions of culture. Previous suppositions about unitary and clearly bounded organic cultural wholes have been widely recognised as no longer tenable. However, curiously, a constant bedfellow of essentialist notions of cultures – the idea of the incommensurability of cultures manages to survive. In this context, incommensurability refers to the argument that different cultures give rise to differing world views which cannot be evaluated or even compared because each is uniquely itself.

Within the English debates, the complex of issues about the relationship between thought, culture and language seemed to congeal around the sometimes buried but always present theme of incommensurability – which can be a matter of the capacity for understanding evident between minds as much as between cultures, and always mediated by some communicative form. The issue of incommensurability appeared in educational debates by introducing the notion of relativism – which acknowledged the diversity of cultures and languages in multi-class/cultural settings at the same time that it problematised the idea of communication across difference.

In Britain, during this period, the desire to address the needs, particularly of working and lower middle-class pupils, shifted the attention of educators and researchers to the particularities of the culture and language of these pupils. As the idea of 'different but equal' appeared in an educational climate oriented toward empowering previously silenced voices, the idea of 'commensurability' began to be perceived negatively as a search for universals through a denial of difference, or as a hegemonic practice geared towards making the views of the dominant class appear as normative. Notwithstanding the strong educational gains of that period, I want to argue that an important opportunity was missed to explore the issue of incommensurability as a means to address the deeper intellectual issues that arose in the course of the debates over language and culture, to make the question of commensurability and incommensurability the starting point and not the end of the investigation into the dynamics of cultural and linguistic diversity and change.

The issue of incommensurability, and the controversies surrounding it, strike at the heart of questions about cultural and linguistic identity and the possibility of dialogue across different interpretative or conceptual frameworks. On the one hand, it challenges the idea that common measures, sets of standards, or 'criteria of rationality' exist with which to understand and evaluate others. On the other hand, it raises the question of what happens when divergent cultures or languages do come into contact – of how, or indeed, if, it is possible to translate a set of ideas, beliefs, and values from one conceptual framework into another (see Winch, 1977; Gellner, 1982; Lukes, 1982; Geertz, 1973, 1983).

The notion of incommensurability is often taken to involve both incompatibility and incomparability of different cultural groups. The idea that the conceptual frameworks of disparate cultures or languages are incomparable, moreover, frequently carries with it the further implication that such frameworks are not mutually expressible – i.e., that there are no terms used in one culture that can be equated in meaning and reference with any terms or expressions in the other (Putnam, 1981, p114), and that, therefore, communication itself is impossible. This view also tends to presume or encourage a view of cultures or language users as integrated wholes. This notion of cultures, however, downplays distinctions between members of the same culture as well as the possibility that the distinctions between different cultures do not necessarily differ in kind from the distinctions between members of a single culture. The strong form of relativism which this view of incommensurability implies is also challengeable on the ground that it leaves unresolved the question of how individuals from different cultures/linguistic groups determine that they *are* different – or indeed the same – if not by communicating with one another.

The uptake in liberal pluralist educational discourses of the idea of cultures and languages as 'incommensurable' can be traced to the anthropologist Franz Boas. Boas maintained that cultures were integrated wholes comprised of 'almost accidental' accretions of elements – the products of the history of the people, the influence of the regions through which it passed in its migrations, and the people with whom it came into contact (Boas, quoted in Stocking, 1974, p5).

Boas' ideas on culture were taken up by his student, Ruth Benedict, whose book, *Patterns of Culture,* reiterated Boas' belief in cultures as historically constituted articulated wholes and not as biologically transmitted complexes of behaviour. In her study of three 'primitive' cultures she argued:

They are travelling along different roads in pursuit of different ends, and these ends and these means in one society cannot be judged in terms of those of another, because essentially they are incommensurable. (Benedict, 1935, p161)

INCOMMENSURABILITY AND ENGLISH EDUCATION

The theme of incommensurability found its way into debates over English education, as a number of complex ideas related to this theme were explored by educators and researchers alike. The practice of literary criticism came under particular scrutiny for its perceived bias, associated with F R Leavis, toward an appeal to a single universal framework of values and beliefs (see Mulhern, 1981; Burgess and Martin, 1990), deemed by its critics to be merely the imposition of elite culture as part of a broader hegemonic practice. It was also during this period that language and linguistics became a focus of the attention of teachers and researchers, and the familiar shift in emphasis in

English teaching away from the 'standard bearers of the cultural tradition' (teachers and texts), towards the 'producers of culture' (pupils, their talk and their writing), also took place (see Inglis, 1971; Shayer, 1972; Mathieson, 1975; Abbs, 1980; Allen, 1980; Ball, 1982). By stressing variety of language uses and relevant language situations as well as speech and linguistic variation, the renewed focus on language promised to help rid English teaching of the problems associated with literature and literary criticism, e.g., the dominance of textual analysis, the appeal to 'universal' truths and the 'inherent elitism' of the consideration and responses given to literary works, and the perceived lack of relevance of literary critical language and 'high' culture to the lives of working-class pupils.

Challenges were made to literary criticism and, in particular, F R Leavis's claim that his critical determinations regarding a literary text were derived from an 'overt' and 'collaborative' interplay of judgements. His critics underscored the implicit value system of traditional literary culture operating within such 'open' exchanges and suggested that *in the absence of a consensus of values amongst participants,* Leavis's approach and his literary critical method collapsed. As Perry Anderson wrote:

The central idea of this epistemology – the interrogative statement – demands one crucial precondition – a shared stable system of beliefs and values ... If the basic formulation and outlook of readers diverges, their experiences will be incommensurable. (Anderson, 1968, p50)

Educators in the 1960s and 1970s were not, of course, faced with a morally or culturally unified group of pupils. Nor was this a time when unity in the pedagogic context was a particular priority – for it was pupils' *diversity* that mattered. For radical educators, any calls for cultural consensus or common standards were viewed as attempts to mask the hegemonic power of the dominant culture. Within this conception, support for egalitarianism went hand in hand with support for cultural relativism as the two came to be perceived as mutually dependent. Paradoxically, though, support for the equal 'right to be heard' began to appear alongside support for the idea that cultures were different enough as to make communication unlikely.

Conservative arguments, on the other hand, sought to protect British society with a Tradition that was not treated as the rightful possession of all members. This exclusionary attitude offered no hope or desire for cultural consensus or common ground – on the contrary, it explicitly refused to consider such an aim.

Although they appeared to be occupying opposing positions, both the radical emphasis on *strengthening subordinate cultures* and the conservative tendency toward *reserving access to high culture* to an educated cultural elite, resulted in their joint commitment to the idea of incommensurability. Ultimately, the gulf between right and left in some respects was not so great. I want to argue that one of the reasons for this is that common to both radical and conservative theorisations of culture and cultural traditions was a tendency to assume their *protective* function. This almost exclusive emphasis on the protective role of culture encouraged a view of cultural traditions that, regardless of political position, *overlooked their intellectual, organic function, i.e., as the means by which individuals consciously or impassively maintain and or transform their beliefs and practices both within their own and with respect to other cultural traditions.* In downplaying the internal transformative abilities of all cultural traditions, dominant and subordinate alike, the issue of cultural change tended to be reduced on the radical side to a question of political power alone, the assumption being that both cultural change and stability were solely a by-product of class struggle. As a result, cultures came to be viewed more as ends in themselves than as ever-evolving organic structures.

But while this view of culture and communication was designed to honour cultural and linguistic *diversity,* it also eliminated the crucial issue of *meaning* from discussion – and the question of how, why or indeed, if, individuals or groups within the same or different cultural/linguistic backgrounds come to inhabit different world views. Basil Bernstein, of course, did investigate this issue and crucially and uniquely determined that the social ran through the mind. In the end, important questions remained unanswered, for example, what were the sources of cultural meanings and how interpretable were different orientations to meanings that obtained between individuals and social groups, i.e., was successful cross-cultural, cross-lingual communication probable, and, if so, how might it be accomplished?

Important and relevant insights into the role of linguistic and cultural processes in structuring experience can be found in the philosophical writings of the 18th and early 19th century German thinkers, Herder and von Humboldt, both of whom directly or indirectly informed the contributions of Boas, Sapir and Whorf. I would argue that their writings suggest a previously unrecognised intellectual point of origin for the conflicting interpretations that were present in the debates over the English curriculum and that continue to appear in educational debates over linguistic and cultural diversity. For although the conflicts that emerged in these debates are primarily perceived as warring educational and socio-political discourses, I believe they must also be interpreted as the persistence of debates over the enduring issue of incommensurability.

Herder maintained that as each individual and culture developed toward the reflection of a whole, they sought a unity in communication with one another while retaining their diversity at the same time. Despite Herder's stress on *unity* in diversity, however, his belief that human languages and cultures were always 'locally grown' makes him one of the earliest thinkers to advance a notion of linguistic and cultural relativism (Herder, 1784–91, p194), suggesting an incongruity in his thinking.

Herder's apparent 'paradoxical thesis' of unity in diversity has been recently criticised by writers who argue that although Herder claimed to recognise the possibility of cultural extension, by venerating the local and the traditional, he established a notion of relativism that could be appealed to by liberalism and fascism alike (cf Young, 1995). But while it is the case that Herder's notion of 'unity in diversity' contains a dynamic tension that appears to encourage a politically malleable form of cultural relativism, a closer examination of Herder's ideas challenges such a reading.

For Herder, individuals and cultures were constantly developing in interaction with others; they were therefore not eternally imprisoned within their languages or their cultures. At the same time that Herder emphasised the historical and linguistic character of 'world views,' he simultaneously acknowledged the existence of standards of mutuality amongst divergent linguistic and cultural groups which would in the end lead to what he termed, *Humanität,* the ultimate recognition of unity in diversity.

For Herder, *Humanität* was not achieved through the progressive unfolding of humankind toward some ultimate truth, but through the interwoven histories of individual nations and cultures. Cultural and linguistic traditions were not simply the reflection of a fixed set of accumulated practices or beliefs, they were the outcome of a continuous 'living dialogue,' a continuous process of becoming which, like the human organism, by its very nature merged the new with the old and the old with the new (Herder, 1764; and see Barnard, 1965). The themes of interaction, transformation and continuous becoming that appear repeatedly in his writings suggest that all individuals and cultures are always only partially formed; moreover, their existence is always simultaneously influencing and being influenced by a particular historical moment.

Herder's idea of history as *transformation through interpenetration* is crucial to contemporary understandings of culture and of the relationship between thought and language. The notion of 'interpenetration' must, however, be distinguished from the current organic metaphor of 'hybridity' (cf Hall, 1992; Bhabha, 1994). It is not concerned with the identification of *new* cultural crossbreeds; rather it indicates the activities of evolution and synthesis brought about through particular *existing* world views structured in and by language.

For Herder, language is the medium whereby both diversity and unity are realised. Different languages and cultures are an outward sign of different experiences shaped by local features of the environment – and consciousness is a function of the interaction of reason/language with a given experience. But the fact that individuals perceive the world from a particular cultural and linguistic perspective, does not imply the impossibility of achieving unity. It simply implies that any unity will always be partial and impermanent and that it will not be a unity of 'perfect parts' but a unity of particulars always capable of being united, at times in harmony and other times in struggle. Herder held that it was possible for the whole to appear differently for each individual and still be a whole. Herder's unity was thus not perceived as the sum total of the necessarily continuous and coherent parts of an objective world.

Rather than proposing a variety of distinct and incommensurable cultures which are 'windowless' in relation to one another and thus incapable of reinterpreting or re-evaluating themselves through others, Herder suggested that cultures and languages are conjoined in history (Herder, 1784–91, p393). This suggests their potentiality, at least, to intersect, overlap and have an effect on one another.

Like Herder, von Humboldt understood that language constructed the 'world view' of its native speakers. However, unlike Herder who viewed this relationship as more phenomenological in kind, emphasising the interpretive, dialogic nature of the formation and exchange of cultural meanings, von Humboldt viewed the structuring of language over experience more in Kantian terms. For von Humboldt, it was the particular grammatical structure, operating like a Kantian category of the mind, which, once established in any language, constrained the possibilities of thought for the speakers of that language (von Humboldt, 1836; Mueller-Volmer, 1990). Von Humboldts's belief that language mediated the subject and the objective world led him to compare grammatical systems and to conclude that some languages mediated this relationship better than others (von Humboldt, 1836, p216).

INCOMMENSURABILITY TODAY

More recent contemporary philosophical debates centred around hermeneutics have elaborated positions which both challenge and extend the terms of the relativism/universalism dichotomy. Within these debates, Gadamer most approximates Herder's position by emphasising the non-contradictory relationship between history, tradition and critical reflection. Like Herder, Gadamer views human consciousness as endlessly becoming, though subject to the effects of history and culture – this he describes as 'effective historical consciousness' (Gadamer, 1975, pp267–274). According to Gadamer, the task of effective historical consciousness is the 'fusion of horizons', his metaphor for the interpretive understanding that occurs between individuals and cultures. It is in the interpretive process of understanding that individuals gradually come to self-conscious awareness of the preconceptions and prejudices that constitute their world views against the newness of other views. For Gadamer individuals belong to traditions, histories and languages; it is only in attempting to understand themselves in dialogue with others that they become reflexively aware of their contingency.

Habermas has criticised Gadamer for denying that the context of tradition serves at the same time as a site in which truths are systematically distorted (Habermas, 1977). Habermas contends that language must also be viewed as a medium of domination that serves to 'legitimate relations of organised force'. He criticises Gadamer, and the hermeneutic endeavour, for reducing social inquiry to the interpretation of meaning, of 'sublimating social processes entirely to cultural tradition' (Habermas, 1977, p361 and see McCarthy, 1978, p183; Bernstein, 1985, pp20–25). He insists that tradition, or the 'lifeworld', be viewed as intrinsically related to other societal processes which are not manifested completely in language. Habermas thus argues for the linkage of the cultural and linguistic with the social, political and economic and in particular, their relationship to labour and relations of power.

Habermas specifically sets out to address the problem faced by modern society when the communicative integrity – the very means of internal coherence – of the lifeworld comes under threat leaving it in a fragmented, alienated and culturally differentiated state. He suggests that under such a threat, individual members of modern society develop and engage communicative reason all the more, seeking and learning new ways to realise reflexively their intersubjectivity in different degrees of solidarity.

Habermas moves beyond both Gadamer and Herder by proposing a context-transcendent as well as a context-dependent account of this process. He maintains that 'the supposition of a common objective world is built into the pragmatics of every single linguistic usage' (Habermas, 1992, p138) and, drawing, in part, on Chomsky's theory of generative grammar, Habermas attempts to disclose the set of universal conditions presupposed in all communicative action.

Habermas's proposition of universal pragmatic presuppositions of communication is intrinsically related to his fear that the 'colonisation of the life world' has created modern societies where individuals have become 'communicatively' alienated from themselves and one another. For Habermas, this alienation and fragmentation carries with it both a potential emancipation, in the sense that individuals are freed from traditions that bind, and a loss of self, in that they can no longer rely on a shared sense of 'communitas.' For Habermas, the emancipatory potential can only be realised if individuals learn, discursively, to make the transition to greater universalism. For Habermas, this does not imply a loss of self or individuality, but an increase in the strength of diversity in unity (Habermas, 1992, p140).

Habermas's universal pragmatics both displays affinities to and distinguishes him from Herder and Gadamer, and contributes to the exploration of the notion of unity in diversity in several ways, but all three attempt to demonstrate the inter-connection between self-knowledge and knowledge of an-other whilst at the same time emphasising that the unity brought about in dialogic communication does not do away with difference (or the individual) but instead confirms it.

What do these deliberations have to say to us about multilingualism and the dialogic? Firstly, contemporary accounts and research designs concerned with multilingualism must take on as fundamental a notion of the dialogic that does not confine languages to the realm of the 'equally valid' but somehow still locked into their own incommensurable worlds of meaning. Such a position – though once a useful part of a rearguard action aimed at Western domination and /or apparently irretractable power relations played out in the realm of language, not only turns the fact of late modern social fragmentation into the 'communicative alienation' Habermas fears, it also belies the facts of dynamic social change through human agency and the proliferation of cultural hybridity with which, in language studies, we are becoming increasingly aware. Second, the implications of abandoning the dominance of the notion of incommensurability are for research that, for example, we can include in our description of speech communities those inevitable elements of change, code-mixing, cultural crossing, not as surprises or deviations from the notion of organic, traditional unity, but as expected features of one language's dialogue with other languages – a dialogue motivated by meaning across cultures.

REFERENCES

Abbs P (1980) 'The reconstruction of English as art', *Tract*, 1, The Gryphon Press, pp4–31

Allen D (1980) *English Teaching Since 1965: How Much Growth?* Heinemann Educational Books

Anderson P (1968) 'Components of the national culture', *New Left Review*, 50, pp3–55

Ball S J (1982) 'Competition and conflict in the teaching of English: A socio-historical analysis', *Journal of Curriculum Studies*, 14, 1, pp1–28

Barnard F M (1965) *Herder's Social and Political Thought*, Clarendon Press

Benedict R (1935) *Patterns of Culture*, George Routledge and Sons

Bernstein R (1985) 'Introduction', in R Bernstein, *Habermas and Modernity*, Polity Press, pp1–32

Bhabha H (1994) *The Location of Culture*, Routledge

Burgess T and Martin N (1990) 'Teaching English in England, 1945–1986: Politics and practice', in J Britten, R E Shafer and K Watson, *Teaching and Learning English Worldwide*, Philadelphia: Clevedon, Multilingual Matters, pp7–38

Gadamer H-G (1975) *Truth and Method*, Sheed and Ward

Geertz C (1973) 'The impact of the concept of culture on the concept of man', in C Geertz, *The Interpretation of Cultures*, New York: Basic Books, Inc, pp33–54

Geertz C (1983) ' "From the native's point of view": On the nature of anthropological understanding', in C Geertz, *Local Knowledge: Further Essays in Interpretive Anthropology*, New York: Basic Books, pp55–70

Gellner E (1982) 'Relativism and universals', in M Hollis and S Lukes, *Rationality and Relativism*, Basil Blackwell, pp181–200

Habermas J (1977) 'A review of Gadamer's Truth and Method', in F Dallmayr and T McCarthy, *Understanding and Social Inquiry*, Notre Dame, Indiana: University of Notre Dame Press, pp335–363

Habermas J (1992) 'The unity of reason in the diversity of its voices', in J Habermas, *Postmetaphysical Thinking*, Polity Press, pp115–148

Hall S (1992) 'New ethnicities', in J Donald and A Rattansi, *'Race', Culture and Difference*, Sage Publications and Open University, pp252–259

Herder J G (1764) 'On diligence on the study of several learned languages', in E A Menze and K Menges, *Johann Gottfried Herder, Selected Early Works, 1764–1767: Addresses, Essays and Drafts; Fragments on Recent German Literature,* University Park, PA.: The Pennsylvania State University Press, pp29–34

Herder J G 1784–1791 (1800) *Outlines of a Philosophy of the History of Man,* New York: Bergman Publishers

von Humboldt W F 1836 (1988) *On Language: The Diversity of Human Language – Structure and its Influence on the Mental Development of Mankind,* Cambridge University Press

Inglis F (1971) 'How to do things with words: a critique of language studies', *English in Education,* 5, 2, pp74–84

Lukes S (1982) 'Relativism in its place', in M Hollis and S Lukes, *Rationality and Relativism,* Basil Blackwell, pp261–305

Mathieson M (1975) *The Preachers of Culture,* George Allen & Unwin Ltd

McCarthy T (1978) *The Critical Theory of Jurgen Habermas,* Cambridge, MA: The MIT Press

Mueller-Vollmer K (1990) 'From sign to signification: the Herder-Humboldt controversy', in W Koepke, *Johann Gottfried Herder,* Colombia South Carolina: Camden House, pp9–24

Mulhern F (1981) *The Moment of the Scrutiny,* Verso Edition

Putnam H (1981) *Reason, Truth and History,* Cambridge University Press

Shayer D (1972) *The Teaching of English in Schools 1900–1970,* Routledge and Kegan Paul

Stocking G W (1974) *The Shaping of American Anthropology 1883–1911: A Franz Boas Reader,* New York: Basic Books

Winch P(1977) 'Understanding a primitive society', in F Dallmayr and T McCarthy, *Understanding and Social Inquiry,* Notre Dame, Indiana: University of Notre Dame Press, pp159–188

Young R J C (1995) *Colonial Desire: Hybridity in Theory, Culture and Race,* Routledge

Rethinking the Bilingual Learner

ROXY HARRIS, Thames Valley University

This paper proposes a rethink or re-assessment concerning the implications behind the use in British educational contexts, in the late 1990s, of terms such as 'bilingual learner', 'ethnic minority pupil', 'pupil with English as an Additional Language' and so on. It suggests that educators have much to learn from the theoretical work developed within the field of British Cultural Studies, and will seek to develop this thinking drawing on empirical data elicited from a British urban secondary school context. This material indicates that for many adolescent pupils there is a much more complex relationship between language, ethnicity, culture and social identity than the terms cited above customarily seem to imply. This may, consequently, open up new ways of looking at questions of language, pupils and learning both in terms of school policy and classroom practice.

The paper draws substantially on thinking about the nature of school provision for 'bilingual', 'ethnic minority' pupils in Britain which was discussed in Leung, Harris and Rampton (1997) and Harris (1997). This earlier work sought to examine the overall approach to these pupils in terms of language and ethnicity in the light of substantial theoretical developments in the field of British Cultural Studies over the last two decades, highlighting, in particular, the work of Bhabha (1994), Gilroy (1987), Hall (1988, 1992), Mercer (1994) and Hewitt (1991, 1995). The broad argument advanced was that while there had been undoubted advances from generally assimilationist to generally multicultural approaches in the education of pupils from the 'visible' ethnic minorities, the underlying ideology remained one of positioning these pupils as permanent outsiders in the British nation state, and that consequently it had been difficult for British educators to develop equitable and effective approaches for language provision in multilingual and multi-ethnic settings. This difficulty was particularly marked in respect to the debate about what approach to language in schools additional targeted (generally known as Section 11) funding should provide.

There seem to be a number of interrelated problems. First, there appear to be inadequate approaches and underfunding in provision for the teaching of those pupils who have limited experience of, and/or proficiency in, English language because they have lived a significantpart of their lives in environments where English is not the most regularly used language. Secondly, there seems to be at best patchy funded provision for either the teaching of the minority languages or for seriously attempting to institute long-term bilingual education programmes even in locations where demographic factors make such programmes highly feasible. Thirdly, there appears to be limited thinking about what kinds of funded provision need to be available for the teaching of subject-specific Standard English literacies to 'visible' minority pupils, whose fundamental patterns of language use are rooted in the local vernacular Englishes of their neighbourhoods, but who have widely varying levels of competence in, and affiliation to, their inherited family and community languages. Finally, this earlier discussion suggested that part of the difficulty in formulating arguments to move beyond the impasse outlined above lay in weak theorising by British educators linked with scanty empirical evidence about what they might mean when they refer to bilingual, ethnic minority pupils and what kinds of curriculum approach might be needed, particularly in the area of language. This lack of clarity was attributed to 'Romantic Bilingualism':

... the widespread practice, in British schools and other educational contexts, based on little or no analysis or enquiry, of attributing to pupils drawn from visible ethnic minority groups an expertise in and allegiance to any community languages with which they have some acquaintance. (Harris, 1997)

THE RESEARCH

The school

The work reported in Harris (ibid.) was developed from written pupil data obtained from a Year 9 class in a West London secondary school in the early months of 1996. For the purposes of this paper we will call the school Blackhill. Blackhill is a secondary school with more than 1,400 pupils. The

School's own 1996 analysis claimed that 20% of the students were white and that 78% were of 'Asian origin'. In addition 'only 19% of students stated that English was the principal language used at home'; and 'Asian languages are the most predominant, with almost 50% of our intake using both Punjabi and English in conversation everyday' (Blackhill School, 1997).

Outline of the research approach

This study seeks to collect deeper empirical evidence for the propositions advanced in 1996. Between December 1996 and July 1997 research was conducted with a Year 10 class at Blackhill (about a third of whom had been members of the Year 9 class which had featured in the 1996 research). Data was collected during approximately 40 visits to the school.

The class

As mentioned earlier, the research was conducted with a year 10 class at Blackhill School at times when they were timetabled to be studying GCSE English. There were 31 pupils in the class (reduced to 30 when one boy left the school at the end of the spring term), 17 girls and 14 boys. All but four members of the class had strong connections with a South Asian ethnicity, in many cases combined with an East African one. 16 pupils claimed to have used Panjabi language with their families before they first attended school, 9 claimed Gujarati, 1 Kurdish, 1 Mauritian French Creole, 1 Swahili, 1 Urdu. Only two pupils in the class claimed to have spoken nothing but English with their families before they first attended school. None of the pupils in the class was white.

Researcher's role

I adopted four main research roles. First, *participant/observer* in the classroom. This occurred in two ways: (i) when I taught a short unit (3 lessons) on linguistic diversity; (ii) on occasions when pupils called on me for assistance with individual or small group work when their class teacher was busy with other pupils, or when the class teacher had to leave the classroom to pursue other duties. Secondly, *observer/participant* in the classroom which occurred in the many lessons when I watched and listened, commenting briefly when occasionally invited to do so by the class teacher. Thirdly, *general observer* as a regular visitor to the school. Fourthly, *ethnographic interviewer* when I conducted individual interviews with all thirty pupils in the class.

DATA SOURCES

Pupil language survey

All 31 pupils in the class completed a modified version of the Linguistic Minorities Project's Secondary Pupils Survey of linguistic diversity. The modifications made were slight. Principally, the many cartoon-like illustrations in the original were dispensed with as were occasional archaic references such as to the assumed study of Latin by many pupils. However, this survey retained virtually word for word the 60 survey questions of the original.

Informant written project

Along with the language survey and the short taught unit (3 lessons) on language diversity in Britain, the pupil-informants were asked to work on a two-part project entitled Language Use in My Life to be completed during the Easter holidays 1997 and handed in immediately afterwards. The first part of the project involved them producing an open-ended piece of writing – 'Language use in my life'. All 30 pupils returned this writing.

Informant taped project

For the second part of the Language Use in My Life project the pupil-informants were given blank 60 minute audio cassette tapes and asked to compile recordings in any way they wished which they felt illustrated typical language use in their everyday lives. Twenty-two pupils compiled tapes and submitted them (see Sebba, 1993, for an example of informant autonomy in the collection of taped data). A further six pupils, who did not submit tapes, handed in written reconstructions of what they said were typical examples of some of the conversational exchanges which occurred in their lives.

Informant interviews

Following the elicitation of the rich data collected by the above means, all thirty pupils were interviewed individually for between 30 and 60 minutes each. The interviews were taped. The tenor of the interviews was shaped by the fact that I was someone whom at least a third of the pupil-informants had seen in their English classes and around the school during the spring term of 1996. Additionally, all of them had seen and interacted with me inside and outside these classes intensively from December 1996 until the period of the interviews in May to July 1997. They were quite clear that I was someone who was interested in their patterns of language use. The starting point for each interview was that I had been interested in what they had said about their language use in their survey questionnaire, written project and compiled tapes but accepted that all these sources of information were intrinsically limiting and wanted to give them a chance to expand on some of the points they had made there. In these senses then, the individual taped interviews had an ethnographic quality. I was very familiar to the informants, and conducted the interviews in a conversational style formulating my questions and prompts in an open-ended way which made it clear that I was there to listen to their perceptions rather than to 'get answers' to set questions.

SOME PRELIMINARY OBSERVATIONS ON 1997 BLACKHILL SCHOOL RESEARCH

At this stage it is possible only to make some preliminary observations on the outcomes of the research. However, it is clear that the pupil-informants depicted themselves in terms of their language, culture and ethnicity in ways which accorded strongly with the anti-essentialist thrust of the work of the British Cultural theorists mentioned earlier.

Culture and ethnicity

Twenty-eight of the 31 pupil-informants were born in Britain and have lived all their lives here and in their routine characterisations of themselves plainly resisted the notion that they were outsiders to British society or unfamiliar with its language and culture. And yet such a notion was a central tenet of the original Local Government Act 1966, Section 11, rationale for funding Local Education Authorities (LEAs) for:

> *... special provision in the exercise of any of their functions in consequence of the presence of substantial numbers of immigrants from the Commonwealth whose language and customs differ from those of the rest of the population.* (Tomlinson 1983)

and has recently been restated:

> *... to support the cost of employing additional staff to help minority ethnic groups overcome linguistic and other barriers which inhibit their access to, and take up of mainstream services.* (OFSTED, 1994)

A serious question, therefore, for educators, is how to move beyond the simplistic designation of these pupils as 'Asians' and 'bilingual learners'.

In Leung, Harris and Rampton (ibid, p66) attention was drawn to what Bhabha (1994) noted was the way in which particular ethnic groups come to be constructed into a permanent 'otherness': 'An important feature of colonial discourse is its dependence on the concept of "fixity" in the ideological construction of otherness'.

Gilroy (1987, pp59–61) supported this view in making specific reference to some of the ways in which routine discourses within the British nation state act to exclude permanently certain ethnic minority groups from what counts as Englishness or Britishness. This practice, which he identifies as ethnic absolutism, 'views nations as culturally homogeneous communities of sentiment'.

According to Hall (1988), what is necessary is to begin to see members of minority groups as active participants in the creation of vibrant 'new ethnicities' and not passive inheritors of fixed ethnicities, identities, cultures and languages. This helps to explain why the pupil-informants in the present research were so resistant to wholesale unambiguous identification with either essentialised 'Asianness' or essentialised 'Britishness'. Mercer (1994) is one of many cultural theorists to suggest how this approach can be more easily understood using the concept of diaspora to see that such young people retain both real *and* imaginary Asian identities along with unmistakably British identities. In this respect he sees them as actors in the creation, in Britain, of 'emerging cultures of hybridity, forged among the overlapping African, Asian and Caribbean diasporas ...' (p3). Hall (1992, p310) in a comprehensive formulation proposes the notion of 'translation' which:

describes those identity formations which cut across and intersect natural frontiers, and which are composed of people who have been dispersed forever from their homelands. Such people retain strong links with their places of origin and their traditions, but they are without the illusion of a return to the past. They are obliged to come to terms with the new cultures they inhabit, without simply assimilating to them and losing their identities completely. They bear upon them the traces of the particular cultures, traditions, languages and histories by which they were shaped. The difference is that they are not and will never be unified in the old sense, because they are irrevocably the product of several interlocking histories and cultures, belong at one and the same time to several 'homes' (and to no one particular 'home'). People belonging to such cultures of hybridity have had to renounce the dream or ambition of rediscovering any kind of 'lost' cultural purity, or ethnic absolutism. They are irrevocably translated ... They are the products of the new diasporas created by the post-colonial migrations. They must learn to inhabit at least two identities, to speak two cultural languages, to translate and negotiate between them. Cultures of hybridity are one of the distinctly novel types of identity produced in the era of late-modernity, and there are more and more examples of them to be discovered.

Patterns of language use (orientation)

In the same way, in describing and analysing their patterns of language use the pupil-informants refused the neat binary opposition between English language and 'Asian home/community' languages, in which they are regularly positioned as outsiders in relation to the former and insiders with regard to the latter (cf OFSTED, 1994, Section 11 rationale). Hewitt (1991) suggests, usefully, that, in fact, urban youth in Britain in their everyday patterns of language use assist in the 'destabilisation of ethnicity'. He also argues that an integral, but often overlooked, aspect of their language appears in their use of what he calls a 'local multi-ethnic vernacular' or a 'community English' which is the 'primary medium of communication in the adolescent peer group in multi-ethnic areas' (p32).

Certainly, the pupil-informants in the present study asserted that they were most linguistically comfortable and confident with a local urban spoken English while simultaneously retaining a weaker but nevertheless continuing relationship with a 'home'/'community' language such as Panjabi or Gujarati. Hewitt (1995, p97), offers a theoretical framework of considerable explanatory power when he refers to:

> *the obliteration of pure language forms deriving from a single cultural source, evident in some inner city areas (in the UK) and ... the diasporic distribution of communicative forms which, whilst generated from and based in local communities, nevertheless reach out and extend lines of connection in a global way. The local penetration and mixing of language forms evident in some urban settings in the UK should, in fact, be seen perhaps as a reflex of the broader linguistic diasporic processes.*

Patterns of language use (evidence from the research data)

From the research outlined earlier some preliminary but insistent factors have already emerged and several of these will now be briefly illustrated under a number of summary headings as follows:

English is the most frequently and confidently used language and the language of choice in most domains

Although most of them had strongly utilised languages like Panjabi and Gujarati in their early years, one of the strongest assertions made by the pupil-informants, without exception, was that they were now most confident and competent in the use of English.

> *I speak it [English] more fluently than I do my own language and I find it much easier because I've always been learning it since I was in nursery so I find it much easier talking in English than I do in Gujarati.* (N.B. [girl], interview)

'Slang' is identified as an important component of routine speech in English

Space does not permit a discussion of the potential dissonance implied by the use of the phrase 'my own language' in the previous quotation. However, the research data shows that the pupil-informants identified themselves significantly with the use of what they called 'slang' in their use of English (cf Hewitt's 'local multi-ethnic vernacular' or 'community English') as the girl just cited put it:

> *... with the teachers like I won't talk like I'm talking to my friends like I would ... put with the teachers like some of the time Standard English with a bit of ... slang in it and at home and with my friends I talk in slang all the time because you ... don't want to talk in Standard English with your friends because you're always with them and you would sound kind of funny if you talk in Standard English.* (N.B. [girl], interview)

Ambiguous relationship with, and limited claimed expertise in 'home'/'community' language

Few of the pupil-informants expressed an unambiguous identification with their 'home'/'community' language and none claimed anything approaching their expertise and competence in English. Here, there is space to consider only a few of the interrelated issues.

(i)   The competence question

In general the pupil-informants felt themselves to be seriously limited in their competence in their 'home'/'community' language. In particular, while many claimed reasonable levels of expertise in receptive 'understanding' skills, far fewer claimed equivalent levels in speaking skills and virtually none said that they possessed any reading or writing expertise at all.

> *I understand it [Panjabi] but I don't know how to speak it ... reading I can't read it, speaking it's just I know the basic stuff maybe and understanding it I understand the language there are only a few bits that I don't understand ... I can't write it.* (N.S.R. [boy], interview)

(ii) Fragmented 'home'/'community' language use with parents

None of the pupils said that they relied exclusively on languages such as Panjabi or Gujarati for sustained communication with their parents, although in a few cases they attempted to do so, either where one parent or the other possessed limited English, or particularly wanted them to use these languages.

… it's like at home like when I speak to my mum I speak English to her and my dad … [I] speak Panjabi and I feel like o.k. and sometimes I have difficulty like speaking Panjabi there's some words I can't say it in Panjabi and so it would be like in English and Panjabi and when I speak to my dad it'll be like I'll be speaking English and he won't answer me [he'll] feel like answering but I won't speak Panjabi but I think we probably speak more English at home like me and my sister and my um me and my mum and dad but when they're together they do speak Panjabi when they ask us questions, it'll be in Panjabi … yeh but we don't [answer in Panjabi]. (P.S. [girl], interview)

(iii) Consistent use of 'home'/'community' language with grandparents to show respect

Almost all the pupil-informants reported that they made consistent and willing efforts to communicate in the 'home'/'community' language with their grandparents and some other older relatives, and that they did so in order to show them respect.

I still talk it [Gujarati] with my grandparents … because they don't understand anything else and like it's a show of respect as well and just like even to my uncles like olders you have to talk in Gujarati unless they talk in English. (K.M. [boy], interview)

(iv) Supplementary school attended to learn 'home'/'community' language but discontinued

The overwhelming majority of the pupil-informants said that they had at some time attended supplementary school classes to learn 'home'/'community' language, but in all cases they had discontinued their attendance while finding it extremely difficult to explain why they had stopped. This was particularly interesting where informants said that they would now like to learn their 'home'/'community' language but were at a loss to suggest how this might occur without participation in one of the available community classes.

I didn't enjoy the lessons [community-based Gujarati classes] I just didn't feel like I was, I don't know, I just didn't like it, I don't know why I … I just stopped going. (S.C. [girl], interview)

(v) 'Home'/'community' language use encountered in fragmented form

Typically, as indicated above, the informants described their encounters with their 'home'/'community' languages as occurring in fragmented ways in a variety of domains. This pattern might, for example, occur in relation to:

- music and films

  I think I can [understand Hindi language films] I mean it's ... also the visuals but you can understand it and I think that um it's sometimes like the words sound similar and then you just get the gist of it I think. I mean the last time I watched one I did understand it. I was confused at some parts. (A.D. [girl], interview)

and on the Hindi language music accompanying the films:

  oh no no no it's I don't understand the songs that's just I think it's all about love most of them. (A.D. [girl], interview)

- religion

  Understanding it [Panjabi] I'm quite good at it but if it was like something some big words like in um like when you go to the temple where you hear the music and stuff it's like I can't understand it. (G.K. [girl], interview)

- travel to parental 'homeland'

  when I went to India once I couldn't understand what they were saying cos like they were speaking properly and I would just speak like slang type Panjabi. (D.U. [boy], interview)

Naturally, caution should be exercised in interpreting this research for two principal reasons. First, as indicated earlier the comments made here are preliminary considerations on a substantial body of rich data. Secondly, the data itself is mainly self-report in nature. Also, it is important to be clear that due to limitations of time and space here, it has been necessary to 'flatten out' the research data somewhat. In other words, in the class there were a few pupil-informants who claimed considerably more 'home'/'community' language competence than was general and there were one or two who claimed no 'home'/'community' language competence at all. However, in the spirit of the theme of this study *Rethinking Language Education,* it is perhaps worth assuming that its findings have some wider salience and making speculations on some possible implications arising from it.

Rethinking the bilingual learner: some tentative proposals

Both Bourne (1989) and Levine (1990) have pointed out the dangers of the oversimplified use of the term bilingual learner in British educational contexts and the accompanying absence of consistent well-funded policy and practice towards pupils categorised in this umbrella way. Hitherto, Section 11 funding has been the main source of funded provision in this area and, given that it is subject to short-term government decisions, is both uncertain and has an increasingly unclear rationale; certainly its rationale (see OFSTED, ibid) appears to exclude the kinds of pupil quoted earlier while purporting to include them. In other words its notion of bilingual learner seems to be cast firmly in terms of the learning of English by those who are unfamiliar with it. It might now be more fruitful to imagine, in the light of the research reported in this chapter, an approach to language education policy, practice and funding developed around the following categories of 'bilingual' learner, perhaps using Rampton's (1990) formulation to ask searching questions related to their linguistic expertise, affiliation and inheritance:

(A) The 'new' arrivals

These pupils may be relatively recent arrivals in the country possessing a limited acquaintance with and low levels of expertise in the English language together with little familiarity with contemporary British cultural and educational practices.

(B) The low-key British bilinguals

(i) Pupils born and brought up in a multilingual home in a British urban area. They have regular routine interaction with family and community languages other than English without claiming a high degree of expertise in these languages. They are entirely comfortable with the discourse of everyday English, particular local vernacular Englishes and with contemporary British cultural and educational practices. They have, however, along with fellow pupils of all ethnic backgrounds, including white British ones, difficulty in reproducing accurate and fluent written

Standard English in the preferred written genres favoured in specific school subject disciplines.

(ii) Pupils born and brought up in British urban areas but who enter early years schooling with a dominant spoken language proficiency in a 'home'/'community' language and not in English.

(iii) Pupils born in another country who enter the British schooling system sometime between the ages of 5 and 16 and appear to gradually move from the 'new' arrival to the low-key British bilingual category.

(iv) Pupils of Caribbean descent who perhaps constitute a special case in terms of their patterns of language use.

(C) The high-achieving multilinguals

These pupils have a good level of expertise or an untapped potential to acquire expertise rapidly in (a) 'home'/'community' language(s) other than English.

The argument, then, is that specific funding ought to be made available to enable the development of high quality pedagogic approaches, materials and in-service and initial teacher training to meet the differing needs of pupils in each of the categories outlined. Despite the obvious limitations of trying to create such crude categories, what is being suggested here is that they offer the beginnings of a debate about a possible new basis for the funding of more precise and justifiable approaches to language education which are positive about the existence of bilingual and multilingual groups and individuals in British society and British schools. They also bear some relationship to the research findings reported in this chapter and to the useful developments in cultural theory which are too often neglected by linguists and educators. Encouraging this debate to develop may well constitute a useful first step in rethinking language education for our times.

REFERENCES

Bhabha H (1994) *The Location of Culture*, London: Routledge

Blackhill School (1997) Unpublished information document

Bourne J (1989) *Moving into the Mainstream: LEA Provision for Bilingual Pupils*, Windsor: NFER/Nelson

Gilroy P (1987/1991) *There ain't no Black in the Union Jack*, London: Routledge

Hall S (1988) 'New ethnicities', in A Rattansi and J Donald (eds) (1992) *'Race', Culture and Difference*, London: Sage/Open University, pp252–259

Hall S (1992) 'The question of cultural identity', in S Hall, D Held and T McGrew (eds) *Modernity and its Futures*, Cambridge: Polity Press/Open University, pp274–316

Harris R (1997) 'Romantic bilingualism: time for a change?' in C Leung and C Cable (eds) *English as an Additional Language: Changing Perspectives*, Watford: NALDIC

Hewitt R (1995) 'The umbrella and the sewing machine: Trans-culturalism and the definition of surrealism', in A Aalund and R Granqvist (eds) *Negotiating Identities*, Amsterdam: Rodopi, pp91–104

Hewitt R (1991) 'Language, youth and the destabilisation of ethnicity', in C Palmgren et al (eds) *Ethnicity and Youth Culture*, Stockholm: Stockholm University, pp27–41

Leung C, Harris R and Rampton B (1997) 'The idealised native-speaker, reified ethnicities and classroom realities', *TESOL Quarterly*, 31, 3, pp543–560

Levine J (ed) (1990) *Bilingual Learners and the Mainstream Curriculum*, Basingstoke: Falmer Press

Mercer K (1994) *Welcome to the Jungle*, London: Routledge

OFSTED (1994) *Educational Support for Minority Ethnic Communities*, London: Office for Standards in Education

Rampton B (1990) 'Displacing the "native speaker": expertise, affiliation and inheritance', *ELT Journal*, 44, 2, pp97–101

Sebba M (1993) *London Jamaican: Language Systems in Interaction*, London: Longman

Tomlinson S (1983) *Ethnic Minorities in British Schools*, London: Heinemann Educational Books

Programme Evaluation in Diverse EAL Contexts

PAULINE REA-DICKINS, University of Warwick

No one would question the role of research in language education, in spite of a recently expressed view that much of educational research is a 'desperate waste of time'! (Alan Smithers at the 1997 British Association of Science). In his response (*Guardian Education,* 16.9.1997), Roger Murphy sees the problem as one of 'policy-makers disregarding findings because they wish to apply their own prejudices and political ideologies rather than to pay attention to evidence'. It seems to me that the 'problem' is not confined to research and that there are similar dilemmas, albeit different in kind, surrounding the role and use of evaluation in educational settings. Educationists are under increasing pressure to demonstrate 'results', e.g. evidence of improved pupil performance, and to adopt educational options based on value for money (VFM). One effect of this is a narrowing of understanding of roles for evaluation in the curriculum; another is reflected in the ways in which curriculum evaluation is actually implemented. In this paper, through an analysis of distinctions between evaluation and research, I examine potential contributions that evaluation can make to a specific language education programme. Evaluation is more than a cost benefit analysis and the compilation of test results. It is argued that in 'rethinking language education', it is relevant to take account of the different roles that evaluation has to play in this process which are identified here in terms of four purposes: 'accountability', 'developmental', 'awareness-raising' and 'managerial'.

DEFINITIONS

The Shorter Oxford English Dictionary offers us the following definitions:

Evaluate: *to work out the value of; to find a numerical expression for to reckon up, ascertain the amount of; to express in terms of the known*

Research: *to search into (a matter or subject); to investigate or study closely An investigation directed to the discovery of some fact by careful study of a subject; a course of critical or scientific enquiry*

The differences emerging here have to do with coming up with a judgement about the worth of something, and providing evidence for this, in the case of evaluation; the focus in research on the other hand is on discovery: close and critical enquiry. In line with the former view, earlier definitions of educational evaluation focused on the merit of a programme or course. For example, Tyler, (1949, pp105–106, cited in Hopkins, 1989, p3) views evaluation as:

> *the process of determining to what extent the educational objectives are being realised.*

Early views present a judgemental definition of evaluation, as a largely objectives-driven undertaking, associated with the conventions of experimental design. Others have promoted a view of evaluation grounded in professional practice of an illuminative and responsive rather than recommendatory nature (e.g. Stenhouse, 1975; Parlett and Hamilton, 1976). This developmental position is clearly captured by Cronbach and colleagues (1980, cited in Nevo, 1986, p16) who describe an evaluator as 'an educator (whose) success is to be judged by what others learn' (p11) rather than a 'referee (for) a basketball game' (p18) who is hired to decide who is 'right' or 'wrong'. In the domain of language education, Brown (1989, p223) provides Weir and Roberts (1994) with their working definition of evaluation as:

> *the systematic collection and analyses of all relevant information necessary to promote the improvement of the curriculum, and assess its effectiveness and efficiency, as well as the participants' attitudes within a context of particular institutions involved.*

The various perspectives on evaluation reflect different models for evaluation. We have, for example, goal-free evaluation (Scriven, 1967), the objectives model (e.g. Tyler, 1986; Weiss, 1972), the illuminative approach (e.g. Parlett and Hamilton, 1976), responsive evaluation (e.g. Stake, 1975; Guba and Lincoln, 1981) and the connoisseurship of Eisner (1985). Analysing these approaches, we arrive at a view of evaluation as thus multifaceted, with the *potential* to make judgements and recommend, to evaluate effectiveness and efficiency, and to contribute to curriculum improvement and development. Changes in goals for evaluation have also been accompanied by a shift in methodology away from the empiricist tradition towards

> *a paradigm of choices emphasising multiple methods, alternative approaches and ... the matching of evaluation methods to specific evaluation situations and questions.* (Patton, 1981, cited in Norris, 1993, p51)

Research is a systematic and planned activity, albeit characterised in a variety of ways. It may be concerned with hypothesis testing or hypothesis generating, be exploratory, explanatory or confirmatory in design, may be qualitative or quantitative, make selections from a wide range of investigative procedures and use of primary and secondary sources. It may be called pure research, classroom research, basic research and so forth. What characterises all good research is that it is principled, asks relevant questions, and should be able to 'generate new information or confirm old information in new ways' (Hatch and Lazarton, 1991, p13). Research, then, is about extending knowledge and contributing to theory.

The relationships between research and evaluation have been raised elsewhere (education literature, e.g. Norris, 1990; in language education, e.g. van Lier, 1988; Mitchell, 1990; Mackay, 1991). The dimensions of methodology, purposes and goals, utilisation, and timing are analysed next.

METHODS, UTILISATION AND CONSTRAINTS

There is overlap between evaluation and research in terms of potential for shared methodology. Early evaluation tradition focused on measurable outcomes in relation to preordained objectives and implied a positivistic approach. The emergence of 'naturalistic', 'responsive' and 'utilisation-focused' evaluation advocated flexibility in methodology with choice of paradigm sensitive to the particular information requirements of the stakeholders. However, this choice may be constrained in evaluations, by sponsors who impose requirements for certain types of data, e.g. test results or survey findings, and are suspicious of evidence in the form of 'changes in attitude' or observation-led case studies.

The purposes and goals of evaluation and research are, however, quite distinct. The responsive dimension of evaluation, in addressing the needs of stakeholder requirements, highlights the *utilisation* function of evaluation in professional practice. Here evaluation feeds into decision making and has, unlike research, immediate utility for policy shaping and is expected to be influential in short-term decision making. In evaluation the 'focus is on intended use by intended users' (Patton, 1990, p122) with 'utilisation-focused evaluation plans for use before data are ever collected' (ibid, p122). Immediately, differences with research objectives become apparent, with a concern in research for contributing knowledge within a discipline. This is not to say that research does not inform policy, nor that it is uninfluential in determining classroom practice. The point is that it is not required to do so: the purpose is different as are the questions posed.

MacDonald (1987, p42) writes of this key difference between the two undertakings: Who asks the questions? The researcher is able to 'select his questions, and to seek answers to them', thereby enjoying greater autonomy. Evaluation, on the other hand, as the study of implementation (e.g. Fitzgibbon, 1996; Pawson and Tilley, 1997), is undertaken for an identifiable client group(s), other than the academic discourse community, who may have different requirements, interests and stakes. Kiely (work in progress) signals that evaluation, unlike research, may examine relationships between different elements of a programme (e.g. aims, teachers' views, policies on method, learners).

Issues of timescales raise further differences, with evaluation more concerned with 'immediate' issues relevant to current practice and practical problems. This makes for tighter time constraints in evaluation studies; and contrasts with more extended timescales for research, and the absence of externally imposed deadlines in order to feed into decision making. There is also less rigid obligation in research to report findings; with more latitude available to research on format and audience.

In summary, research primarily seeks contributions to knowledge. Contributions to praxis (if indeed a concern) are often secondary. Evaluation, on the other hand, is grounded in professional practice and is expected to provide information that will feed into decision making, planning, action, or change.

OPERATIONALISING EVALUATION AND RESEARCH

Background context

One of the initiatives of the Minority Group Support Services (MGSS) of Coventry City Council arose from evidence of underachievement of some pupils in its schools (both mono- and bilingual), i.e. performance below the national and city averages. In an area of the city with a high density of learners for whom English is an Additional Language (EAL), The Early Years Intervention Project (EYIP) was introduced to address this underachievement and target the English language development of pupils, in the age range 5–7 years old, in Key Stage 1 of the National Curriculum (Reception, Year 1 and Year 2). Each of the nine project schools has a full-time language support teacher, with 28 bilingual/multilingual classroom assistants (CAs) distributed across the schools.

To support the EYIP goals, the CAs work alongside the language support teacher and monitor on an individual basis each child's use of language. This language is sampled, and recorded in writing on a daily basis, and feeds into the Language Development Record compiled for each child. Model Assessment Profiles, designed for each Key Stage, are used to determine the level (A–E) of a child's language proficiency on entry to school and against which achievement is measured at different points in the school year. Other measures are used to provide data for administrative purposes, and all schools participate in the Key Stage 1 National Curriculum assessments.

Within this wider EYIP project, a small-scale research and evaluation project is in progress.[1] In relation to the assessment of learners with EAL this is investigating the systems in place and the validity of some of the procedures used in both the formative and summative assessments of the targeted learners with EAL. In particular, it is focused on approaches to language sampling and the development of learner profiles as well as the different curricular contexts in which formative learner assessment is implemented.

---

1   A joint project between MGSS (Chris Shearsby and Sandra Howard) and the University of Warwick (Sheena Gardner and Pauline Rea-Dickins).

STAKEHOLDERS AND THEIR STAKES

The stakeholders

The stakeholders in this project include the funding agencies who support the EYIP, the LEA, the project management team and their staff who provide training for the teachers, the teachers themselves (language support teachers, school coordinator for the project, the CAs), school heads, parents of the targeted learners and the learners. To these we may add the researchers. In terms of obvious power, some of these stakeholders are more important than others: the more important ones make the decisions and take action while the less important are those affected by those decisions. Yet, each set of stakeholders has certain specific demands in relation to aspects of the assessment process and its related procedures.

Identifying the stakes

Some of these stakes are reflected in the range of questions listed below.

1 Is the intervention project leading to better results for the targeted learners?

2 Does the project represent 'value for money'?

3 What improvements can be made in the way language is sampled and how the language samples are recorded?

4 How can the Model Assessment Scales be modified or changed that might result in more curricular-related features and a better discrimination of levels?

5 What should be included in the training programme provided for the language support teachers and the CAs in relation to language sampling, and how these samples are recorded and used?

6 What is the relationships between the data presented by the CAs to the teacher and the samples recorded by the teacher (e.g. balance of emphasis on linguistic and functional categories)?

7 What is the relationship between the EAL language data gathered by CAs and a child's use of language in specific curricular tasks in, say, English and Maths?

8 What can we learn about learner performance on the different assessment
   data sets available with reference to learner progress?

Matching stakes to stakeholders

The concerns of administrators and funding bodies who are in the business of
selecting among course options and balancing information against cost are
reflected in 1 and 2 above. Thus, relevant evaluation design and procedures
should be in place to provide this type of information. However, the
programme manager, those responsible for shaping classroom methodology
and activities, and the teacher trainers want to know how to improve and
develop their systems and procedures and to provide appropriate training for
those charged with the implementation of the programme. These stakeholders
have clearly identified professional tasks to be accomplished, implicit in 3–5
above, and require that an evaluation of these curricular contexts yield data to
inform their decision making, planning and action. Thus, evaluation is
expected to provide some of the 'solutions' *and* within strict timescales
determined by the school year. Additionally, there is the expectation that the
curricular-focused enquiry, with teacher engagement in this process, will lead
to both curriculum and staff development. The interests of language education
researchers are reflected in the last three questions on the list, and are
explained somewhat differently. In their case the context provides the
opportunity to engage critically in aspects of theory in relation to knowledge
in areas of language testing, discourse analysis and classroom-based child
language development. There is no requirement of research to generate
knowledge about programme implementation.

The first five questions above reflect stakeholder requirements for
particular data sets which have an immediate and short term utilisation focus,
i.e. the use of findings within the lifetime of the project. The research stake in
the project connects with issues of assessment and the research study will seek
to explain teachers' perceptions of language and language proficiency implied
through the language sampling and learner profiling. In examining language
data derived from curricular-based assessment and standardised procedures,
issues of validity and ethicality of assessment procedures will also be
addressed. Thus, the expectation of the research is to contribute to knowledge
about the context and conditions of assessment for EAL learners and not
directly to any short-term action or recommendation.

In a project of this kind, the use of assessment can raise 'other' questions such as test validity questions (leaving aside (!) questions fundamental to child first and second language acquisition and the use of the Level 1 to support Level 2 language development). For instance, how is the domain of assessment defined? To what extent do the assessments have curricular validity? For any given test procedure, do differences in levels of test or test item difficulty vary according to the first language of those who take the test? To what extent does background knowledge support or inhibit learner performance? Where assessment schemes identify levels of language attainment, how are such levels fixed? What operational validity do such levels have in relation to learner 'access' to the National Curriculum? How do the learners themselves construct the domain of standardised assessments within the school curriculum? Implicit in all these questions is the need for validation studies. These are not the questions that evaluation can readily answer, constrained by time, stakeholder demands, and resources.

The roles for evaluation

The Early Years Intervention Project illustrates four functions for evaluation within language education programmes.

A *judgemental* dimension is shown with standardised tests used to measure progress, even where there may be disenchantment with the actual measure itself, i.e. used in the absence of a better alternative. Educational administrators and other professionals are often forced into 'accountability bonding' because funding, or continuation of funding, is contingent upon providing quantifiable information. Evidence is also sought for the VFM of alternative models for raising achievement. In connection with the Reading Recovery programme, for example, SCAA analysed intervention schemes which took place between 1992 and 1994 and established that the average annual cost per pupil under the Reading Recovery Scheme was £1,030, with children achieving six months above the control group; under phonological teaching, children achieved three months above the control group at a cost of £581. Management is often required to produce VFM data, to link costs to measurable achievements in order to demonstrate the cost benefits of their proposed scheme.

Developmental evaluation represents concerns of teachers and curriculum managers who share common ownership of current and future curriculum development. Specific tasks and feedback mechanisms can facilitate curricular improvements (e.g. improved ways in which language is sampled and recorded). This requires stakeholder participation, that is the engagement of professionals (e.g. the language support teachers, classroom assistants and mainstream teachers) in the critique of the curricular practices leading to action in the form of collaboratively refined classroom procedures. Evaluation thus can be action-oriented and supportive of curriculum development goals.

It has long been argued that development within the curriculum is contingent upon an *awareness* of the workings of the classroom (Stenhouse, 1975; see also van Lier, 1988). In the EYIP, therefore, the CAs, the language support and the class teachers need to be provided with opportunities to develop a deeper understanding of the tasks they are involved in as a basis for contributing to project improvement. The awareness goal in the EYIP is to develop a personal knowledge base for the CAs. Evaluation has therefore the potential to stimulate professional involvement and development.

Evaluation is also a *management* activity, and takes up the concerns of managers and key staff for regular information and knowledge in order to plan strategically, with data from evaluation activities feeding into this process. A corollary of this is the need for clear frameworks for evaluation data to feed into.

CONCLUSION

In this paper, I have attempted to tease out some distinctions between evaluation and research, in that they have somewhat different yet complementary contributions to make in the field of language education. I have exemplified four roles for evaluation through reference to a specific language education project. The *accountability* dimension is identified with providing results, frequently of a measurement-based kind, and judging programme effectiveness against results and costs. *Developmental* evaluation functions as a means for stimulating curricular improvements; it is closely linked to the concept of *awareness raising* and the professional development of those individuals invested with the responsibility for the implementation of educational programmes. Evaluation also provides data for *managing* developments of different kinds within the curriculum and it informs decision making. Although evaluation may be seen as an extension of research, sharing methodologies, procedures, and skills, distinct characteristics of evaluation are its action orientation in terms of shaping decision making, policy and practice.

When rethinking roles for evaluation in language education, it may be useful to categorise the different demands or 'stakes' in terms of (i) the marketplace and associated accountability requirements; (ii) curriculum innovation and implementation perspectives; and (iii) research and development functions. Each stakeholder group has an interest in different kinds of information. These need not be mutually exclusive, but frequently can be problematic, bringing evaluation sharply into the political arena. The status of the evaluation and stakeholder expectations may present a major dilemma for the evaluator: Is the evaluation one of compliance to the sponsor to validate the status quo? Is it one of seeking information which may challenge existing policy and practice?

I have argued that what sets aside evaluation from research activity is its purpose, its audience, and the needs of these stakeholders for utilisation-focused enquiry which are of immediate practical use to them in refining practice. As suggested elsewhere:

> *For their process of decision making, LEAs (and schools) need to have available to them much more research and evaluation. In particular they need to be able to get rapid evaluations of initiatives as they develop ...*
> (Sanday, 1993, p42)

From this perspective, evaluation contributes to a theory of practice, to knowledge about implementation, which is distinguishable from the contributions that research makes to a discipline. But, herein resides another dilemma. The findings from narrowly focused research studies, implicit in some of the questions on assessment raised earlier, are crucially important to the accurate interpretation of evaluation findings. This suggests the need for a closer analysis of evaluation within an ongoing research agenda in the development of language education.

ACKNOWLEDGEMENTS

I thank Sheena Gardner and Richard Kiely for helpful feedback on an early draft of this paper.

REFERENCES

Brown J D (1989) 'Language program evaluation: a synthesis of existing possibilities', in R K Johnson (ed) *The Second Language Curriculum,* Cambridge: Cambridge University Press, pp222–241

Eisner E (1985) *The Art of Educational Evaluation,* Lewes: The Falmer Press

Fitz-Gibbon C T (1996) *Monitoring Education,* London: Cassell

Guba E C and Lincoln Y S (1981) *Effective Evaluation,* San Francisco: Jossey-Bass

Hatch E and Lazarton A (1991) *The Research Manual, Design and Statistics for Applied Linguistics,* New York: Newbury House Publishers

Hopkins D (1989) *Evaluation for School Development,* Milton Keynes: The Open University

Mackay R (1991) 'How program personnel can help maximise the utility of language program evaluations', in S Anivan (ed) *Issues in Language Programme Evaluation in the 1990s.* Anthology Series 27, Singapore: Regional Language Centre, pp60–71

MacDonald B (1987) 'Evaluation and the control of education', in R Murphy R and H Torrance (eds) *Evaluating Education: Issues and Methods,* London: Harper and Row Publishers

Mitchell R (1990) 'Evaluation of second language teaching projects and programmes', *Language, Culture and Curriculum,* 3, 1, pp3–18

Nevo D (1986) 'Conceptualisation of educational evaluation', in E House (ed) *New Directions in Educational Evaluation,* Lewes: The Falmer Press

Norris N (1993) *Understanding Educational Evaluation,* London: Kogan Page

Parlett M and Hamilton D (1976) 'Evaluation as illumination: A new approach to the study of innovative programmes', in G V Glass (ed) *Evaluation Studies Review Annual,* 1, Beverley Hills, California: Sage, pp140–157

Patton M Q (1990) *Qualitative Evaluation and Research Methods,* 2nd edition, London: Sage Publications

Pawson R and Tilley N(1997) *Realistic Evaluation,* London: Sage

Sanday A (1993) 'The relationship between educational research and evaluation and the role of the local education authority', in R G Burgess (ed) *Educational Research and Evaluation for Policy and Practice?* London: The Falmer Press, pp32–43

Scriven M (1967) 'The methodology of evaluation', *Perspectives of Curriculum Evaluation,* Aera Monograph Series on Curriculum Evaluation, 1, Rand McNally & Company, pp39–83

Stake R E (1975) *Evaluating the Arts in Education: A Responsive Approach,* Columbus, Ohio: Charles E Merrill

Stenhouse L (1975) *An Introduction to Curriculum Research and Development,* London: Heinemann Educational

Tyler R (1986) 'Changing concepts of educational evaluation', *International Journal of Educational Research,* 10, 1, pp1–113

van Lier L (1988) *The Classroom and the Language Learner,* London: Longman

Weir C and Roberts J (1994) *Evaluation in ELT,* Oxford: Blackwell

Weiss C (1972) *Evaluation Research: Methods of Assessing Program Effectiveness,* Englewood Cliffs, NJ: Prentice Hall

Processes of MFL Speech Production and their Curricular Implications

DAVID A WILKINS, University of Reading

It has become largely a truism in the field of foreign language teaching that, since the aim of language teaching is to enable people to learn a foreign language, a prior understanding of the nature of foreign language learning is essential before a suitable approach to teaching can be decided. In this paper I do not wish to challenge the rationality of this argument, but to suggest that the views of language learning on which current practice tends to be based are too narrow and do not give full recognition to the complexity and variety of the mental processes which actually operate in the production of speech or writing in a foreign language.[1] The reasons for our failure to acknowledge the full nature of these processes are themselves complex. They are consequences of among other things the simplifying assumptions typically made in the construction of models of language and language behaviour. They also reflect genuine problems faced in trying to conduct empirical research into processes that may by definition be unobservable. I will explore the extent to which it is in fact now possible to make relevant observations concerning processes involved in speech production and report some initial, informal research which, it can be argued, demonstrates that existing models are unsatisfactory as a basis for language teaching practice. I will suggest that in so far as approaches to the teaching of foreign languages are justified by reference to such models, they need to be modified to take account of the true state of affairs.

---

1   It is interesting to note, for example, that Ellis's (1994) survey of research into second language acquisition dedicates only 10 of its 700 or more pages to how learners use their L2 knowledge, though, as he points out, cognitive theories of acquisition are often simultaneously theories of use (Ellis, 1994, pp393–403).

SOME CURRENT IDEAS AND THEIR LIMITATIONS

Let me start by describing some characteristics of what I might call idealised second language speakers. Like fully mature monolingual speakers they have knowledge of the language system that they are using and on the basis of this knowledge can construct utterances (perhaps sentences) in the foreign language. This knowledge is not conscious, hence the preference in the linguistic literature to refer to it as *competence,* but it enables speakers to select lexemes, to modify their form if necessary, to arrange them in sequences and to give them some phonological realisation, all with the purpose of conveying meanings which will express their intentions. These speakers are not like L1 speakers of the same language because they do not yet deploy a language system which is identical to that of the L1 target (if it ever will be). Nonetheless they operate the system in fundamentally the same way. That is to say, they possess a rule-governed system through which they are capable of producing novel utterances in the foreign language.

Although this is referred to above as an 'idealised view', the assumption, if only implicitly, in much of the recent literature is that this is indeed the core process by which speech is produced in a foreign language. A substantial, probably dominant proportion of all empirical and theoretical research carried out into second language acquisition in recent years has been dedicated to discovering how, over perhaps years of learning, this underlying competence develops and on what principles. Much of this research has been associated with concepts derived from theoretical linguistics and to the exploration of the relevance to second language acquisition (SLA) of Chomsky's Universal Grammar and of the Principles and Parameters theory. Other research has been founded on the notion of *interlanguage,* that is, the idea that the learner possesses an evolving language system which is seen as the basis for speech production. An acceptance of the idealised view was quite explicit in the influential work of Krashen reported in the 1970s and 1980s. He argued that the initiation of speech in a second language could only take place from within the 'acquired system' and that any other kind of learning could not modify the underlying system itself although it could be used to monitor and, under certain conditions, change the output from that system.

There are, of course, alternative views, though none that have generated a comparable volume of empirical research specifically dedicated to SLA. One that has in the last few years begun to have an impact in the language teaching and applied linguistic literature suggests that the learner's competence is to a significant degree based on a variety of what may be loosely called *prefabricated sequences* (here used as a cover term for *idioms, fixed phrases, partially productive sentence stems* and *collocations*).[2] These may be sequences that have been learned from the beginning as fixed, unanalysed chunks. Alternatively they may be sequences that have become so familiar through frequent need and use that they are no longer composed by the more general linguistic processes. It has been argued that spoken, conversational output, at least, is primarily constructed on the basis of such sequences with the more orthodox compositional processes playing a secondary role. There is a real problem in finding objective and non-arbitrary ways of defining and identifying such units and of distinguishing sequences that are actually processed as fixed sequences by speakers and that are therefore psycho-linguistically significant from those that are merely frequent in occurrence in the language, but probably few would deny that they play some role in language output.

It is not difficult to identify language teaching practices which can be associated with these two views of the nature of linguistic knowledge and of its use in actual speech although these practices have not necessarily been justified in the first place by reference to specific theoretical stances. A widespread characteristic of *communicative language teaching,* for example, is the attempt to reproduce in the classroom activities which capture all the essential conditions of meaningful linguistic communication. This is done through the use of simulations, games, information transfer and other techniques often broadly characterised as *task-based learning.* Where such activities are preceded by linguistically focused forms of language teaching, they may be seen as simply promoting the integration of different aspects of linguistic knowledge and as increasing fluency in the language. But for some they provide the only essential conditions for foreign language learning on the grounds that engagement in the meaningful and purposive use of language is not only necessary but also sufficient for the operation of the natural language acquisition processes. That is to say, exposed to and engaged with language in this way, learners will develop the kind of underlying rule-based competence referred to earlier. It is even claimed by some that the development of this competence is unaffected by direct language teaching.

---

2   These are discussed briefly in Ellis (1994, pp84–88). A comprehensive review is provided by
     Weinert (1995). See also Ellis (1996).

By contrast the emphasis on the role of prefabricated sequences may find echos in some forms of *(notional-)functional language teaching.* The syllabuses followed for foreign language teaching in British schools show a strong influence of the notional-functional approach developed by the Council of Europe projects from the 1970s onwards. These syllabuses attach considerable importance to forms of language needed for the exercise of common functions of language and for participation in everyday spoken interaction. In practice this has meant that in the first few years of language learning (the learning of French in almost all cases) particular emphasis is laid upon role-plays, dialogues and question-and-answer sessions with a high proportion of routinised behaviour, that is, sequences in which use can be made of utterances which are either wholly memorised or which can be used with minimal modification. Presumably such language teaching would find support from those who believe that such fixed sequences play an important role in normal speech processing.

By implying that the two positions sketched above are indeed *in contrast,* we are engaging in the familiar dialectic process whereby we tend to oppose differing viewpoints rather than attempt to reconcile them. This is perhaps a necessary part of the process whereby we explore fully the implications of a given theoretical perspective, but it has its dangers when it also forms the basis for some kind of applied linguistic practice, the teaching of a foreign language, for example. There is very little justification for pedagogy to follow theory in this blind way. The problem is that without direct evidence of the kinds of knowledge that speakers of a foreign language have and of which knowledge they make use in producing speech and how, we have no way of knowing whether one of these views is the correct one, whether both are in fact correct and reconcilable or whether, indeed, the picture is more complicated still. The fact is that virtually no research has been conducted into the cognitive processes in which L2 speakers engage when they produce an utterance and into the kinds of skills and knowledge that actually contribute to that performance. If we had a better understanding of these matters it would enable us to judge in what domains learners' competence needs to be developed. The belief that has motivated this paper is that there may well be not one, economically describable competence that underlies performance, but a variety of competences which may contribute together to the forms that the speaker's utterances have. At the very least we need to address the issue directly in order to obtain what evidence we can.

AN EXPERIMENTAL ELICITATION TECHNIQUE

Is it possible to find objective evidence concerning the cognitive processes involved in second language speech production? One major SLA researcher at least had doubts.

> *It may prove impossible to find empirical evidence to prove what sorts of knowledge underlie different kinds of interlanguage performance.* (Tarone, 1988, p75)

It is clear that the processes themselves cannot be directly observed. This leaves two alternatives: either we must find ways of inferring from performance evidence and associated theorising what unobservable processes have been responsible for the output observed, or we must use the producers themselves as witnesses to what has taken place. Neither is unproblematic. It is far from certain that reliable inferences can be drawn from performance evidence and we cannot be sure that what producers tell us actually reflects adequately the processes that have taken place. In any case, speakers themselves cannot know what *unconscious* processes are taking place. Nonetheless it is the latter option that seems to me to offer us the best hope of making some progress in understanding the nature of the processes involved and it is on this that I have collected some initial informal evidence as a basis for the design of a possible, more rigorous research programme.

The use of data from learners' introspective accounts is by no means new in second language research. *Retrospective* accounts have been widely used for research into learning strategies. *On-line* accounts have been used in research into comprehension. In the former case, subjects are expected to reflect on their learning experiences over relatively long periods of time. In the latter case think-aloud protocols are prepared which are held to provide evidence of comprehension processes, though there has been criticism that the technique interferes with normal processing. Neither, as it stands, is suitable for research into language production especially speech production. Retrospective accounts are too distant from the moment of production for subjects to be able to retrieve accurate information. On-line accounts cannot be provided simultaneously with the act of production itself. This is not to say that producers' introspections cannot be tapped at all. Current research into written composition processes includes computer software-based techniques which capture all modifications made by the writer to a text and permit the researcher to interview the producer to investigate the motivations behind the changes that were made.[3] This research, however, tends to be concerned more with discoursal features of text production than with processes in the encoding of conceptual meaning.

The data collection reported here uses an experimental technique whereby subjects are engaged in an unprepared L2 (French) conversation which is of short duration (3 or 4 minutes) and which is recorded. The recording is subsequently replayed to the subject. One utterance in the conversation is then focused on and the subject is asked to report in the L1 (English) on all the mental processes by which the content and form of that utterance were arrived at. The technique requires that the researcher can readily and promptly identify an utterance which will provide interesting insights. It is also inevitable that the subject's introspections benefit from some prompting and that care has to be taken that the subject does not respond simply according to the researcher's own agenda. This is not intended to be the place for either a full-scale report or an evaluation of the technique, but one positive thing that did emerge was that under these conditions subjects retain for active recall a good deal of relevant information about their mental activities during or in the seconds immediately preceding the production of their utterance. In this particular instance the subjects were three comprehensive school learners of French. They were in their sixth year of secondary schooling and were all at the end of their first year of an A-level course. There is no assumption that they were representative of all learners of French. They were relatively successful language learners and were chosen by their teacher (who did not know either the purpose of the study or the technique to be used) who had been told only that the subjects should be articulate in English. After a brief introductory exchange with the researcher, the subject was asked to recount some episode in her/his life which had made a strong impression. It was from this part of the exchange that the utterance that formed the basis for the analysis was to be taken.

SOME DATA

In this paper I am not primarily concerned to evaluate the feasibility of the technique. Suffice to say that on the basis of this limited, informal feasibility study I am convinced that speakers' active recall within a short time-span can

---

3   Work in progress at the University of Reading is reported in Spelman Miller (1998).

provide useful insights into the processes by which speakers produce utterances in a second language and further that those insights deserve careful consideration for their possible implications for language learning. For the moment let me focus on some broad indications that are clearly provided by the data obtained. The data will be reported under the following headings:

> Proceduralised knowledge: prefabricated sequences
> Proceduralised knowledge: compositional processes
> Declarative knowledge
> Use of the L1
> Other comments

PREFABRICATED SEQUENCES

Even at this relatively advanced level, subjects are clear that certain strings forming either part of or whole utterances were produced as chunks, that is to say were retrieved as wholes and were not the result of compositional processes. Typical examples cited were:

1 *J'aime beaucoup ...*
2 *Je suis allé ...*
3 *J'ai une soeur qui s'appelle Vicky*

Of (1) the speaker said, 'the reason that phrase came was because that's sort of the basic learning that's really been drummed into you when I was a lot younger ... it always comes back first and then you want to elaborate on it'.

(2) '... is just a phrase that is so much instilled in you I just know it'. Of particular interest in this case is the phonology. The liaison of the /z/ of *suis* before *allé* is performed without the slightest hesitation or, apparently, awareness. Liaisons elsewhere are usually much more tentatively produced or are omitted altogether.

For (3) the subject reports the researcher's enquiry as to whether he had a sister as being 'like a trigger sentence' and agreed that 'that sentence just came out straightaway'. In response to the question of whether this was the sort of sentence that he had said before, he responded 'a lot', and as to whether this was in oral work in class, 'exactly'.

It may not be entirely accidental that each of the above phrases begins an utterance with a first person Subject. All subjects reported that in many such cases they would not have been able to process the form as readily if either the Subject or the tense of the verb had been different. This provides added confirmation that, although these forms are unconsciously produced, they are not the product of a rule-governed process. As suggested above they also regularly reported that the availability of these forms stemmed from the heavy insistence on routinised language performance in the early years of their learning of French. Thus, in order to distinguish prefabricated sequences from other sequences that are produced by unconscious processes, it is necessary to tap into the subjects' awareness of their previous language learning experience.

COMPOSITIONAL PROCESSES

I refer to the production of any (part of a) string by direct retrieval from underlying linguistic competence as a compositional process. This may include the successful identification or inclusion of a grammatical element or of a lexical item. Not everything is therefore strictly compositional. By definition these are the processes that will be least of all accessible to introspection and will be most taken for granted by the speakers. As noted above, it is only the subject's knowledge of his or her previous learning experience that may differentiate some such strings from those produced as prefabricated sequences, since either may be produced with little or no consciousness of processing. The relation with declarative knowledge is discussed in the next section.

By the absence of comment from the subjects and by their generally consistent performance in respect of certain grammatical features, it can be inferred that major sentence constituents are generally ordered unproblematically. A number of lexico-grammatical elements are placed and mostly formed with facility, e.g. preposed articles, subject pronouns, auxiliary verbs, demonstratives, prepositions, possessive adjectives. The considerable similarity between English and French where many aspects of sequencing are concerned probably accounts for the subjects' facility in operating these systems. However there is also evidence of rule-based processing in one instance where the two languages differ. One subject produces the following examples involving adjective placement.

4 *une île grecque*
5 *j'ai ma voiture propre ... ma propre voiture*
6 *les pays étranges*

(4) receives no comment from the subject and is one of a number of instances (noted in all three subjects) showing that the sequence N + Adj is strongly established. Indeed so strongly is it established that when he wishes to refer to his *own* car (requiring the use of the word *propre* in the exceptional pre-nominal position) he places it after the noun but then corrects himself in recognition that in post-nominal position *propre* means *clean*. Similarly, although (6) is not correct target French, it orders noun and adjective in the regular way. What is striking about this is that the subject actually initiates this sequence in English:

7 *I wanted to say **foreign** countries so that was more a case of thinking the two words and then putting them together*

But the 'putting together' actually takes place in French following the now well-mastered rule.

Another subject provides other evidence that self-correction is not necessarily made on the basis of declarative knowledge, i.e. that monitoring can take place using judgements from within the second language system:

8 *j'étais ... mm ... J'avais douze ans*

Asked whether she corrected herself because she remembered that with expressions of age the verb *avoir* is used she replied, 'no, it's not really remembered it's, it's more when you say it of when you know you think perhaps it sounds strange so you go on and correct yourself afterwards'. There seems to be clear reference here to a grammatical intuition based on under-lying competence.

DECLARATIVE KNOWLEDGE

Declarative knowledge is defined here as any kind of knowledge however arrived at and however organised which has not been proceduralised. It may thus be some kind of explicit, conscious grammatical rule, but it could equally be some mnemonic device or procedure, a memorised paradigm, some meta-linguistic reasoning procedure (the conscious use of analogy, for example) or any other comparable aid to deciding the form of the output. There is ample evidence that the subjects use declarative knowledge.

In relation to (8) above the subject indicates that the problem is finding the appropriate form for the past tense *(imparfait)* of the verb *avoir*. 'Well that tense hasn't been so much sort of drummed into us so mm I think you have to really think about it first ...' In trying to find the appropriate form, she unfortunately substitutes the imperfect form of *être,* a not uncommon confusion. The same subject also says:

9   *If you had a more complicated sentence then it would, say, with the tenses if you had to say I had had I would say **I had had** and then convert it to English (error for French) ... that wouldn't come naturally*

This clearly implies the existence of some kind of conscious retrieval system. The rote learning of numerals has a clear effect on processing:

10 *Obviously one to ten is fine it's between ten and twenty that the problems come in ... sometimes even now I have to go through my head sort of from one to thirteen...*

11 *elle travaille comme ... comme ... representif*

Without the subject's own evidence here one might conclude that in (11) the hesitation was caused by the search for an appropriate lexical item, but the speaker's observation reveals what appears to be a classic case of Krashen-style monitoring:

12 *the pause ... I remembered ... that when you're talking about someone's job you don't say **un**... so I consciously stopped myself saying it*

Use of the L1

It is clear that many utterances or parts of utterances are initiated in English. These may be anything from individual lexical items to whole predicates:

13 *Pour une voyage ... compagnie de voyage
I was trying to say 'travel-agent'
Thinking in English? 'Yeah'*

14 *Au moment*
   Probably just said, 'at the moment' to myself, so it is translated

15 *Elle travaille comme representif*
   That came as an English sentence beforehand

16 *I was searching for her age in English*
   i.e. conceptualisation requiring calculation carried out in English but 'no translation'

Conceptualisation in English is often allied to declarative knowledge:

17 *J'etais mm mm j'avais douze ans*
   *You have to really think about it first and that does go to English first in your head and then then it's converted to French cos in English it's **I was** but you say **j'avais***

OTHER COMMENTS

Other comments made by the subjects show an awareness of factors influencing their output. These include the benefits of earlier focused learning: 'we've done that' and the desire to produce language that is not too English-sounding: 'that's trying to make it sound more French than you know really sort of basic GCSE French', 'I think I'm a bit worried about it sounding really English ... you don't want to sound too English'.

The experimental situation itself stimulated reflection by the subjects on the nature of their own knowledge and skill:

18 *It's strange the way some things are now embedded I can just recall straightaway and other things they're there but I have to think about them more ... and they're not ... the other level where I'm going straight through the English*

The subject seems to be suggesting that there is a level of awareness or of cognitive effort which comes between wholly proceduralised knowledge and dependence on initiation in the L1 probably accompanied by use of declarative knowledge.

DISCUSSION

A proper consideration of both the value and the limitations of investigating speech processes by use of speakers' self-reports must be deferred to another occasion. The technique is never likely to be sufficient to support a comprehensive theory of second language speech production. Nonetheless I would suggest that, even on the basis of the limited and insufficiently representative evidence presented here, there is a prima facie case for saying that speech output draws not on a single underlying proceduralised linguistic competence but on a variety of competences which frequently operate and interact even within the same utterance or within the same linguistic unit. The initiation of speech may be in the first or the second language; linguistic elements may be retrieved and combined as unanalysed chunks, from wholly internalised L2 knowledge, from various kinds of declarative knowledge including mnemonic systems, from direct associations between L1 and L2 forms and from more general cognitive processes such as the use of analogy. Control of any one part of the language system will not be simply *either* a matter of *automatic* production from internalised rule *or* the wholly conscious application of explicit knowledge of the language system. What is more, there may also be intermediate levels of control which being neither wholly conscious nor wholly automatic require different levels of cognitive effort and attention to achieve speech output. And, to repeat, any individual utterance is likely to be the consequence of the operation of several of these processes.

I suspect that the reader will say that this is only to state what any language learner or indeed speaker of a foreign language already knows. If that is so, we might ask why the possible significance of this state of affairs has not been more explicitly considered in either the research or the pedagogic literature. It may be because many of these processes have been perceived as actually inhibiting the development of 'real' competence in the L2 and therefore as needing to be discouraged. While agreeing that the ultimate aim of language learning will be to proceduralise language knowledge to the extent that the learner's time and circumstances permit, I would argue that the dependence of virtually all learners, even to the most advanced levels, on all the processes that have been referred to above demands that we should regard those processes not as handicaps but as part of the learners' resources. There is every reason to argue that if these processes are going to be used, then it is to the language learner's benefit that they should be used as effectively and efficiently as possible.

It may be becoming clear now why I regard what we may be able to discover about production processes as having *curricular implications*. I assume a foreign language learning context in which contact with language is limited in time and is restricted to the instructional environment, that is, is largely unavailable outside the classroom. At one end of the spectrum of views of communicative language teaching is the position that the necessary and sufficient condition for language learning is the opportunity for communicative engagement in the language. The evidence is that while in theory this might enable learners to develop a linguistic competence, in practice that competence and the consequent performance would be severely limited in scope by the poverty of the experience, quantitatively and qualitatively, that the classroom can provide. Given that most learners will have developed conceptual and cognitive abilities that go well beyond what can readily be expressed with such a limited competence, the availability of other mechanisms to service language performance should be seen as a very positive factor. If learners can call on declarative knowledge of the L2, knowledge of communicatively useful fixed phrases and even perhaps knowledge of the way in which the forms of the L1 may be related to forms of the L2, their capacity to express the meanings and social functions of language will be significantly extended. It is in my view important to recognise that over a long period of time the engagement of processes based on the L1 and on declarative knowledge makes available to the speaker communicative resources of far greater range and complexity than what will be available solely from proceduralised language knowledge.

A language curriculum that recognises this will find a place for activities which encourage the learner to focus on aspects of the language system, to become aware of important characteristics of that system and to be able to make use of them even before they have become fully internalised. The learner's resulting experience of language will be a mixed one. Of course it will include the now familiar communicative activities, it will embrace fixed phrases of high social and textual utility, but it will also encompass activities which deal explicitly with the language system, which aid the learner to develop control of specific aspects of that system, which draw attention to significant differences between the L2 and the L1 and which may well in the process stimulate the learner's intellectual curiosity about a language (and culture) that is different from the L1.

The mixed experiences of language that will result from such an approach will not simply be a mushy eclecticism as has sometimes been suggested, but a rational reaction to a fuller understanding and appreciation of how people produce a second language and of the way in which language teaching can actually promote communicative capacity by taking account of that understanding.

REFERENCES

Ellis N (1996) 'Sequencing in second language acquisition', *Studies in Second Language Acquisition,* 18, 1

Ellis R (1994) *The Study of Second Language Acquisition,* Oxford: Oxford University Press

Krashen S (1981) *Second Language Acquisition and Second Language Learning,* Oxford: Pergamon

Spelman Miller K S (1998) 'Aspects of written text production: A study of on-line writing on two tasks', in U Schuurs and G Jeffrey (eds) *Literacy in a Second Language: L2 reading and writing skill,* Amsterdam: Amsterdam University Press

Tarone E (1995) *Variation in Interlanguage,* London: Edward Arnold

Weinert R (1995) 'The role of formulaic language in second language acquisition', *Applied Linguistics,* 16, 2

PART III
LITERACIES IN SCHOOL AND SOCIETY

New Literacy Studies:
Hobbesian Fears and Utopian Desires

BRIAN V STREET, University of London

THE 'PROBLEM'

My 'problem' stems from the anthropological observation that a visiting Martian might be surprised at the extent to which arcane debates about literacy, language and learning appear in the public domain in contemporary British and American society. Popular newspapers and tabloids as well as the 'quality' press, and also television and radio seem full of accounts by 'experts' of their own piece of the struggle over the meanings of literacy and in particular the acquisition of literacy: phonics vs whole language, code-based vs meaning-based reading, cognitive and situated models of literacy. Although my own interest has mainly been in uses rather than acquisition of literacy and my own part in the debate has been about social practices associated with reading and writing, rather than psycholinguistic conflicts over the grapheme/ phoneme relationship, I am intrigued by the way in which these debates have taken on a social character of their own. Other academics working in other niches of the intellectual horizon may go a lifetime without their debates appearing in the headlines of the *Independent on Sunday* newspaper (1993) or splashed across full-page spreads of the *Sunday Times* (1994): so it is a matter of intellectual and social history why this should be the case with respect to literacy and language in education. That this may appear common sense to some – 'literacy is the basics, the ground on which other social practices in modern society rest' – attracts my attention even more. What counts as common sense in one culture and in one era may indeed be arcane or ideologically fundamental in another. And there have certainly been many times and places where that view of literacy has not been the received wisdom.

So, what is the 'Literacy debate'? I do not intend to outline it in detail here, as my interest is more in explaining the current representations of it and Wray (1997) has recently provided a clear summary of the issues. According to Wray the debate can be traced back through a quarter of a century:

> *... yet still appears to centre around two polarised positions. Chall (1967) set the terms of the debate as being on the one hand between those who advocated a code-based approach to teaching reading and on the other those who emphasised the place of meaning.* (Wray, 1991, p161)

This basic divide seems to remain, even where the terms may have shifted somewhat, to conflicts between 'Phonics' and Whole Language/'Real Books', (Goodman, 1996, 1998; Willinsky, 1990; Meek, 1991); the role of 'Phonics' in the UK National Curriculum (Dombey, 1998; Beard, 1993); whether written alphabetic knowledge is best learned 'naturally' (Willinsky, 1990) or through formal delivery (OFSTED, 1996); and to a distinction between 'autonomous' and 'ideological' models which I suggested in 1985 and which has recently been adapted for teachers in adult literacy programmes (Fiedrich, 1996, reprinted in LAC, 1997). Many researchers, including Wray himself, have tried to propose a 'balanced' approach and most teachers probably combine use of 'real' materials and learning for meaning, with workshop-type sessions on particular problems of the phoneme/grapheme relationship. Nagy and Anderson (1999) have recently argued on theoretical grounds that phonemic awareness requires both practice in 'natural' conditions and some explicit instruction. Research suggests that 'it should be considered an outcome, rather than a cause, of learning to read' (p2): they resolve what appears a paradox in the Literacy Debate by postulating 'a reciprocal relationship' between phonemic awareness and learning to read: although the concept of phoneme is essential to the alphabetic insight, letters provide a scaffold for the development of this difficult concept. It is the process of beginning to learn to read that draws the child's attention to letters, sounds and their relationships, enabling the insight which unlocks the system' (p2). In other words, formal learning of the phoneme/grapheme relationship – what is popularly known as 'phonics' – is not enough: learners also learn through practice and use. But neither is practice and use sufficient, as some Whole Language proponents suggest: some formal learning is also necessary. This, then, is the sense in which language and learning theory lead to a 'balanced' approach.

Some recent 'balanced' approaches, however, may not be quite as even-handed as the term suggests. A recent book that claims to offer 'balanced perspectives' provides an object lesson in how ideological arguments are disguised behind the supposedly detached and neutral discourse of the autonomous model of literacy. Roger Beard, (1993, p1) cites favourably Chall's (1967, 1983) claim that 'overall, code-emphasis approaches produce better results in the teaching of early reading'. According to Beard, this is 'not a surprising conclusion because the English writing system is an *alphabetic* one ...' thereby apparently rejecting the 'balanced' view of the character of alphabetic systems put forward by Nagy and Anderson above. Although the book claims to provide a 'balanced approach' to the phonics (or code-emphasis) and whole language (or meaning emphasis) approaches, it is quite clear that its editor and the selection of chapters leans towards the former: the term balance here does not refer to the balance of articles in the book, which mainly privilege a phonics and skills-based approach, but indicates that this book is intended to 'balance' the influence of the whole-language and child-centred view, which has clearly held sway for too long. This notion of 'balance' represents probably the dominant discourse in current policy documents (LTF, 1997; TTA, 1997; DfEE 1998), which frequently claim that 'research shows' a phonics approach to be best and blames falling standards of literacy on the strength of the whole-language, meaning-based movement of the 1970s and 80s.

The debate itself, then, is almost always loaded, despite the frequent claims to scientific knowledge, objectivity and common-sense truths about the nature of language and literacy. The debates and the discourses in which they are represented need both locating and explaining. In this paper I shall attempt to apply to it some insights from recent anthropologically-oriented views of literacy, that are coming to be known as the 'New Literacy Studies'. I will firstly explain what NLS refers to, detail some of the theoretical ground and understandings of language and literacy on which it stands and pursue the implications of these new approaches for the problem posed. Finally I will suggest ways in which educational policies around curriculum and teaching may be affected by these developments. This is not so much to 'resolve' the debate as to shift the ground on which we consider issues of language and literacy in the first place.

NEW UNDERSTANDINGS OF LANGUAGE AND LITERACY

The New Literacy Studies (Gee, 1991; Street, 1984, 1993) consist of a series of writings, in both research and practice, that treat language and literacy as social practices rather than technical skills to be learned in formal education. The research requires language and literacy to be studied as they occur naturally in social life, taking account of the context and their different meanings for different cultural groups. The practice requires curriculum designers, teachers, and evaluators to take account of the variation in meanings and uses that students bring from their home backgrounds to formal learning contexts, such as the school and the classroom. NLS[1] emphasises the importance of 'culturally sensitive teaching' (Villegas, 1991) in building upon students' own knowledge and skills (Heath, 1983; Heath and Mangiola, 1991).

The new research and practice are based upon new ideas about the nature of language and literacy. In turn the research has reinforced and developed these ideas (Collins, 1995). There are two major tenets to this new thinking: (a) the notion of 'Social literacies'; (b) that language is 'Dialogic'.

'Social literacies'

This phrase (Street,1995) refers to the nature of literacy as social practice and to the plurality of literacies that this enables us to observe. That literacy is a social practice is an insight both banal and profound: banal, in the sense that once we think about it is obvious that literacy is always practised in social contexts and that even the school, however 'artificial' it be accused of being in its ways of teaching reading and writing, is also a social construction. The school, like other contexts, has its own social beliefs and behaviours into which its particular literacy practices are inserted. The notion is, in this sense, also profound in that it leads to quite new ways of understanding and defining what counts as literacy and has profound implications for how we teach reading and writing. If literacy is a social practice, then it varies with social context and is not the same, uniform thing in each case.

I have described this latter view as an 'autonomous' model of literacy: the view that literacy in itself has consequences irrespective of, or autonomous of,

---

1   NLS here refers to the New Literacy Studies. Since the article was penned, the UK government's policy – the National Literacy Strategy – has also come to be referred to as NLS.

context. In contrast with this view, I have posed an 'ideological' model of literacy, which argues that literacy not only varies with social context and with cultural norms and discourses regarding, for instance, identity, gender and belief, but that its uses and meanings are always embedded in relations of power. It is in this sense that literacy is always 'ideological' – it always involves contests over meanings, definitions and boundaries and struggles for control of the literacy agenda. If that is true, then it becomes harder to justify teaching only one particular form of literacy, whether in schools or in adult programmes – or at least the justification needs to be made explicit. If literacy is seen as simply a universal technical skill, the same everywhere, then the particular form being taught in school gets to be treated as the only kind, as the universal standard that naturalises its socially specific features and disguises their real history and ideological justifications. If literacy is seen as a social practice, then that history and those features and justifications need to be spelled out and students need to be able to discuss the basis for choices being made in the kind of literacy they are learning.

Recently there has been some elaboration of key concepts in this field, such as the notion of 'multiple literacies', literacy events and practices, social, community and individual literacies. I will briefly indicate the issues and outline my own position. One of the major tenets of the New Literacy Studies has been that literacy is not a single, essential thing, with predictable consequences for individual and social development. Instead there are multiple literacies that vary with time and place and are embedded in specific cultural practices. Examples of variation in literacies have included Heath's (1983) account of three literacies associated with three communities in the Piedmont Carolinas – Roadville, Trackton and Maintown literacies; my own (Street, 1985) account of three literacies in an Iranian village (schooled literacy, 'Qoranic' literacy and commercial literacy); Barton and Ivanič's (1991) account of 'community literacies' in the north of England; descriptions of schooled and sub rosa literacies amongst adolescents in the US by Shuman (1993), Camitta (1993) and Bennet and Sola (1994); and Besnier's (1996) analysis of the literacies associated with sermons and with letter writing in Nukulaelae.

Recently concern has been expressed regarding this pluralisation of 'literacies'. Wagner argues that this creates a new reification in which each literacy appears a fixed and essential thing. I have argued that there is a danger of associating a literacy with a culture where current anthropological perspectives suggest fragmentation and hybridity in both domains (Street,

Culture is a Verb, 1993). Kress sees the claim for plurality of literacies as paradoxical for NLS since it implies a stability in each literacy that such researchers explicitly reject:

*This paradox only exists if in the first place we assume that language is autonomous, unaffected by the social, and therefore **stable**. If we assume that language is **dynamic** because it is constantly being remade by its users in response to the demands of their social environments, we do not then have a need to invent a plurality of literacies: it is a normal and absolutely fundamental characteristic of language and of literacy to be constantly remade in relation to the needs of the moment; it is neither autonomous or stable, and nor is it a single integrated phenomenon; it is messy and diverse and not in need of pluralising.* (Kress, 1997, p115)

Although I agree with Kress in principle, and indeed this argument reinforces the point I am making here about dynamic models of language and literacy, I think that for strategic reasons it has been important to put forward the argument regarding plurality. I have found particularly in development circles, where agencies present literacy as the panacea to social ills and the key ingredient in modernisation, the dominant assumption has been of a single autonomous literacy that is the same everywhere and simply needs transplanting to new environments. In order to challenge this view and to focus on the specificity and dynamic character of literacy, the notion of multiple literacies has played an important role.

There is, however, another sense in which the plurality of literacies has come to be used and here I agree fully with Kress: he argues that this second sense comes from the metaphorical extension of the concept of literacy to other *domains* of social life, such as computing, politics etc. One even hears of emotional literacy. Apart from glib and lazy rhetorical usages, Kress also sees these extensions as flawed in that they fail to see language as just one of many modes of communication.

*Because it is seen as **the only real mode** as the most highly developed, the one that sustains thought and rationality, all other modes of communication, or for that matter, all cultural **systems**, have to be described as being literacy. This devalues the term, so that it comes to mean nothing more than 'skill' (as in keyboard skills) or competence. It* *also prevents the possibility of examining the actual function of other systems as systems in their own right.* (Kress, 1997, p115)

This then raises the question of the boundaries of what is included under the term 'literacy', which Kress and I would agree is a multiple and complex of phenomena, including print, text as block, letters, text as genre, letters as sound, media layout etc. I would just add that recent debates about 'multi-literacies' (cf New London Group, 1996) seem to imply a similar reduction of the concept of literacy to a given channel – in this case the multi in multi-literacy seems to refer to whether the particular literacy is in the visual, media or print domain as though each were a separate literacy. I would prefer to think of literacies as some complex of these domains that varies with context, so that the mix of visual, print and other aspects depends upon cultural and contextual features. Computer literacy, for instance, is not a new single literacy but involves different uses of oral and literate channels in different situations: there is no one phenomenon called Computer Literacy and the term can be misleading in both research and policy terms.

I have preferred for research purposes, if not immediately for policy purposes, to work with the concept of 'literacy practices'. This term enables us to specify the particularity of cultural practices with which uses of reading and/or writing are associated in given contexts. Within a given cultural domain there may be many literacy practices i.e. not one culture one literacy. By literacy practices I mean not only the observable behaviours around literacy – Heath's 'literacy events' – but also the concepts and meanings brought to those events and which give them meaning. Strictly speaking, then, the literacies referred to above – Heath's three Piedmont communities and their different literacies; the Iranian village literacies; community literacies in the north of England; schooled and out of school literacies, etc – are best thought of as literacy practices. It is sometimes clumsy to refer to, for instance, 'schooled literacy practices', especially in contexts where policy makers and the media are still working with an autonomous model of literacy that scarcely gives credence to out of school literacies anyway. There the specification of the dynamic and culturally-specific and valued character of local literacies requires still the pluralisation, despite Kress and others' reservations. But in situ, when one is dealing with the particular forms of reading and writing and their meanings to different groups of people, the concept of 'literacy practices' becomes the key term.

From this perspective one may ask what are the literacy practices at home of children whose schooled literacy practices are judged problematic or inadequate. From the school's point of view those home practices may represent simply inferior attempts at the real thing: from the researcher's point of view those home practices represent as important a part of the repertoire as different languages or language varieties. Viewing them as literacy practices can help both perspectives to address exactly what such literacy involves and, from a pedagogic point of view, what is there to be built upon if the aim is to help such people to add dominant literacy practices to their linguistic repertoire. Whilst 'literacy practice' may traditionally refer to classroom behaviours, the term 'literacy practices' allows us to adopt a broader and more culturally relative perspective and thereby to see and value varieties of literacy practices that we might otherwise miss and that would certainly remain marginalised through such lack of attention.

Dialogic language

New theories of language closely associated with those regarding 'social literacies', focus upon the nature of language as a continually negotiated process of meaning making as well as taking. In this research tradition, it is viewed as always a social process, as interactive and dynamic (Volosinov, 1973; Hymes, 1977; Halliday, 1978). For Bakhtin (1981), language is both centrifugal and centripetal, in the sense that users are always struggling to extend its boundaries and meanings as well as working within prescribed limits; and it is 'dialogic' in the sense that it is always in dialogue – language, even when employed silently by single individuals, is always part of a social interaction, whether with imagined others or with the meanings and uses of words that others have employed at other times and places. As Bakhtin states, 'words come saturated with the meanings of others'. Again this view of language might appear commonsensical at one level – we all know that languages vary, whether that means the differences between French and English, or at a more local level between different dialects, creoles and patois. But the implications of this stance, like that of 'social literacies', are at the same time profound. If language is always contested, negotiated and employed in social interaction, then the appropriateness of particular uses and interpretations have likewise to be opened to debate: it becomes impossible to lay down strict and formal rules for all time and the authority of particular users – whether teachers, grammarians or politicians – becomes problematised. We all, as it were, take possession of language again rather than being passive victims of its entailments.

The implications of this view of language are only just being felt in applied studies (cf the work and publications of the British Association for Applied Language Studies (BAAL)). With respect to education and schooling in particular, these perspectives have recently been conveyed through the notion of Critical Language Awareness (Fairclough, 1995) which argues that learners should be facilitated to engage in debates about the nature and meaning of language, rather than be treated as passive victims of its 'structural properties'. This includes learning some metalinguistic terms, but a more inclusive set of such terms, learned for a different purpose than those often put forward by state institutions, such as the recent TTA document on English in the Initial Teacher Training Curriculum for Primary Schools (TTA, 1998) or the National Literacy Strategy (DfEE, 1998). It is to the basis of these dominant views of language, expressed in popular media and through state institutions, that I now turn, to explore reasons why the new, dialogic and social interpretations of language outlined above remain unpalatable in these contexts.

HOBBESIAN FEARS

In recent years there has, indeed, emerged a deep resistance to the above theories and their implications for education. These fears are expressed so powerfully and at such deep psychological levels, that they may be characterised as 'Hobbesian' in the sense that they seem akin to the fear of chaos and disorder that the seventeenth century English philosopher Hobbes argued justified particular forms of government (Hobbes, 1651/1976). Without a contract with a sovereign authority, in the form of the king or an autocratic ruler, and the rules they instituted, society would not exist as life would descend into a primal struggle of all against all: it is government that creates the conditions in which these natural tendencies are restricted and moderated in the interests of all, thus facilitating society and establishing the conditions for relatively harmonious social life. Although philosophers would argue that Hobbes' account of the bases for political authority is in fact logically worked through from observation of the specific character of capitalist society with its focus upon market forces (cf MacPherson, 1976, p38), it is Hobbes' graphic account of the behaviour of men in a hypothetical state of nature that has caught the popular imagination (Hobbes, 1651, ch XIII). The state of nature is a typical seventeenth century trope – excited perhaps by the experience of Civil War – in which the philosopher's logic is followed through in concrete imagery. Hobbes imagines what it would be like if all restraints were removed: every man would constantly be open to violent invasion of his life and property by other men and civilised life itself would be impossible:

> *no Culture of the Earth ... no Arts; no Letters; no Society; and which is worst of all, continuall feare, and danger of violent death; And the life of man, solitary, poore, nasty, brutish, and short.* (Hobbes, 1651, ch13, p62)

'No Letters' indeed. The trope persists in much twentieth century discourse upon literacy, as evidenced in the newspaper records and policy documents cited above. As with government more generally, so with regard to modes of communication, it seems, we need a model of language that institutes formal authority, the autocratic rule of the old grammarians and schoolteachers who keep in check the tendencies of both language and literacy to anarchy. The new theories of language and literacy represented by NLS, with their privileging of variation, difference and challenge to authority, appear to replicate Hobbes' State of Nature where there are no Arts, no Culture and no Letters. If followed through in teaching and education they would lead to disorder in the classroom and inability to communicate in social life. Indeed, much of the literature in the popular press about 'progressive' teaching methods cites as evidence of its dangers the fear of social breakdown, of students' lack of discipline, and employers' worries about the inability of their new employees to communicate – to speak and write the language in ordered ways. Life in this state would indeed then be 'nasty, brutish and short'.

These fears can also be interpreted in terms of another, analogous set of images, offered by the anthropological literature on boundaries and classification, purity and danger. This begins from the famous Durkheim and Mauss (1903) text *Primitive Classification* which argued that categories in nature and in society were socially constructed not just given in the design of the world. The ways in which, for instance, colour or animal life or the organisation of time and space were divided up varied from one society to another; they were social not natural categories. In linguistic terms a development of this perspective has been the classic 'Whorfian hypothesis' which argued that the ways in which a given language divided up categories and drew boundaries between them helped determine how it was possible to think about them. The classification of snow, or of colour, or of animal species, determined how speakers of that language could perceive the items in the natural world designated as snow, colour, or different animal types. The hypothesis is generally known for its unprovability: since any research on this issue has to be conducted through linguistic media, it is impossible to test fully the claims. In any case the 'strong' version is evidently overstated, since categories are more nuanced, most people in the world speak a number of languages so they can shift and overlap between categories and because lexical classification is not the only means of experiencing phenomena – visual, and non-linguistic resources are now recognised to play a bigger part than was recognised at the time.

Nevertheless, a 'weak' version of the Whorfian hypothesis, complementing the Durkheimian thesis on social classification, probably remains the epistemological ground in which anthropology as a discipline exists (as well as new linguistic theories such as Critical Discourse) – if knowledge is rooted in linguistic and social classification, then we cannot presume our own categories are natural or universal and we cannot presume to understand other people's accounts of the world, until we enter their worlds, their language, their classification scheme. Hence the need for comparative ethnographers who will research these different worlds. Hence, though, the fear expressed in popular imagination about items and issues that transgress a given society's boundaries and categories. It is this fear too that new theories of language and literacy have to contend with.

Mary Douglas (1966), writing in the 1960s, extended these insights to the understanding of our own mundane classifications, which she associated with deeper affective attachments to order and disorder. The terms clean and dirty, which are used in much of western society as though they designate natural categories, determined by criteria derived from such scientific principles as germ theory and contagion, are she suggests equally 'social' not natural. The organising of the home, the kitchen, the body in terms of avoiding dirt and creating cleanliness, are better described in social terms as attempts to create order out of disorder, using the linguistic and social resources of a given culture. Dirt is not an essential, natural category: dirt is matter out of place. If we extend this insight to the perception of language that dominates many institutions in our own society – notably those of government and of education – we might have a further explanation for the emphasis there on the rules of language and on teachers and students having to learn inventories of categories – word lists, grammatical terms, etc – as though these were the essence of language. The boundaries between order and disorder are the spaces where danger lurks according to Douglas, and culture is obsessively concerned with protecting itself from the natural state – disorder – by emphasising the purity of categories and drawing firm boundaries between them. In linguistic terms this fear of disorder and of boundaries and focus on the purity of categories and classificatory types, leads to an obsessive attention to rules, to 'proper' language use, such as standard in lexis, grammar and pronunciation. Again, as with Hobbesian fears discussed above, contemporary society's obsessive attention to language and literacy and to the minutiae of rules that supposedly govern them, can be interpreted as a fear of disorder and an almost sacred attention to purity.

These, then, may offer some explanation for why the apparently arcane debates amongst scholars regarding phonics, real language, dialogic inter-action and ideological models of literacy, emerge in the public domain with such surprising force in contemporary society. The explanation, then, lies not with the true underlying natural order of language and literacy as essential categories, but in the Hobbesian fears and cultural boundary making that are evoked by the new less categorical and less essentialist theories of language and literacy. These new theories open up and provisionalise features of life long held fixed and sacred and that have previously been carefully guarded by officially or unofficially appointed wardens in the institutions of state. The intensity of the debate makes sense if we recognise that it is more about the fear of disorder – Things Fall Apart – than about linguistic theory.

UTOPIAN DESIRES

However, the fear that things might fall apart is not simply held by arch conservatives and those assumed to be on the political Right in the current debates over traditional and progressive teaching methods. We all have a stake in order, in Hobbes's notion of government, in being able to communicate. The desire to privilege the dialogic, contestable and social nature of language and literacy, to live with diversity, still entails its own struggle: it is the struggle of all Utopian movements, with the order and constraint within which freedom and variation are possible. Utopian desires too are tempered by the reality that social life, including language and literacy practices, is patterned and persistent even amidst its rich diversity. One way of adjusting this patterning to the flux, ambiguity and uncertainty that our researches honestly tell us we must face when dealing with language and literacy is through theory: to make explicit the theory on which our actions are based and to follow through the implications of that theory, enables us to maintain order and authority without descending to authoritarianism. Following Popper (1957), scientists generally accept that a theory is only as good as its ability to account for more facts than other theories, that it cannot be 'proved' forever but that once it has been falsified by a better theory, it has to be abandoned. Theory, then, provides a hold on a given state of flux, but it has to be recognised as provisional, it provides an 'as if' state of suspension without which there is indeed chaos. For scientists since Popper this seems less of a problem than it sometimes does for languages and literacy workers, with the constant evoking of Hobbesian fears about living with a theory of diversity. In the area of ecology and environment, for instance, scientists have persuaded the public that diversity, as Darwin demonstrated, is the root of creativity and development of species. In the field of language and literacy, on the contrary, there seems a deep fear about abandoning some of the sacred fixities of lexis and syntax, a rigidity of species has set in. In the UK the National Curriculum has privileged 'standard' more than its earlier advisers considered wise (cf Cox, 1996) and recent proposals for what teachers should know have focused on narrow grammatical detail at the expense of social or critical understanding of language in use (ITT/TTA/DfEE), whilst the definitions of 'Literacy' seem to narrow with every public commission (cf LTF).

The new theories of language and literacy that I have characterised as the New Literacy Studies, have adopted a more Popperian stance, in the sense that they are only as good as their current evidence and that they are only provisional views of a complex field of vision. NLS, then, will have to change as more research and experience falsifies their cherished tenets. This scientific perspective on NLS matches well with the constructivist view which suggests that language and literacy, as social constructs, are always provisional and contested in themselves, just like the theories about them. The difficulty for those who subscribe to these new theories is whether they can live with that degree of provisionality and doubt. As lecturers, how do we respond when our students demand more firm and fixed accounts of the language and literacy realities we encounter; as teachers, how do we respond when learners demand that we act with authority, tell them what is right and wrong linguistically, and 'deliver' language and literacy as we might any other commodity from the supermarket. As researchers how do we respond when other researchers tell us they 'know' what is the truth of language, how it is learned, what is the relation of sound and sign in alphabetic writing systems and what are the rules for production and competence in different languages? As human beings how do we cope with our own desires for order and fear of disorder, at a time when our social training and theories of knowledge suggest that the notion of disorder offers a better account of reality (cf chaos theory)? Living with provisionality and uncertainty, allaying our Hobbesian fears, may be the key epistemological ground for making any use at all of the new theories.

IMPLICATIONS FOR RESEARCH AND PRACTICE

These are considerable. Both researchers and practitioners – and many of the best people in this field do both these days (Cochran-Smith and Lytle, 1993) – have to acknowledge the fears and desires that come with investigating and reflecting on language and literacy: we are not just neutral observers, but social beings already inscribed with culturally-influenced manifestations of the deeper fears and desires that influence all human life. The fears and desires associated with language and literacy, then, are not simply those of a reactionary and self-interested elite, as many 'progressive' educators might believe, but are built into the process of learning and studying themselves and are true across the political spectrum. Advocates of the NLS may have felt that their approach has meant going against the grain, challenging dominant 'ways of knowing': but it may be that the grain is not simply that of a 'dominant' society with which they can feel romantically in conflict but that of their own deepest desires and fears. We all have to live with the psychological and social consequences of the new theories. What then are the practical consequences for educationalists of recognising these principles and difficulties? I have spelt out some of these in more detail in a recent article in *English in Education* (Street, 1997) and here just summarise briefly what I think follows for curriculum, pedagogy and assessment from adopting the broader view of literacy developed here.

Curriculum and assessment that reduce literacy to a few simple and mechanistic skills fail to do justice to the richness and complexity of actual literacy practices in people's lives. If we want learners to develop and enhance the richness and complexity of literacy practices evident in society at large, then we need curriculum and assessment that are themselves rich and complex and based upon research into actual literacy practices. These in turn require models of literacy and of pedagogy that capture that richness and complexity. What teaching methods are appropriate to this new understanding of literacies remains open to debate, although some interventions have already suggested some parameters for the debate: that teaching, whatever form it takes (e.g. whole class; student-centred; phonics; 'real' books) has to be able to take account of the variation in literacy practices amongst students and to give value to their different backgrounds and the different literacies they employ in their home contexts. An emphasis on 'real' uses of literacy and attention to the contexts of use appears more likely to follow from these tenets than focus on 'artificial' or formal features of supposed universal literacy. If English standard is agreed as important, then from this perspective the justification needs to be presented and students need to be able to discuss alternatives and know when it is appropriate to use them (cf Fairclough on *Critical Language Awareness,* 1995), a position that corresponds to recent work on the role of 'argument' in the science classroom (Driver et al, 1994; Mitchell, 1996).

The emphasis is on appropriateness, a key concept in the Ethnography of Communication (cf Hymes, 1977), rather than a pure concept of 'correctness' that dominates much formal thinking on language and literacy (Heath and Mangiola, 1991). The NLS, then, does not eschew the focus on standard or deny the value of 'grammar' and whole class teaching: it intervenes in those debates at a different level than the simple polarities set up in current media representations. Because it is rooted in research as well as practice, NLS implies a teaching method that likewise facilitates for students and teachers alike the development of provisional models that help them to describe, observe and analyse different literacies rather than just learning and teaching one literacy as given. In Heath's terms (1983), teachers and students become 'ethnographers', exploring the various meanings and uses of literary in the social context of the school and its surrounding communities. In Street and Street's terms (1991), 'schooled literacy' becomes one amongst many and students are encouraged to research its place in the spectrum of literacy practices in which they engage.

Recognition of 'the richness and complexity of actual literacy practices' has provided the basis for a number of new approaches to classroom practice, of which I will cite just a few which I hope could act as inspirations for further research and development. Heath and Mangiola (1991) were commissioned by the National Education Association in the USA to develop a classroom text that would help teachers address 'the literacy needs of the culturally and linguistically diverse students who now populate our schools'. The resulting text offers detailed case studies of 'successful cross-age tutoring programs' where students who had been failing and dropping out were trained to tutor young elementary students in reading. The dramatic success of such programmes in terms of teacher attitudes and pupil improvement in literacy skills was put forward as a model for teacher-research collaboration in the area of language and literacy diversity and it would be fruitful to explore the possibilities of adapting the model to the UK situation.

A research project in Brisbane Australia, explored the complexity of home and school literacies, in this case focusing more on locality and class than on language and ethnicity (Freebody et al, 1995). A team of researchers funded by the Department of Education, studied 'Everyday literacy practices in and out of schools in low socio-economic urban communities', observing in close detail the linguistic behaviour around texts both at home and at school in order to establish the relationships between them. Important implications were drawn out for pre-service and in-service programs, notably attuning teachers more to local literacies and challenging dominant stereotypes about children's ability to learn and use literacy. For purposes of this paper, a major finding that challenges the romantic perception of NLS as simply a way to critique dominant practices, is that:

> *With respect to the home-school relationship, our findings do not lead to any grounds for privileging home versus school literacy practices. Rather they lead to recommendations concerning the more effective mutual recognition of these practices in both sites.* (Freebody et al, 1995, pxxii)

These examples suggest a challenge for educators in the UK likewise, where the new theories of language and literacy outlined above, have been well understood for over a decade (Brookes and Hudson, 1982). For instance, research into community literacies has been conducted by a team of researchers from Lancaster University and their work has been particularly influential in adult literacy work (Barton and Ivanič, 1991; Hamilton and Barton, 1998). But the combination of ethnographic-style research into everyday literacy practices and constructive curriculum development and pedagogy, that is beginning to characterise the adult field in many parts of the world, has not penetrated so deeply into the school or into teacher training in the UK. Indeed, the present media and policy representations of literacy draw upon tropes rooted in less culturally sensitive models of language and literacy. The task, then, appears to be twofold: to challenge the dominant representations of literacy; and to develop collaborative research projects that look at the actual literacy practices of both home and school, with a view as Freebody states, to 'effective mutual recognition of these practices in both sites'. For the data thus collected to be fed into teacher training programmes and into curricula and pedagogy requires some change in dominant representations. If this paper has contributed in a small way to such a change, it will have served its purpose.

NOTE

Parts of this paper have been published in *English in Education*, NATE, 31, 3, Autumn 1997.

REFERENCES

Baker J, Clay C and Fox C (eds) (1996) *Challenging Ways of Knowing in English Mathematics and Science*, London: Falmer Press

Baker D (1996) 'Children's formal and Informal school numeracy practices', in Baker et al (eds) (1996) *Challenging Ways of Knowing in English Mathematics and Science*, London: Falmer Press, London

Baker D and Street B (1993) 'Literacy and numeracy', *International Encyclopaedia of Education*, Oxford: Pergamon, pp3453–3459

Bakhtin M (1981) *The Dialogic Imagination* transl. M Holquist and C Emerson, Austin: University of Texas Press

Barton D and Ivanič R (1991) *Writing in the Community*, Sage

Basic Skills Agency (BSA) (1997) *International Numeracy Survey*, London: Basic Skills Agency

Beard R (ed) (1993) *Teaching Literacy: Balancing Perspectives*, London: Hodder & Stoughton

Black S and Thorp K (1997) *Literacy Practices and Linguistic Choices*, Australia, NSW: Northern Sydney Institute of TAFE

Bloome D (1989) *Classrooms and Literacy*, Ablex: NJ

Brookes A and Hudson R (1982) 'Do linguists have anything to say to Teachers?', in R Carter (ed) *Linguists and the Teacher*, London: Routledge

Cochran-Smith M and Lytle S (1993) *Inside-Outside: Teacher Research and Knowledge*, New York: Teachers College Press

Collins J (1995) 'Literacy and literacies', *Annual Review of Anthropology*, 24, pp75–93

Cope B and Kalantzis M (eds) (1993) *The Powers of Literacy: A Genre Approach to Teaching Writing*, Brighton: Falmer Press

Cox B (ed) (1998) *Literacy is not English*, Manchester: Manchester University Press

Dombey H (1998) 'What's Wrong with Phonics?' in B Cox (ed) *Literacy is not English*, Manchester, Manchester University Press

Douglas M (1966) *Purity and Danger,* London: Routledge

Driver R, Asoko H, Teach J, Mortimer E and Scott P (1994) 'Constructing scientific knowledge in the classroom', *Educational Researcher,* 23, 7, pp5–12

Durkheim E and Mauss M (1903) *Primitive Classification,* trans. R Needham, Cohen and West, 1963

Fairclough N (ed) (1995) *Critical Language Awareness,* London: Longman

Feidrich M (1996) *Literacy in Circles?* Working Paper No 2, London: Action Aid

Freebody P (ed) (1995) *Everyday Literacy Practices in and out of School in Low Socio-Economic Urban Communities,* Australia: Brisbane Department of Education

Freebody P, Gee J, Luke A and Street B (1997) *Literacy as Critical Social Practice,* Brighton: Falmer Press

Gee J (1990) *Social Linguistics and Literacies: Ideology in Discourses,* Brighton: Falmer Press

Gee J (1991) 'The narrativization of experience in the oral style', in C Mitchell and K Weiler (eds) *Rewriting Literacy: Culture and the Discourse of the Other,* New York: Bergin and Garvey, pp77–102

Goodman K (1996) *Ken Goodman on Reading: A common-sense look at the nature of language and the science of reading,* Ontario, Canada: Scolastic

Goodman K (1998) 'The reading process', in V Edwards and D Corson (eds) *Encyclopaedia of Language and Education,* Netherlands: Kluwer Academic Publishers, pp1–8

Halliday M (1978) *Language as Social Semiotic,* London: Edward Arnold

Hamilton M and Barton D (1998) *Local Literacies,* London: Routledge

Heath S B and Mangiola L (1991) *Children of Promise: Literate Activity in Linguistically and Culturally Diverse Classrooms,* Washington DC: National Education Association

Heath S B (1983) *Ways with Words,* Cambridge University Press

Hobbes T (1651) (1976) *Leviathan or the Matter, Forme and Power of a Commonwealth Ecclesiasticall and Civill,* edited with introduction by C B MacPherson, London: Penguin

Hymes D (1977) *Foundations in Sociolinguistics,* London: Tavistock

Independent on Sunday (1993) 'Illiterate England', 7 February, p19

Kress G (1996) 'Internationalisation and globalisation: Rethinking a curriculum of instruction', *Comparative Education,* 32, 2, pp185–196

LAC (1997) 'Two different theoretical approaches to literacy and their implications for adult literacy programs', *Literacy across the Curriculum,* 12, 3, pp4–5

Lemke J (1995) *Textual Politics: Discourse and Social Dynamics,* London: Taylor and Francis

Levine K (1998) 'Definitional and methodological problems in the cross-national measurement of adult literacy: the case of the IALS', *Journal of Written Language and Literacy,* 1, 1, Amsterdam: John Benjamins

Maybin J (1993) *Language and Literacy in Social Practice,* Open University Press

Meek M (1991) *On Being Literate,* London: Bodley Head

Mitchell S (1996) *Improving the Quality of Argument in Higher Education,* School of Education, Middlesex University Report and Evaluation Series

Nagy W and Anderson R (1999) Metalinguistic awareness and literacy acquisition in different languages', in D Wagner, L Venezky and B Street (eds) *Literacy: An International Handbook,* New York: Garland

Oakhill J, Beard R and Vincent D (eds) (1995) 'The contribution of psychological research', Special Issue of *Journal of Research in Reading,* 18, 2, Oxford: Blackwell

OECD (1995) *Literacy, Economy and Society: Results of the First International Adult Literacy Survey (IALS)*, Ottowa, Canada: OECD/ Statistics

Popper K (1957) *The Poverty of Historicism*, London: Routledge and Kegan Paul

Reynolds D and Farrell S (1996) *Worlds Apart: A Review of International Surveys of Educational Achievement Involving England*, London: OFSTED/HMSO ('OFSTED 1996')

Rogers A et al (1994) *Using Literacy: A New Approach to Post-literacy Materials*, Report on a research project. ODA Technical Report

Saxena M (1991) *The Changing Role of Minority Literacies in Britain: A Case Study of Punjabis in Southall*, Lancaster: Centre for Language in Public Life

Saxena M (1994) 'Literacies among Punjabis in Southall',"in M. Hamilton, D Barton and R Ivanič (eds) *Worlds of Literacy*, Philadelphia: Multilingual Matters

Street B (1993) *Cross-Cultural Approaches to Literacy*, Cambridge University Press

Street B (1995) *Social Literacies: Critical Approaches to Literacy in Development, Ethnography and Education*, London: Longman

Street B (1998) 'Social Literacies', in V Edwards and D Corson (eds) *Encyclopaedia of Language and Education*, Netherlands: Kluwer Academic Publishers, 133–142

Street B (ed) (1993a) 'The New Literacy Studies', Special Issue of *Journal of Research in Reading*, 16, 2, Oxford: Blackwell

Street B and Street J (1991) 'The schooling of literacy', in D Barton and R Ivanič, *Writing in the Community*, Sage, p143–166

The Sunday Times (1994) 'The dangers of illiteracy', 10 April, p10

Villegas A M (1991) *Culturally Responsive Teaching*, Princeton, NJ: ETS

Volosinov V N (1973) *Marxism and the Philosophy of Language*, Orlando: Academic Press

Whorf B (1959) *Language, Thought and Reality*, Cambridge Mass: MIT Press

Willinsky J (1990) *The New Literacy: Redefining Reading and Rriting in Schools*, London: Routledge

Wray D (1997) 'Research into the teaching of reading: A 25-year debate', in K Watson, C Modgill and S Modgill (eds) *Education Dilemmas: Debate and Diversity*, 4 'Quality in Education', London: Cassell

Recent proposals for literacy in UK schools

Committee for Linguistics in Education (CLIE) (1997) Recommendations to the Teacher Training Agency', *BAAL Newsletter*, 55, Spring, pp 17–19

DfEE (1998) *National Literacy Strategy*

Literacy Task Force (LTF) (1997) *A Reading Revolution: How Can We Teach Every Child to Read Well?* Preliminary Report of LTF published for Consultation, February

Teacher Training Agency (TTA) (1998) *Initial Teacher Training: English*

Bilingualism with and without Biliteracy; Biliteracy with and without Biculturalism

Arturo Tosi, University of London

Terminology and context

Terminological confusion and the context of language education serve as the starting point for this discussion. Terms such as bilingualism and some of its cognates have been much used in academic research and discussions over the past twenty years: yet not only are they still used loosely in the research literature, but they are often employed in a conflicting manner as well. It is noticeable, for example, that their meanings have evolved from a narrow to a broader sense, and this has posed new problems of distinction and specification. This is why language scholars increasingly feel the need to define these terms while, at the same time, policy makers and administrators are more inclined to indulge in their ambiguities.

In this paper I will refer to the classic distinction between *natural bilingualism* (e.g. the alternative use of two languages in the natural environment) and *balanced bilingualism* (the equivalent mastery of two languages); and I will adopt the concept of *biculturalism* when I need to refer to the ability to operate competently within two separate cultural environments. Despite the political misuse, and subsequent semantic deterioration, I still find this term useful to describe tendencies of culture loss or maintenance in bilingual communities, where speakers who have some experience of two cultures, are inclined to cultivate and to develop only one of the two alternative identities, or vice versa a combined or hyphenated identity.

My other preliminary considerations concern the context of language education in Britain. It is now widely acknowledged that the fact that English has become the dominant world language is a source of advantages and disadvantages (Quirk, 1987).

Both English as a mother tongue and English as a second or additional language can benefit from empirical research and national experiences of many industrially advanced societies where literacy and education are widespread. For the teaching of modern foreign languages we can draw from that inexhaustible laboratory of ideas and experiments that is provided by the scholarship and the business of English as a foreign language (EFL). The fact that the spread of English language in the world is the major factor in the development of bilingualism means that our British scholars have at their disposal massive data and access to direct observations of how bilingualism develops in diverse social and educational settings.

Last but not least, Britain has firmly established its connection with Europe, which is not only a unique forum for the study of bilingualism and biliteracy, it is also a formidable laboratory of bilingual education for future generations.

Suffice it to remember that international education, which began in the early 1960s with an even number of French-medium and English-medium schools, today in Europe alone has a few French-medium, but several hundred English-medium schools. Their teachers, who are all almost invariably native speakers of English, devote much time and effort to train pupils of different nationalities and cultural backgrounds, to become fully operational in English without losing competence in the language and loyalty to the culture of their national tradition (Tosi, 1991).

By contrast with this formidable background and experiences of language education, it is noticeable that in Britain most people demonstrate a marked disinclination to learn other languages and that the education system is reluctant to invest in an innovative and forward-looking policy of modern language education (Quirk, 1987).

In this paper I set out to examine some of the recent justifications of this monolingual philosophy. More specifically I intend to compare some of its effects in the two areas of language education that claim equal concern with the development of bilingualism (e.g. in the sense of adding competence in a second or foreign language to the first or native tongue). One area is natural bilingualism, which usually attracts limited school support, and the other area is foreign language education, where more national resources are invested to develop biliteracy with the ability to operate competently with the target culture.

My argument is that the failure in motivating learners to achieve a more rewarding mastery of other languages stems from the same misconceptions that are used to promote monolingual superiority in one sector, which have spread and invaded the other sectors of language education.

BILINGUALISM WITH AND WITHOUT BILITERACY

For the school population that comes from an ethnic minority bilingual background, the development of high levels of literacy in the home and community language should not be assumed to be automatic. This is because the natural bilingualism that emerges from the home-school language switch, involves fluency in communicative skills for family and community use, which, not being supported in primary education, usually develops in these young children the skills of reading and writing in the school language only. As adolescents, their involvement in the minority language and culture may still be very strong, but as they have acquired the skills of reading and writing in one language alone – English – the new dominant language is allowed to interfere with the other language phonetically, lexically and semantically. In this case the code-switching from the minority language speeds up the drift to monolingualism, especially when the new generations become aware of its distance with the standard language spoken in the country of origin (Tosi, 1986). With the school focusing on literacy and academic competence in English language only, while assigning to community organisations the responsibility to develop literacy in the standard variety of the other language, bilingualism is often transitional and biliteracy is generally absent. (For a discussion on the related issue of language shift, see Clyne and Kipp, 1997, and Mobbs, 1997.)

There are some arguments that have been used to justify this approach to minority language education in British multicultural society. These need to be made explicit, as they increasingly seem to be misconceptions about pupil motivation and teacher professionalism.

The value of natural bilingualism

There is a widespread belief in most schools that this form of language competence can never develop into a real educational advantage for children, as their everyday use of a different language at home interferes with the learning of the school language, and this in turn hinders fluency and literacy in English. Even the MOTET project, which was set up to investigate the benefit of primary bilingual education in Bradford, did not succeed in challenging this view (Fitzpatrick, 1987).

Early biliteracy

When community organisations seek collaboration and coordination with LEAs either to use school space or to coordinate teaching methods, or indeed to monitor pupils' progress, community teachers are often faced with the unwritten rule that pupils should not be taught mother tongue literacy in primary education, as this may hinder the development of literacy in English (this was one rule of the LEA that ran the Mother Tongue Project in Bedford – Tosi, 1984).

Cultural content

The argument that classes of community languages would lose their 'community' dimension in mainstream education (once provided by the school in the modern language curriculum) was introduced by Sir Keith Joseph (1984), Secretary of Education, and since then it has demoted the status of these languages without succeeding in promoting motivation for learning and literacy.

Classroom pedagogy and teacher professionalism

The argument, that minority community languages could be offered in the mainstream curriculum, provided that they are taught according to the pedagogy and professionalism of other modern languages, and in established foreign languages departments, was also introduced by the Secretary of State and then endorsed by the Swann Committee in 1985 (*Education for All*, 1985).

This last point is worthy of specific attention, as there is more than one educational objection to this argument.

Firstly, the syllabus and materials of foreign language pedagogy focus on practical transactions that may be useful to foreign language learners, but are less relevant to children from bilingual backgrounds. Secondly, phrases and formulae of foreign language communication are often based on the standard models of the target country, and they overlook the community based repertoire of bilingual children, who are born and brought up in a different country and may feel that their home language is stigmatised by the choice of the standard norms of another country. Thirdly, as for the choice of the cultural content, if the community language teacher follows the criteria of foreign language pedagogy, the realia and memorabilia chosen from the target country may prove to be unpalatable stereotypes for learners who feel emotionally involved with the values of a different country (Royal Society of Arts, 1985).

All these diverse circumstances point in one direction: that the apparent efficiency of community language teachers working with a foreign language syllabus does not actually meet the needs of bilingual learners. Quite the opposite: these young people usually feel stigmatised by an approach which assumes in their bilingual background the same neutrality as that of the monolingual learner of foreign languages. Indeed, the cost of this policy and pedagogy in dealing with natural bilingualism can be as high as to transform provision for community language teaching into an agency of language shift rather than maintenance. But there is another price to pay. Schools are less encouraged to believe in the value of bilingualism as an intellectual resource, especially when natural bilinguals do not seem to progress, despite the most advanced materials and methodologies adopted in the mainstream education. Society as a whole has lost the rare opportunity to capitalise on a profitable area of language education and literacy: especially where investment could involve non-European languages, which today are increasingly important for work and business, while the training of monolingual speakers of English to develop these skills has proved extremely costly and difficult.

BILITERACY WITH AND WITHOUT BICULTURALISM

If we now turn to the other area of language education – foreign language education – where more time and effort are spent on training monolinguals to develop high levels of fluency and literacy in a non-native language, we find that the combination of biliteracy and biculturalism usually involves a costly and demanding operation in every education system. This is either because of the limited linguistic experiences and cultural involvement available in formal education, or because of the distance between cognitive operations and communicative uses in L1 and L2, or both.

In Britain, however, such difficult but crucial investments remain below the European standards, because of some widespread misconceptions that still dominate the policy and practice of our foreign language education. These too need to be made explicit.

Optimal age

The 'French in Primary Education' project (Burstall, 1970), which failed to demonstrate the advantages of early foreign language instruction, had the effect of jeopardising this innovation, undervaluing the benefits of early fluency in a second or foreign language, and reinforcing the misconception that monolingualism is the ideal condition for cognitive development.

Since then another generation of school pupils has been struggling with unfamiliar structures and vocabulary, having to cope with the unpalatable sounds of foreign pronunciation and intonation at a later stage. The lack of a good early rapport with a foreign language, and the prejudice that its learning was too exotic and therefore more suitable for small children or for girls, has managed to put off large sectors of young people, especially those who see it as disrespectful of traditional Britishness and its masculine heritage (Quirk, 1987).

Language choice

Following the so-called rationalisation of foreign language education in the early eighties, French took over many Italian and Russian positions, and more recently German and in some areas Spanish ones as well. This lack of alternatives has increased a traditional sense of insularity among the new generations without succeeding in spreading a new love affair with our neighbours.

Certainly a great number of students who enrol to read German, Italian or Spanish in my university, Royal Holloway, admit that the main reason for their choice was their disenchantment with French; while the gifted learners who start the study of a second foreign language at university, criticise the fact that they could not take them up in schools that taught exclusively or predominantly French.

Motivation

To counterbalance this disinclination to learn foreign languages, some major efforts were made in the past ten years to shift the focus from general cultural and intellectual advantage to the practical skills connected with the job market and income earning. Some people are saying that we are now approaching the end of this utilitarian fashion: thus, perhaps, this is the right time to ask how the bilingual profiles of our future generations of graduates will compare with the bilingual training of other young Europeans. I shall draw on my own experience of language learning and teaching at university.

Foreign languages as a vehicle of scientific knowledge

For the undergraduates and postgraduates who read science or technology the consultation of texts for keeping in touch with scientific advance – say in French or German – is normally out of the question. Likewise access to original texts in the area of humanities, especially those disciplines that have shaped our European heritage, that is to say in Greek, Italian, or Spanish – in addition to those already mentioned – are out of reach. Yet the mastery of these languages, which for most has not been achieved at school, is now highly valued in our undergraduate programmes. Subseqently, more and more students spend much time and curriculum resources from their modular degree programmes in, for example, history or music, struggling with the rudiments in languages, where they achieve a basic mastery of everyday communicative use that is little if at all useful for an academic purpose.

Foreign languages for literary and cultural studies

For those students who study the language, literature and culture of a foreign country, substantial retraining in practical oral and written language skills is also required. This of course detracts time from the study of crucial aspects of the foreign culture, as well as from other and more rewarding cognitive and academic uses of the target language. We hear of many cases where the lecturers cannot use the target language as a medium of instruction, for the paradoxical reason that students will never learn enough of the set books to pass the exams for their degree. We are told that this happens not only where there are many beginners, but also in many university departments, where an A-level in French is the norm rather than the exception.

As in the case of support for early bilingualism or that of foreign languages in primary education, or that of using a second language as a medium of instruction if at all possible in school, or at least at university, we must acknowledge that there is a profound and long-term problem. If we are to evaluate the factors of our limited success, it is hard to hold the language teachers responsible for lack of professionalism, or the learners for lack of motivation: there are just too many signs that the recommendations of researchers have been undervalued, and that some of their pedagogical guidelines have been misinterpreted.

CONCLUSIONS

It seems that over the past two decades, the responses given by policy makers to parents, teachers and researchers have contributed to the emergence of a spurious dichotomy, based on the allegedly diverse value of two forms of bilingualism. One form involves the addition to English of another European language, with precedence given to the languages of powerful economies; another form involves ethnic minority languages, whose fluency and literacy are still little appreciated in terms of education and community life, and their currencies quite wrongly undervalued in terms of international relations.

This distinction between high status and low status forms of bilingualism has been a source of much parental confusion, of tensions in families and in schools, and of some major pedagogical misunderstandings in the field of language education. It has also taught some negative lessons about the kind of society and world we live in. The equation:

$$\text{one language} = \text{one culture} = \text{one national identity}$$

is an image of reality that no longer corresponds to what can be seen today in Britain or in the rest of Europe.

It is difficult, therefore, not to speculate that some of the misconceived messages sent to celebrate monolingual superiority, aimed at one sector of the school population – minority bilingual background pupils – have matured into adverse and possibly unexpected results with English monolingual children in the other field of language education.

To conclude, there is certainly more than one area where researchers and practitioners involved in these two sectors of language education could establish a fruitful collaboration, aimed above all to remove some of the old misconceptions that have informed policies and practices in the past two decades. Here are some examples of rethinking set out to meet today's needs of multilingual and multicultural Britain in Europe.

1 *There is a correlation between individual motivation for language learning and public respect for domestic and foreign languages.* Treating minority community languages like the cultural heritage of 'others' that has no place in the education for all, encourages the thinking that the learning of foreign languages and cultures is an act in favour of other people rather than of the learners themselves.

2 *There are enormous advantages in early instruction and literacy, whether we teach monolingual pupils to learn a foreign language, or bilingual background children who study their home and community language.* When children are taught from the early stages of their school experience a language different from their normal medium of education, they develop natural skills and positive attitudes that most find it extremely difficult to acquire later on (Baker, 1988).

3 *Fluency and literacy in a non-native language are of great benefit to the mastery of the native language, as well as to general communication skills.* Such enrichment becomes visible when the speaker is faced with real life situations, and the advantage should not be confused with any short-term impact in the learning or use of the school language (Cummins, 1979).

4 *The academic use of another language – its use as a medium of instruction – provides the most effective means for progressing and advancing its mastery.* This principle applies to all language learners, including those with a bilingual and with a monolingual background. Programmes of foreign languages in many education systems in Europe have already introduced some forms of 'bilingual education', where the target language is used as a medium of instruction, rather than being taught within the traditional time frame of the foreign language curriculum (Baetens Beardsmore, 1982).

5 *Teaching and examination syllabuses should differentiate between the communicative skills for personal interaction in everyday use, and the*

more sophisticated abilities for cognitive and academic use. This reform was originally suggested by the scholars of bilingualism and minority languages. Subsequently it has become adopted by international schools, and now it is increasingly debated as a desirable curriculum development of foreign language education in many education systems. This type of development should be most attractive in a country like Britain, where native speakers of English cannot usually improvise the academic use of another language, transferring discourse strategies and vocabulary from their mother tongue, like most speakers of Romance, Germanic or Slavonic languages can often do, after a basic communication course in another language of the same family.

REFERENCES

Baetens Beardsmore H (1982) *Bilingualism: Basic Principles,* Clevedon, Avon: Multilingual Matters

Baker C (1988) *Key Issues in Bilingualism and Bilingual Education,* Clevedon, Avon: Multilingual Matters

Burstall C (1970) *French in the Primary School,* Slough: National Foundation for Educational Research in England and Wales

Clyne M and Kipp S (1977) 'Trends and changes in Home Language use and shift in Australia, 1986–1996', *Journal of Multilingual and Multicultural Development,* 18, 6, pp 451–473

Cummins J (1979) *Bilingualism and Special Education: Issues in Assessment and Pedagogy,* Clevedon, Avon: Multilingual Matters

Education for All (1985) The report of the Committee of Inquiry into the education of children from ethnic minority groups chaired by Lord Swann, London: HMSO .

Fitzpatrick B (1987) *The Open Door,* Clevedon: Multilingual Matters

Joseph Sir Keith (1984) Address given by the Secretary of State to the School Council Conference on 'Materials for Mother Tongue Teaching to Children of Migrants' sponsored by the European Communities

Mobbs M (1997) *Children's Other Languages: Expertise, Affiliation and Language Use among Second Generation British South Asian Pupils,* NALDIC Working Paper, Watford: National Association for Language Development in the Curriculum

Quirk R (1987) 'English is not enough', *The Times Higher Educational Supplement,* 11 December

Royal Society of Arts (1985) *Diploma in the Teaching of Community Languages.* Scheme document and syllabus, London: Royal Society of Arts

Tosi A (1984) *Immigration and Bilingual Education,* Oxford: Pergamon Press

Tosi A (1986) 'Home and community language teaching for bilingual learners: Issues in planning and instruction', *Language Teaching,* January

Tosi A (1991) 'Language in international education', in P Jonietz (ed) *World Yearbook of Education: International Schools and International Education,* London: Kogan Page

Literacies and Epistemologies in Primary Education

Roz Ivanič, University of Lancaster

The 'rethinking' to which I want to contribute concerns language for learning: language in its role of providing children with tools for developing their knowledge and understanding. I will be showing how children at Key Stage 2 encounter, reproduce and recombine the visual and linguistic characteristics of the texts to which they have had access both in and out of school, and hence become party to a variety of views of knowledge. In doing so I will on the one hand celebrate the diversity and inventiveness of children's creative re-combinations, but on the other draw attention to the ways in which children can reproduce representational resources without questioning the views of knowledge inscribed in them. To do this I will draw on examples from the research in which I am currently involved, collecting and analysing a longitudinal sample of independent project work on a range of topics by children in Years 4–6. I will end with some recommendations for a language pedagogy which includes helping children to examine critically the representational resources which they are encountering and re-producing in their own work. The aim of such a pedagogy would be for learners to become players in the communicational landscape, drawing upon only those representational resources which they understand to be of benefit to the world in which they live.

In this paper I will be arguing that, within the literacy practice of doing a school project, children are encountering, reproducing and creatively recombining a variety of representational practices: both a variety of alternatives from within what might broadly be called 'literacy for learning', and others from vernacular literacies such as comic reading and personal letter writing.

INDEPENDENT PROJECT WORK

I am using the term 'independent project work' to refer to a particular type of task set in some schools, requiring children to select a topic (sometimes from a restricted range, for example 'an animal'), to research it, and to write a 'project' containing the findings of their research. What makes this type of work especially interesting to research is that it is relatively unstructured in the sense that the teacher does not control every step of the work. The literacy practices, including the representational practices, on which the children draw vary enormously as they encounter, work with, and re-present material on different topics from a wide variety of sources across the home-school divide.

In the school in which the research team was working this type of work was first initiated in Year 4. At this stage the teacher treated the task as mainly 'in class', setting aside class time for it, helping children to access resources available within the school, and helping the children to carry their projects through to conclusion. However, even at this stage, each child or group of children was relatively autonomous in deciding what to study, how to find out the information, and how to re-present it. She encouraged the children to pursue their projects outside school, setting a precedent for this work being undertaken as 'homework', but did not expect this. In Year 5, this work was set partly to be undertaken in relatively unsupervised time during school hours (when the teacher was busy with other duties) and partly at home. By Year 6, the instructions for the project were given, a deadline was set, and then the children were expected to do their work entirely in out-of-school time.

VIEWS OF KNOWLEDGE

On the basis of an informal study of a large quantity of this work, I have become aware of what seem to me to be many different ways of conceptualising knowledge[1] underpinning the verbal and visual resources on which the children are drawing. Some of these I see as fully fledged 'epistemologies' or 'paradigms' for knowledge (for example, A, G); others are constituent elements of one or more 'epistemologies' (for example, D). Some of them overlap and interact with one another: I am not claiming that stretches

---

1 In what follows I do not distinguish systematically between 'knowledge', 'facts', 'information', 'understanding' and 'truth' although in a more detailed treatment of this topic I would do so.

of discourse can be classified neatly as being underpinned by one rather than another view. However I do want to propose that each of these beliefs about knowledge is identifiable in the visual and linguistic resources the children are deploying. In this section I list these as views A–M, with brief notes about each. This is, inevitably, extremely schematic and, to some extent, idiosyncratic, as 'views of knowledge' are the object of study for philosophers and sociologists of scientific knowledge, and a great deal has been, and can be, written about them. My list is informed partly by the data I have been studying and partly by informal knowledge of work in these fields (for further reading about such issues see, for example, Chalmers, 1978; Latour, 1987; Kuhn, 1996). My aim here is to sketch out some ways in which knowledge can be construed which are relevant to thinking critically about language for learning in general, and children's project work in particular. In the next section I give an example from the children's project work to show how these views of knowledge are inscribed in particular representational practices on which they are drawing.

A. Knowledge is 'given', emanating from authority

This was the dominant view of knowledge in England before 1640, when truth was seen as having divine origin. This view also applies to situations where truth is authorised by the State. The view that knowledge is 'just there' and does not require proof, explanation of how it is known, or critical examination is reflected in a wide variety of practices in pedagogic settings and elsewhere.

B. Knowledge is empirically produced

This view of knowledge entered the lanscape in Europe in the seventeenth century and is associated with empiricists like Francis Bacon when scientific activity burgeoned. The idea of 'objective truth' is closely associated with this view, since there is nothing mysterious about it: scientific experiments are replicable and furnish proof. There is an issue as to who can claim to be a scientist: in many modern approaches to primary school science the children themselves conduct experiments to find out for themselves how things work. However, I suggest that a large proportion of the semiotic resources to which children are exposed treat authoritative adults as the researchers and experimenters, and – worse – often exclude them from the text, resulting in knowledge being presented as described in view A.

C. Facts are facts

This view is an outcome of both views A and B, although the source of truth is different in each case. Knowledge is presented as a set of facts: unquestionable truth. In this view there is no place for uncertainty, no interest in shifting, partial, fluid, provisional or alternative knowledges and understandings.

D. Knowledge is abstract

This is the belief that knowledge is concerned with universal truths – generalised states of affairs and facts about all entities of a type, rather than situated facts about particular cases in specific contexts. The abstracting of knowledge from the context in which it is experienced is, according to Smith (1990), partially a consequence of textualising it in written language.

E. Knowledge is the intellectual property of authoritative individuals or institutions

This attitude often accompanies knowledge that results from scientific activity (view B). It can also accompany view A, when the writers of books presenting knowledge as 'given' are treated as authorities. It seems useful to list it separately, since it is particularly significant in discussions of plagiarism.

F. Knowledge is grounded in (personal) experience

This view of knowledge does not give priority to the findings of authoritative individuals ('scientists'), but rather to the perceptions of individuals, based on experience and situated in context. It depends on 'being there', on the detail available to the senses, and on the interplay of different kinds of knowledge (for example, scientific, practical, perceptual). This view of knowledge embraces difference and ultimately may deny the existence of hard facts. The idea of 'subjective truth' is based in this view of knowledge. In its most extreme form, this is a relativist view of knowledge, which might be criticised as naively romantic. However this view of knowledge is not confined to individuals talking about their own experience, but extends also to formal research which seeks to ground 'knowledge' in people's perceptions and experience, and to look to experience for the legitimation and countering of claims (see view K).

G. Knowledge is socially (and ideologically) constructed

In this view, knowledge is shaped by its socio-political context and by the social processes involved in its construction. It is similar in some ways to view F, in that it denies the existence of 'objective truth', but it differs in that it locates these non-objective knowledges (note the plural) in social processes rather than individual processes. This view of knowledge has been elaborated since the 1950's by sociologists of scientific knowledge, and more broadly by social theory in general, pivotal moments being the publication of *The Structure of Scientific Revolutions* (Kuhn, 1962) and of *The Social Construction of Reality* (Berger and Luckmann, 1966).

H. Knowledge is a packaged commodity

This view of knowledge is of a different order from those mentioned so far. It is more to do with the social and political use of knowledge than beliefs about its nature (see, for example, Bernstein, 1996; Fairclough, 1992 pp 207ff). For example 'sound-bites', which sell convincingly through popular media, are a product of this attitude to knowledge.

J. Knowledge evokes wonder and reverence

This view of knowledge can accompany any of the others, except perhaps view G. It is common in 'higher-brow' documentary forms such as *The National Geographic* magazine, some TV documentaries, and some encyclopaedias.

K. Knowledge requires legitimation

Views of knowledge listed so far differ as to whether the knowledge needs legitimation, and in the type(s) of legitimation conventionally required by each view. In view A, there is no need to provide legitimation, as the authority of the source is sufficient legitimation in itself. View B depends on rational legitimation being provided through replicable research procedures. In view E, knowledge can be legitimised by mention of authoritative individuals. Personal experience constitutes legitimation in view F. (See van Leeuwen, n.d., and van Leeuwen and Wodak, forthcoming, for distinctions among different types of legitimation.)

L. Knowledge can change belief, and/or lead to action

This view concerns the uses rather than the nature of knowledge. Knowledge is deployed for the purposes of persuasion and argument. Some holders of view G reverse the causality, claiming that knowledge is shaped by the rhetorical uses to which it is put.

M. Knowledge is structured and experienced multimodally

This view is concerned fundamentally with the forms in which knowledge is experienced. In this respect it connects with view F, where knowledge is a product of the senses, not just of the mind or of scientific proof. Recently Kress and van Leeuwen (1996, and other publications by these authors) have observed that this view also affects the forms in which knowledge is communicated. Using visual as well as verbal resources for communication is, in itself, a statement about the sources of knowledge and understanding.

AN EXAMPLE FROM PRIMARY PROJECT WORK

In this section I take a single page (Figure 1) from a project on spiders produced collaboratively by three boys, Jim, Ryan, and Scott, at the age of nine. The page is immediately attractive, showing the boys' enthusiastic engagement with their topic, and their creative recombination of elements from several genres. Without detracting from their inventiveness, I want to suggest how the representational resources on which they are drawing reflect if not reproduce some of the views of knowledge described above. In doing so, I refer to the following list of features which are, I suggest, some of the verbal and visual resources which differentiate among views of knowledge and understanding:

- presence or lack of social actors, especially of researchers and observers;
- generic or specific reference to people and things;
- presence or lack of representation of human reactions (perceptions, thoughts, feelings/affect);
- 'conceptual' presentation of universal truth (present tense verbs of being and having in language), or 'narrative' presentation of specific action or personal experience (often past tense verbs for material processes in language);

- representation of agency;
- presence or absence of legitimations, and their types (linguistic realisations only, I think);
- degree of certainty/reality of representation;
- degree of involvement between the producer and the reader/viewer.

I suggest that several verbal and visual features of this representation of knowledge and understanding of spiders show it to be premised on view A. First, the page has no verbal or visual representation of human actors, certainly not as researchers and observers, nor of human agency, so knowledge is presented as 'given' rather than empirically produced (view B), or socially constructed (view G). There is no reference to authoritative individuals as owners of this knowledge (view E). Secondly, the major participants in clause structure, and the main entities represented visually are spiders and their prey: the objects rather than the makers of knowledge. (See van Leeuwen, 1993 and 1996, for a theory of representation which identifies the components of a social practice – in this case, the social practice of constructing scientific knowledge – and seeks to analyse which of these components are represented, and how.)

Views C and D are also clearly in evidence, both in the verbal representation of the spider's actions and in the visual representation of what a spider is like. There are no markers of modality in the language. The verbs representing the actions of the spiders are all in categorical present tense modality (*live, catch, takes, eat*), presenting these actions as unquestionable fact, and as general truths, not situated in time. The diagram showing the parts of *a spider's body* represents a 'state of affairs', abstracted from reality and presented as 'conceptual', theoretical knowledge (see Kress and van Leeuwen, 1996, for the distinction between conceptual and narrative visual represent-ations). The creatures are represented linguistically in generic rather than specific forms – by plurals (*trapdoor spiders, beetles, caterpillars, flies*), and by indefinite singulars (*a spider's body, a rat*): these generic forms contribute to a representation of knowledge which is abstracted from the particular (view D). The relative lack of colour and reality features on this page are also evidence of a view of knowledge as abstract rather than experiential.

These features characterise a very large proportion of all the project work we have studied by this class of 37 children from Year 4 to Year 6. Taken together they present an unchallengeable, objective view of knowledge. I suggest that this is reinforced by features which I associate with view H. In this example the knowledge about spiders is presented as a patchwork of

Figure 1   Page 1 of the Spiders Project

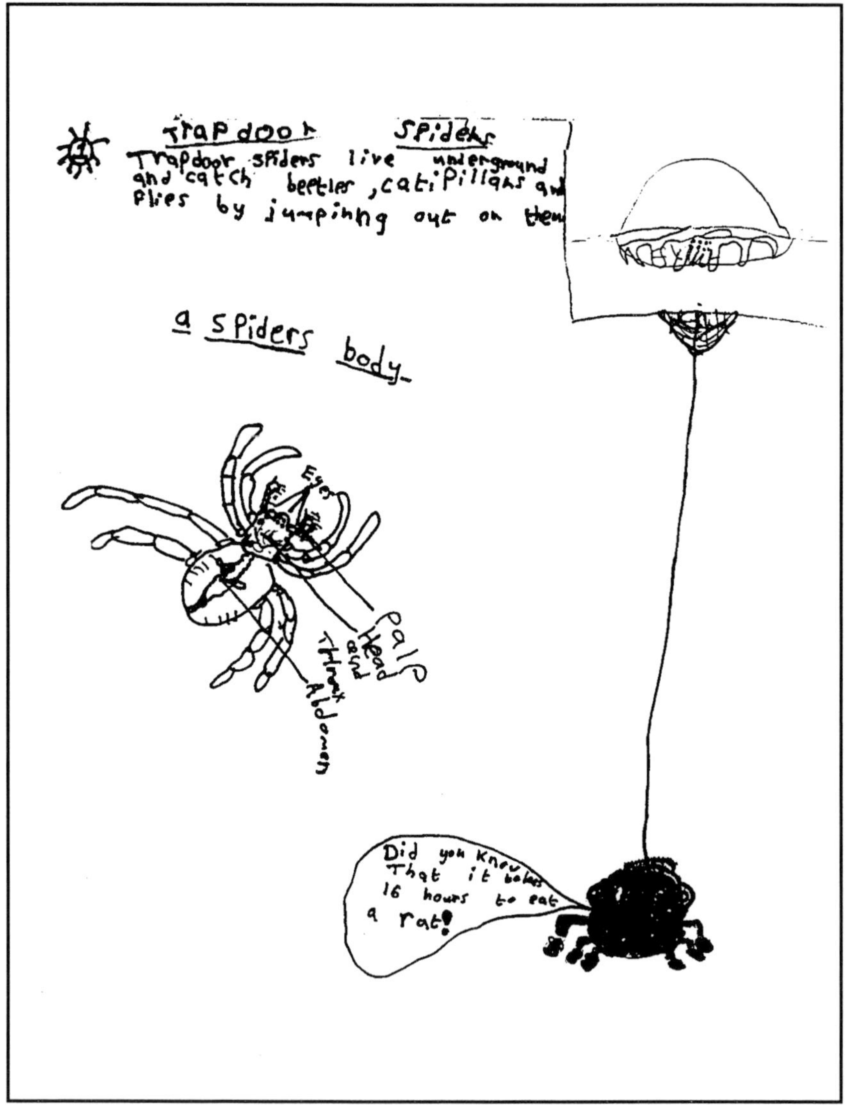

'info-bytes' in verbal and visual form, and as 'fun': the little spider logo surrounding the page number, and the cartoon spider-informant achieve this. While wanting to celebrate children's enjoyment in finding things out and re-combining them in this non-school way, I do not want to do so naively. I suggest that this info-tainment approach to facts in the sources the children are drawing on is a commodification, a turning of knowledge into something to be exploited in the form of – usually expensive – commercially available products. These representational practices were not traditionally found in school books, but are increasingly prevalent in modern sources of information (both print and electronic) in and out of school. The small, fun-size gobbets of information are designed to sell as much as to inform, and may ultimately be detrimental to the development of a critical approach to knowledge. When the children encounter these commodified info-bytes they are, to put it at its worst, serving the interests of the fact-industry. However, when they in turn use some of these techniques themselves, they may, to put it at its best, be breaking down the traditional hierarchies of control over knowledge, as I suggest below.

Knowledge is not dehumanised completely. The capacity to ask about and tell knowledge is attributed to the cartoon spider hanging on a thread on the bottom right of the page, and perhaps by extension to the three boy-authors. The act of knowing is attributed to readers (*Did you know that*). The cartoon spider is a specific, if fictional, spider, in contrast to the generalised spiders drawn and mentioned elsewhere on the page. In this way knowledge is, as it were, brought to life – not left inert on the page as in many versions of views A–E. One might go so far as to see the placing of authority over knowledge in the mouth of the cartoon spider as a challenge to views A–E, making fun of the seriousness of knowledge. Is this an embryo form of view G, perhaps implicitly questioning what counts as knowledge, and who has the right to voice it? I suggest that the critical potential of this form of representation will remain dormant unless it is brought out explicitly in talk around the children's work.

There are hints of other views of knowledge on this page too. The drawing of the trap-door spider's lair in the top right-hand corner is done realistically in pencil, attempting to represent three dimensions, natural variation in shape, and details in the background. In contrast to the schematic diagram of the spider's body-parts, this type of representation can perhaps be associated with view F and view M, where experience of seeing the object of study in reality is significant. Further, the care and interest with which this item is drawn (not visible in the printed copy, but apparent in the original) suggests view J: a sense of wonder and delight in the natural world. But there are no represent-ations of human perceptions or reactions in the language – characteristics associated with view J which do appear in some of the project work (see van Leeuwen, 1995, for the identification and significance of representations of human reactions).

In common with the vast majority of the project work we have examined, this page contains no verbal or visual correlates of views K or L. There is no legitimation nor use of knowledge for rhetorical purposes: it is knowledge unquestioned, knowledge for its own sake.

It is also interesting to note the interactive elements of the messages. The playfulness of the spider logo surrounding the page number and of the cartoon spider have the effect of drawing the reader into the topic. The cartoon spider faces the readers and addresses them directly, using the interactive second person pronoun. This spider is in bright green and red colour, increasing the interpersonal involvement. However, the smallness of the 'info-bytes' increases social distance from the readers, and perhaps from the writers, treating knowledge as relatively detached from them.

I have shown through the detailed examination of one example how the children participate in several, sometimes contradictory, views of knowledge as they encounter, copy, imitate, and creatively recombine a wide range of sources from home and school. I have suggested that a particular view of knowledge as unquestionable truth dominates, and that while there are traces of other epistemologies, they are minimal and marginalised in various ways. While the three boys have taken control over some aspects of knowledge – choosing which facts are interesting and turning facts into fun – I suggest that they are still ultimately subservient to knowledge-as-power under the control of authoritative others.

RETHINKING LANGUAGE EDUCATION: SOME RECOMMENDATIONS

One recommendation may appear to be to avoid independent project work and to control children's encounters with knowledge and knowledge-making processes more closely. Certainly some of the work we saw in the classroom was underpinned by views B, F, K and L, providing a crucial antidote to the predominant views of knowledge I identified above. However, I think that more would be lost than would be gained by taking this implication from our research. Children are learning a great deal from the requirement to research topics independently and to make them their own by re-presenting them in some way. In particular, this type of task encourages them to engage in home and community-based sense-making literacy practices (as described in Barton and Hamilton, 1998) alongside school-based ones. This experience has the potential to carry reading and writing for learning beyond the confines of the classroom into their everyday lives. Many of the independent projects we have studied contain evidence of this. Further, I suggest that any attempt to control children's access to representations of knowledge would be doomed to failure: the views of knowledge I have been identifying are prevalent in school text-books, in commercial information books and in all forms of media presentation to which children have access in and out of school. Far more important, in my view, is consciousness-raising about these issues, both in relation to independent project work and in relation to all the knowledge-presenting sources to which children have access. I suggest that language education should include explicit examination of the role of language and other semiotic media in learning across the curriculum.

Firstly, I suggest that it is important for teachers and, through them, for their students to recognise the way in which many representational practices privilege views of knowledge as unquestionable truth (views A–E), and the way in which literacy practices treat knowledge as a commodity (H). Further, it is important to recognise the way in which children become party to these views of truth through encountering and reproducing mainstream representational practices – in textbooks, on CD-ROMs, on TV etc (see Kress, 1996; Ivanic, 1998; Clark and Ivanič, 1997, esp ch 6). Whether children become critically aware of the views of knowledge underpinning these resources depends very much on the talking and thinking which accompanies their use.

Secondly, I suggest that children should encounter representational practices associated with other views of knowledge to balance the predominant views A–E. This could include reading, and critically examining, sources which present knowledge and understanding in story form, and from a variety of perspectives (as argued by Meek, 1996). It could include undertaking tasks, including independent project work, which involve not just exposition but also argument (views of knowledge K and L – see Andrews, 1995; Costello and Mitchell, 1995, for examples of work of this sort).

Thirdly, I suggest that children should be encouraged to draw on home practices for literacy and learning, including the full range of representational practices they encounter outside school as well as in the classroom and the library. Many home literacy practices have been 'pedagogised' (see Street and Street 1991), and involve the representational practices I have been identifying here as associated with unquestionable, abstract truth. But there are many others which situate learning in the context of everyday needs and interests: the need to know, the need to make sense, the need to keep records, the need to distribute information as part of family or community activities (as shown in Barton and Hamilton, 1998). Examples from our research show children using, for example, family diaries and records, club newsletters, magazines associated with their hobbies, leaflets from trips, community-based publicity. Drawing on these literacy practices might help children to see learning as a part of everyday life, and to link learning with experience.

Fourthly, I suggest that children can be made aware of the social pressures which exist for them to conform to some ways of representing knowledge at the expense of others. Through the representational practices they participate in, children contribute to reproducing particular views of knowledge and not others. The school examination system for most subject areas is likely to reward the use of representational practices associated with certain configurations of views of knowledge A–D and, in later years, K and perhaps L. The representational practices associated with view F are likely to be rewarded in all subject areas in the lower primary school, and in English up to the age of 16. Higher education puts great store on view E, and more on K and L than school education does. Some disciplines operate with views F and G; others don't. It is therefore in learners' interests to be able to enter into the representational practices which will be rewarded by the institutions in which they are studying. If this is done in the context of a critical awareness of the epistemological and other consequences of the selections they make, they may learn also to question the bases of these practices, and ultimately to make responsible choices based on more than just pragmatic considerations. In this way they can become contributors to the shaping of the representational landscape, helping to maintain views of knowledge which they consider to be the most truthful and equitable.

Finally, in our rethinking of language for learning I suggest that it is important to recognise the value of the act of producing rather than just receiving representations of knowledge and understanding. For all my critical analysis of the views of knowledge underpinning the representational resources employed on the page from the 'Spiders project', I want to end by celebrating the diversity, inventiveness and assertiveness that it displays.

Independent projects and some other types of school work provide a special opportunity for children to be designers (in the sense argued by Kress, 1997). Every time children creatively re-combine representational resources for their own purposes they are, at least potentially, taking control over them. Work of this sort gives children the opportunity above all to have the experience of meaning-making: to make knowledge their own in some way. In our study we have observed time and again how important it is for children to have a sense that their re-presentations are worth making: that knowledge is theirs for reshaping, not just someone else's to impose upon them.

ACKNOWLEDGEMENTS

I am grateful to The Leverhulme Trust for funding the two-year research project entitled 'A multi-media corpus-based longitudinal study of children's writing for learning' (Grant No. F/185/AG), from which the data for this paper is taken. This paper, while written by me, is to a large extent based on the work of the project team as a whole, the other members of which are Fiona Ormerod, Nick Smith, Tony McEnery and Jane Collins.

I am indebted to Anne Marshall-Lee for invaluable advice on the development of the section 'Views of knowledge' (pp140–144).

REFERENCES

Andrews R (1995) *Teaching and Learning Argument,* London: Cassell Educational

Barton D and Hamilton M (1998) *Local Literacies,* London: Routledge

Berger P and Luckmann T (1966) *The Social Construction of Reality,* New York: Doubleday and Concentration

Bernstein B (1996) *Pedagogy, Symbolic Control and Identity: Theory, Research and Critique,* London: Taylor and Francis

Chalmers A F (1978) *What is This Thing Called Science?* Milton Keynes: Open University Press

Clark R and Ivanič R (1997) *The Politics of Writing,* London: Routledge

Costello P and Mitchell S (eds) (1995) *Competing and Consensual Voices,* Clevedon: Multilingual Matters

Fairclough N (1992) *Discourse and Social Change,* London: Polity

Ivanič R (1998) *Writing and Identity: The Discoursal Construction of Identity in Academic Writing,* Amsterdam: John Benjamins

Kress G (1996) 'Representational resources and the production of subjectivity', in C R Caldas-Coulthard and M Coulthard (eds) *Texts and Practices: Readings in Critical Discourse Analysis*, London: Routledge

Kress G (1997) *Before Writing*, London: Routledge

Kress G and van Leeuwen T (1996) *Reading Images: The Grammar of Visual Design*, London: Routledge

Kuhn T (1962) *The Structure of Scientific Revolutions*, 3rd edition 1996, Chicago: University of Chicago Press

Latour B (1987) *Science in Action*, Cambridge, Mass: Harvard University Press

Meek M (1996) *Information and Book Learning*, Stroud: Thimble Press

Smith D (1990) *Texts, Facts and Femininity*, London: Routledge

Street J and Street B (1991) 'The schooling of literacy', in D Barton and R Ivanič (eds) *Writing in the Community*, London: Sage

van Leeuwen T (1993) 'Genre and field in critical discourse analysis: A synopsis', *Discourse and Society*, 4, 2, pp193–225

van Leeuwen T (1995) 'Representing social action', *Discourse and Society*, 6, 1, pp81–106

van Leeuwen T (1996) 'The representation of social actors', in C R Caldas-Coulthard and M Coulthard (eds) *Texts and Practices: Readings in Critical Discourse Analysis*, London: Routledge

van Leeuwen T (n.d.) Legitimation, Unpublished lecture notes, London College of Printing

van Leeuwen T and Wodak R (forthcoming) 'Legitimizing social control: A discourse-historical approach', *Discourse Studies*, 1, 1

Home and School Reading Practices in Two East End Communities

ANN WILLIAMS and EVE GREGORY
University of London

Teacher	*Do you want this one or this one?* (offering two books)
Pupil	*This.* (starting to read) *Snow is falling …*
Teacher	*Shall we read who it's by?* (expecting P to join in)
	By Franklin M. Bradley. Illustrated by Holly Keller
Pupil	*Snow is falling …*
Teacher	(pointing to the picture) *What's that there? It's night isn't it.*
	Night...
Pupil	*Night has come and ...*
Teacher	*Snow*
Pupil	*Snow it ...*
Teacher	*Is*
Pupil	*Is falling. It ...*
Teacher	*It ...*

The above extract is part of a reading session that took place in a primary school in the East End of London. The teacher guides the young reader through the text, providing new words, making use of pictures, correcting miscues and introducing the child to the language of books. Yet this teacher, reading so skilfully with the young pupil is neither qualified nor experienced. She is Naomi, a 7-year-old child from Year 2 with her pupil, Aisha, a 6-year-old from Year 1. The school they attend is situated in an area of considerable social and economic deprivation, similar to those investigated recently in a special report on reading standards in inner cities in Britain, which found the reading achievement of children growing up in such areas to be considerably lower than that of their counterparts in more affluent neighbourhoods (Ofsted,

1996). Much of the research into early literacy that has concentrated on such areas has attempted to account for children's early reading *difficulties.* There have been few studies of children such as Naomi, reading so expertly with her young 'pupil', who succeed in spite of difficult circumstances. Naomi was one of the children involved in a recent study carried out in the East End of London which aimed to explore the home literacy practices and the school learning strategies of primary school children from two communities (Gregory et al, 1996). The results revealed some very able children and a rich variety of home literacy practices which were not always recognised nor exploited in the school context.

BACKGROUND

Explanations for teachers' reluctance to dwell on cultural differences in learning practices can be traced to a tradition of educational, linguistic, and social research in which home and school learning practices have been starkly polarised. In the 1960s, one of the major causes of educational failure was deemed to be the cognitive or intellectual deficit suffered by children from poor home backgrounds (Hindley, 1962; Wiseman, 1964; Cullen, 1969), a view embodied in the Plowden Report *Children and their Primary Schools* (1967) which stresses that 'the educational disadvantage of being born the child of an unskilled worker is both financial and psychological' (para 85) and refers to the 'double environmental and genetic handicap' of children living in impoverished areas (para.153) where 'homes provide little stimulus for learning' (para 151) and where children are 'in need of enriched intellectual nourishment' (para 152).

With the early work of Bernstein (1971) and Tough (1973), linguistic deficit was added to the cognitive disadvantage said to be suffered by such children. Tough's oral language tests led her to conclude that children from 'uneducative' (used synonymously with lower social class) homes failed to use spoken English to explain, hypothesise, deduce, inquire, analyse and compare – functions, she argued which were vital for school success. The influential Bullock Report *A Language for Life* (1975) calls upon this research to support its conclusion that there is an indisputable gap between the language experiences that some families provide and the linguistic demands of a school education:

In what we have called the culturally disadvantaged home, a child's language will be limited by certain norms of relationship: there will be less opportunity for him to discuss the reasons for and the likely results of certain decisions. Intentions, possibilities, alternatives, consequences: he will lack occasions to explore these. (5.6)

During the 1980s attention shifted from the child's general linguistic competence to focus on the ability to use one particular type of language: narrative and story. The new deficit hypothesis was that children entering school unfamiliar with written narrative were likely to experience early reading difficulties (Wells, 1985, 1987):

... it is not the reading of stories on its own that leads children toward ... success in school, but the total interaction in which the story is embedded. At first they need a competent adult to mediate as reader and writer between them and the text... (Wells, 1985, p253)

This explanation of deficit was given official recognition in the Cox Report *English from Ages 5 to 11* (1988) whose argument runs as follows: Learning to read demands the existence of certain cognitive and linguistic skills gained primarily through a familiarity with written stories. Parents should read books with their children from their earliest days, read aloud to them and talk about the stories they have enjoyed together (2.3). These 'fortunate' children will become literate more quickly than those whose only experience of books is in school. Children who enter school unfamiliar with stories and books will be unable to handle the symbolic qualities of language needed to learn to read; these children are likely to be from lower social class backgrounds. This 'narrative inexperience' explanation of early reading difficulty still prevails in Britain during the late 1990s. Recent government initiatives to improve literacy will set out to oblige all parents to sign a contract to read regularly with their children (*The Guardian*, 29 July 1997).

Longitudinal and ethnographic research in the USA (Heath, 1983; Michaels, 1986) also polarises home and school learning. According to these studies, explanations for children's early difficulties lie not in the deficit of the family but in the mismatch of learning styles and cultural practices between home and school. Children from 'non-mainstream' (non-middle class) and linguistic and ethnic minority backgrounds enter school unfamiliar with classroom rules of language and learning resulting in low teacher expectation and poor achievement. Finally, ethnomethodological studies on classroom discourse from Australia, the USA and Britain (Baker and Freebody, 1989; Heap, 1991; Gregory, 1993) reveal how some children are systematically excluded from the vital 'story-reading' sessions in the classroom. Through a finely-tuned analysis of moment-by-moment teacher/child interaction, they highlight the hierarchical nature of the relationship between teacher and pupil, in which the pupil must 'bring cultural logic to the interpretation of texts'. This logic however, is cultural logic as the teacher understands it, 'for it is only when the student's logic appears to model the teacher's logic that an answer might stand as an adequate answer and thus count as reading' (Baker and Freebody, 1989).

Such studies polarise home and school learning and promote a 'static' view of learning in which the child arrives in school bringing linguistic and cultural baggage which contrasts sharply with school knowledge and inevitably results in difficulties. Teachers, anxious to underplay differences in home background between children, and obliged by the National Curriculum to promote a common culture (which in reality is that of the majority group), tend not to exploit cultural differences in learning practices of minority groups. A more productive approach to teaching and learning in multicultural classrooms however, might be to take a dynamic view of learning whereby home and school learning practices reinforce each other. In this way children might transform home practices by grafting school learning on to them and teachers might build upon community reading practices in their school lessons. Examples of how this 'dynamic syncretism' might work in practice can be illustrated by some of the findings from our recent research.

THE STUDY

A crucial question we needed to ask in order to investigate possible syncretism was: 'What literacy practices are taking place in homes where the bed-time story might not be the nightly ritual?' Our project (Gregory, Mace, Rashid and Williams, 1996) was carried out over one year in two primary schools in the East End of London, and involved two groups of six children: a Bangladeshi British Sylheti speaking group and a white monolingual English speaking group. The children were recorded reading in school with their teachers and at home with members of their families. Interviews were conducted with family members, with the children and with their teachers both in mainstream school and in mother tongue and religious classes, and the children were observed throughout the year in their schools and community classes. In addition, the good readers in the group were recorded reading with younger, less expert students. The data was analysed using a multi-layering approach which combines both ethnographic and ethnomethodological techniques, the focus moving from the outer ethnographic layer of the social context to the inner layer of individual reading interactions between teacher and pupil.

LITERACY IN THE COMMUNITY

One of the more surprising results of the ethnographic analysis was the extent and diversity of the out-of-school literacy activities of both the children and adults. The intensive nature of the Bangladeshi British children's out-of-school activities can be seen in this extract from an interview between the researcher and a 6-year-old boy, Rashid.

AW   *How many children are there in your class?*
R   *There are 83 children.*
AW   *83 children in your Arabic class! And when do you go to that?*
R   *Seven o'clock to nine o'clock.*
AW   *On?*
R   *A night.*
AW   *Every night?*
R   *Monday to Friday.*
AW   *Monday to Friday! You go for two hours every night! Aren't you tired?*
R   *I don't feel tired.*
AW   *No? And who goes with you? Anybody from your class?*
R   *I go by myself. And some people go from upstairs ... juniors.*
AW   *Are you the youngest then?*
R   *Yes and I'm on the Qur'an.*
AW   *No! How many teachers are there for 83 children?*
R   *There's two.*
AW   *Only two. Who are they?*
R   *One is the Qur'an ... you know, all the Qur'an he can say it without looking.*
AW   *He can? What's his name?*

R   *I don't know. And one is ... he can ... he knows all the meanings.*
AW   *Does he? Does he tell you all the meanings?*
R   *Yes he does.*

Several points emerge from this brief extract from our conversation: first, the large number of young children attending these long and quite demanding classes; second, the number of hours per week the children spend in such classes and third, the relative sophistication of 6-year-old Rashid who is already reading the Qur'an and able to differentiate between the teachers and their respective roles. Rashid was not exceptional. All the Bangladeshi British children involved in the project attended classes at least six days a week (see Table 1). Both boys and girls attended Qur'anic classes in which they learned to read ('qara'a' meaning to 'read' or 'recite by heart') in Arabic. In addition every child attended Bengali classes, often conducted in someone's living room and taught by a parent of one of the pupils. Thus, although the children were not listening to nightly bedtime stories, they were working with written or spoken texts in four languages: spoken Sylheti at home and in the community, written and spoken English in mainstream school, written Bengali in the community literacy classes and written Arabic in the mosque.

While the Bangladeshi British children studied for religious reasons and worked hard at their Bengali literacy, the white monolingual children were also engaged in out-of-school literacy activities. Their home literacy activities however revolved around play: reading comics and children's books, writing letters and diaries and, in the case of the girls, including Naomi, regularly playing 'schools' with their friends or if no friends were available, with imaginary pupils (Williams, 1997).

Table 1   Community class attendance among Bengali British children

Children	*Mon*	*Tues*	*Wed*	*Thurs*	*Fri*	*Sat*	*Sun*
M	B	B	B	B	B	A	A
A	A	A	A	A	A	B	B
Sh	B	B	B	B	A	A	
H	A	A	A	A	B	B	
S	A	A	A	A	B	B	
U	A	A	A	A	A	B	B

B = Bengali class   A = Arabic (Qur'anic class)   Duration of lessons: 2 hours

TEACHERS' STRATEGIES

The influence of school literacy practices was clearly evident in the white monolingual children's out-of-school play. In the case of Naomi, it was possible to quantify the effect of schoolteaching on her own reading practices. The reading sessions between the project children and their schoolteachers, parents and other family members were transcribed and a list of nine strategies used by the 'teachers' to support or 'scaffold' the children's reading was drawn up using a set of categories originally described by Hannon, Jackson and Weinberger (1986). The categories included providing words, insisting on accuracy, providing initial sounds, pausing, prompting etc (see Figures 1 and 2 for list of strategies). Moves made by the 'teachers ' were allocated to one of the categories and the number of moves in each category was expressed as a percentage of the total 'teacher' moves in the session. We recorded Naomi reading with a younger pupil (see extract above) and thus were able to match the strategies she used with those of her teacher. Figures 1 and 2 show the 'scaffolding' strategies used by Naomi reading with the Year 1 pupil and those of her teacher Mrs Kelly reading with a group of children. The two charts bear a remarkable resemblance to each other. Naomi is a skilled reader who has already learnt from her teacher which strategies are needed to decode the text and, what is more, she can use them to help another reader.

Naomi is from what would have been termed a 'disadvantaged' home in the Bullock Report. She lives with her mother and brother in a fifth floor council flat in inner London. There is very little money available for books and no evidence in the flat of the 'artifacts relevant to literacy – the newspapers, magazines, cookery books, notice boards, maps' recorded by Leichtner (1984, p41) in middle-class homes. Yet Naomi is a keen and determined reader. She reads at home and chose an encyclopaedia for her birthday. It is evident that she models herself on her schoolteacher, taking her school reading practices into the home where she is supported by her mother who is pleased and proud of her daughter's progress.

READING AT HOME

The Bangladeshi British children also read diligently at home. Unlike their monolingual counterparts who read with their parents, however, they read with their older siblings. Transcription and analysis of their home reading

Figure 1   Mrs Kelly reading with group

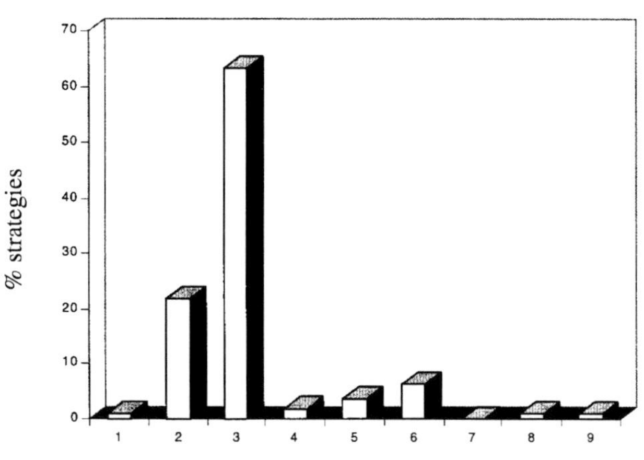

scaffolding strategies (after Hannon et al, 1986)

Figure 2   Naomi reading with Aisha

scaffolding strategies (after Hannon et al, 1986)

Key:

1 Negative comment	4 Pausing	7 Providing initial sounds
2 Insisting on accuracy	5 Prompting	8 Providing auditory clues
3 Providing whole words	6 Splitting words	9 Identifying phonic elements

sessions revealed that the older siblings employed a series of intricate and finely tuned scaffolding strategies to support the young readers. In the initial stages, the scaffolding is almost total with the older sibling providing most of the text. As the child's proficiency increases however, the scaffolding is gradually removed until the child can read alone. We were able to grade the scaffolding strategies as follows:

1 *Listen and repeat:* the child repeats word by word after the older sibling.

2 *Tandem reading:* the child echoes the sibling's reading, sometimes managing only telegraphic speech.

3 *Chained reading:* the sibling begins to read and the child continues, reading the next few words until s/he needs help again.

4 *Almost alone:* the child initiates reading and reads until a word is unknown; the sibling corrects the error or supplies the word; the child repeats the word correctly and continues.

5 *The recital:* the child recites the complete piece (in a similar way to a prayer recital in Arabic). (Gregory, 1998)

The following extract is part of a reading session between Akhlak and his big sister:

	Akhlak	**Big sister**
34		Okhta (this one)
35		*It's*
36	It's a whobber. *Meg*	
37		*Mog*
38	*Mog* catched a fish	
39		*Caught*
40	*caught* a fish	
44	They cook	
45		Cook*ed*
46	*Cooked* a fish	
47		*and*
48	*and* Owl had a rest. Meg was looking	
49		*looked out*

In this extract we see the child and his sister practising 'chained reading': the sibling begins reading, the child continues, reading the next few words until he needs help again; the sibling either corrects or provides the word, the child repeats the correction and continues to read. These home reading sessions were characterised by a very high number of turns and a fluent, fast-moving pace. In many ways, the strategies used by the Bengali British siblings reflect the teaching practices in Bengali and Qur'anic classes in which the young pupils repeat words and phrases after the teacher, mistakes are corrected and the children then repeat the correction until they are fluent.

READING IN SCHOOL

When they arrive in mainstream school however, the Bangladeshi British children often encounter very different reading practices from those to which they have become accustomed at home and in their community classes. The following extract from a reading session between an English teacher and Uzma demonstrates clearly how teacher and child approach the reading lesson with very different expectations of their respective roles.

	Uzma	**Teacher A**
19		OK. Point to the words as you did last time
20	(There) string	
21		*String*
22	*String* (interruption from another child) *String* on the carpet	
23		*String*
24	*String* … On the … upstairs	
25		*Upstairs*

In this short interaction we see the reversal of practices recorded in the Bangladeshi British homes where the sibling leads the reading session and the child continues when and as s/he feels confident. In this mainstream school classroom, however, Uzma herself is expected to initiate the reading. She then reads the word or phrase and hopes that the teacher will provide the next word. Instead, the teacher repeats Uzma's word. Uzma repeats the word again and hesitates, hoping for some support. It is not forthcoming and the teacher merely repeats the word again. Accustomed to the security and the supportive scaffolding of her home reading sessions, it is not surprising that Uzma appears to be unsure of herself and soon falters.

The second teacher involved in the project however, conducted her reading lessons differently. In the extract below Mrs Kelly, Naomi's teacher, is reading with a group of monolingual and bilingual children. It is Susie's turn to read.

Children (Susie, Naomi, Maruf, Tope and Carl)	**Mrs Kelly**
233	Right, OK, Susie's turn. No peeping. Wait a minute Susie. The children aren't ready. OK?
234 Susie *The little girl*	
235 Naomi *skipped*	
236 Susie *skipped along*	
237	*Sorry to interrupt you Susie, just wait one moment. Give Susie about ten seconds to think about it first and then we can help you.*
238 Susie *along....*	
239 Naomi *whistling*	
240 Susie *whistling*	
241	*silly*
242 Susie *silly*	
243	*tunes*
244 Susie *tunes*	
245 Maruf, Carl and Tope *Suddenly*	
246 Susie *suddenly she saw a huge dog*	
247 Tope *er ... dog?*	
(laughter)	
248 Naomi *fast asleep*	
249	*fast asleep*

250	Susie	*fast asleep and under a tree.* *The dog was*	
251	Tope	*really*	
252	Susie	*really a wolf … …(long pause)*	
253	Naomi	*… enough ?*	
254			*although … although*
255	Susie	*although Red Riding Hood* *didn't know that.*	
256	Tope	*Picking*	
257	Susie	*Picking a leaf of grass, she*	
258			*tickled*
259	Susie	*tickled the wolf on the nose.* *He opened one …*	
260			*Now don't actually tell her* *this because I taught you …* *do you remember? If you* *see the letter e and the* *letter a together … can you* *remember the sound?*
261	Carl	*edie … eddie?*	
262			*beady … beady …* *beady eye*
263	Naomi	*Miss, maybe she's picking* *flowers for him*	

Kelly's reading sessions were very much group activities. In the above extract it is Susie's turn to read but the teacher encourages all the children to join in and provide words when Susie hesitates (lines 237–239). When no one can provide the word, then Mrs Kelly intervenes (lines 241, 243, 254). In this way all the children in the group are encouraged to 'scaffold' the reader, using strategies that reflect those used in the Bangladeshi British homes. The reader receives the support she needs and all the children in the group participate actively in the session. The pace is swift and the children clearly enjoy the story. Mrs Kelly uses a wide variety of strategies in her teaching of reading, ranging from imparting knowledge about books to using phonics. She is clearly a very experienced teacher and, having worked in multi-cultural classrooms for many years, ensures that the kind of supportive scaffolding strategies recognised by her Bangladeshi British pupils from the Qur'anic class and their home reading sessions have some part in her reading lessons.

CONCLUSION

In the light of the evidence presented above, we suggest that we need to move away from static views of learning which polarise home and school practices for non-school oriented families, to examine the kind of syncretism that can occur when teacher and child are dynamic learners. We would like to feel that success in early reading is not solely dependent on a child entering school already familiar with its reading practices, nor on parents being able to duplicate school practice in the home, nor even on teachers simply choosing the 'right method' but on the teacher and child building on their shared knowledge to ensure that all children, whatever their home circumstances, have the best possible chance of becoming good readers.

ACKNOWLEDGEMENTS

Family Literacy History and Children's Learning Strategies at Home and at School, ERSC project No. R000221186. Eve Gregory would also like to acknowledge the Leverhulme Trust in supporting this work during 1997.

REFERENCES

Baker C D and Freebody P (1989) 'Talk around text: Construction of textual and teacher authority in classroom discourse', in S de Castell, A Luke and C Luke (eds) *Language, Authority and Criticism*, Lewes: The Falmer Press

Bernstein B (1971) 'A sociolinguistic approach to socialisation with some reference to educability', in D Hymes and J Gumperz (eds) *Directions in Sociolinguistics*, New York: Holt, Rinehart and Winston

Bullock Report (1975) *A Language for Life*, London: HMSO

Cox Report (1988) *English for Ages 5–11*, London: HMSO

Cullen K (1969) *School and Family*, London: Gill and Macmillan

Gregory E (1993) 'What counts as reading in the early years classroom?' *British Journal of Educational Psychology*, 63, pp214–230

Gregory E (1998) 'Siblings as mediators of literacy in linguistic minority communities', *Language and Education: An International Journal*, 11

Gregory E, Mace J, Rashid N and Williams A (1996) *Family Literacy History and Children's Reading Strategies at Home and at School,* ESRC Final Report: R000221186

Hannon P, Jackson A and Weinberger J (1986) 'Parents' and teachers' strategies in hearing young children read', *Research Papers in Education,* 1, 1, pp6–25

Heap J (1991) 'A situated perspective on what counts as reading', in C D Baker and A Luke (eds) *Towards a Critical Sociology of Reading Pedagogy,* Philadelphia: John Benjamins Pub. Corp.

Heath S B (1983) *Ways with Words: Language, Life and Work in Communities and Classrooms,* Cambridge: Cambridge University Press

Hindley C E (1962) 'Social class influences on the development of ability in the first five years', in A G Skard and T Husen (eds) *Child Education,* Copenhagen: Munksgaard

Leichtner H J (1984) 'Families as environments for literacy', in H Goelman, A Oberg and F Smith (eds) *Awakening to Literacy,* Portsmouth, N.H.: Heinemann Educational

Michaels S (1986) 'Narrative presentations: An oral preparation for literacy with 1st. graders', in J Cook-Gumperz (ed) *The Social Construction of Literacy,* Cambridge: Cambridge University Press

Ofsted (1996) *The Teaching of Reading in 45 Inner London Primary Schools* (ref.27/96/D5), London: Ofsted

Plowden Report (1967) *Children and their Primary* Schools, London: HMSO

Tough Y J (1973) *Focus on Meaning: Talking to Some Purpose with Young Children,* London: Allen & Unwin

Wells C G (1985) 'Pre-school literacy related activities and success in school', in D Olson, N Torrance and A Hildyard (eds) *Literacy, Language and Learning: The Nature and Consequences of Reading and Writing,* Cambridge: Cambridge University Press

Wells C G (1987) *The Meaning Makers,* Portsmouth, N.H.: Heinemann Educational

Williams A (1997) 'Investigating literacy in London: Three generations of readers in an East End family', in E Gregory (ed) *One Voice, Many Worlds,* London: David Fulton Publishers

Wiseman S (1964) *Education and Environment,* Manchester: Manchester University Press

PART IV

LEARNERS AND TEACHERS IN THE CLASSROOM

Classroom Discourse and Pupils' Language Use

Lynne J Cameron, University of Leeds

A two-year teacher education project at the University of Leeds involving close work with mainstream teachers at secondary level has revealed detailed insights into the everyday classroom experiences of teachers and pupils for whom English is an additional language (EAL). The project is described in more detail elsewhere (Cameron et al,1996; Cameron,1997).

In this paper, I take a dynamic view of classroom discourse and show how adjustments to teachers' use of language can affect pupils' access to the concepts of the subject area and opportunities for language development. After reporting the context, and the data collection and analysis, I show how teachers' language use can avoid problems that may prevent access to new ideas and how opportunities for pupils to use language may be optimised in mainstream classroom discourse. Detailed analysis of classroom data produces a clearer picture of desirable skills in mainstream teaching that aims at language development alongside conceptual development. In the final section I list some of these skills and suggest that important issues about mainstream language development remain to be addressed.

MAINSTREAM LANGUAGE USE: THE CONTEXT

Current policy in England and Wales requires that EAL pupils receive support for their language development in the mainstream classroom as they study curriculum subjects. The data used in this paper[1] come from a range of subject classrooms in a secondary school in a once-prosperous northern England

---

1   The project school has given permission for classroom data to be used anonymously.

industrial town, now with high levels of unemployment and social deprivation. The school had about 700 pupils aged between 11 and 16, more than 70% of whom used English as a second or additional language. Major home languages were Gujerati or Panjabi. The bilingual pupils were mostly second or third generation British, born in the town, and had attended both nursery and primary schools locally, i.e. they had received between 7 and 11 years of English medium education. There was also a small group of Bosnian refugee children in the school who had arrived very recently, having learnt English as a foreign language.

Of the school staff, only one teacher was bilingual. The school had a small team of language support staff; at the time of the project, this comprised one full-time and two part-time teachers. Mainstream teachers are subject specialists, and have often received very little, if any, language-related initial teacher education. Recent national initiatives have provided sums of money for in-service development, but, as in the case of many schools, the impact on many individuals had been minimal. The mainstream teachers we worked with had not received any in-service training on language development; some of them had worked with the school language support staff in 'partnership' mode (Bourne,1997), but most had not done so, and there was at least one major department in the school which had never taken part in any co-operative work with language support staff (for reasons we were not privy to).

The task facing the mainstream teacher is complex. A typical project class contained pupils at different points in additional language development, with different home languages, and with different levels of literacy, both in English and home language. In addition, there were children with special educational needs and children coping with social and emotional traumas of various types. Specialised language support was focused on those pupils beginning to learn English; but later-stage EAL pupils, whose skills were still developing, received no specialised support.

Discussions with EAL professionals from around the country suggest that this situation, in terms of relative lack of language-sensitive expertise available for advanced EAL pupils in mainstream secondary classrooms, is not unusual.

MAINSTREAM LANGUAGE USE: DATA COLLECTION AND ANALYSIS

As a theoretical framework, I use the non-reductionist levels of Activity Theory: *activity, action* and *operation* (Wertsch,1985), and draw on recent work in language use (Clark, 1996, 1997; van Lier, 1996) and some of the techniques of conversation analysis. *Activity* is concerned with sociocultural context, and the unit of activity has been labelled 'contextual event' by Rogoff (1990, p27) to emphasise that investigation and interpretation must be context-bound. At the level of *actions,* classroom lessons or tasks are possible units of analysis. Actions are directed by the goals of participants, and, from an applied linguistic perspective, both what is done and what is said, i.e. action and interaction, can be examined. *Operations* serve to make an action happen under particular concrete conditions; here utterances or individual acts would be the content of investigation. Classroom action and interaction form the base on which our teacher education enterprise was based. We started from investigation of classroom action, explored related theory and research, and returned to it to try to make changes in classroom practice.

In the first stage of the project, university consultants observed lessons, made and transcribed audio recordings, and carried out the first round of analysis and interpretation. These preliminary interpretations were discussed with the teacher, and a joint interpretation of classroom activity was constructed. This process allowed the teachers to begin to see how their own actions and interactions constrained and constructed opportunities for pupils to engage in action and interaction. We reached a clearer understanding of how pupils' performance in lessons could be influenced by teachers' expectations and use of language, and, conversely, how pupils' performance influenced teachers' expectations and the demands they placed on pupils.

In initial discussions, teachers' concerns about pupils' language were mostly expressed in terms of problems that their pupils seemed to have, such as not knowing enough vocabulary, answering questions with single words or not at all, or not writing enough in response to exam-type questions. Teachers' lack of knowledge, understanding about, and metalanguage for, EAL development made it difficult for them to link what they did in lessons with the reactions of pupils other than rather negatively, through explanations around lack of motivation, shortage of vocabulary, or lack of ability (Cameron, 1997). Very often, it seemed that teachers taught their History or Maths or Science lessons, but felt that pupils were somehow not managing to take part in them as expected. Classroom activity seemed to be perceived as two separate events, one experienced by the teacher and one by the pupils, that overlapped at points but were, on the whole, disconnected.

A dynamic systems view of classroom interaction would suggest that changes in the teachers' knowledge and awareness can lead to changes in practice: increased sensitivity to the conditions of language use, e.g. pupils' current levels of subject understanding and stage of EAL development, and adjustments to action and interaction. Changes in classroom action were grounded in interpretations of classroom reality, and drew on new information from university-based seminars on language and language development. Strategies for classroom action included decisions by a maths teacher to work on lesson introductions and clarity of explanation, and by a drama teacher to try out discussion in first language groups.

Teachers reported back on the outcomes of implementing strategies to their colleagues in later seminars; sometimes, the consultant involved would support this feedback, using classroom transcript data to illustrate practical and theoretical points about language development. This shared linking of ideas and actions, through investigation and interpretation, seemed to pull together the teacher education process in an increasingly concentrated nexus around classroom interaction.

In the next section, I report findings from the analysis of classroom data at different points in the project, looking at how teachers use language to construct and constrain opportunities for language and conceptual development, and at the effects of adjusting language in use.

ADJUSTING MAINSTREAM LANGUAGE USE

Language carries much of the content of subject lessons; as such, it is required to provide access to ideas, the information and ways of thinking that comprise the curriculum subject area. For EAL pupils in the mainstream, the same language use is expected to provide opportunities for language development. It is commonly recognised nowadays that theory which suggests comprehensible input will provide both necessary and sufficient conditions for language development is over-simplified and inadequate, and that pupils need to notice and use language in increasingly complex ways for development to continue (Swain, 1995; Skehan, 1994). Analysis of mainstream classroom language use demonstrates some of the ways in which access to ideas and to language development opportunities can be opened up for pupils through changes in practice.

Language use as access to ideas

As mainstream teachers of a subject specialism, the project teachers were already aware of the need to support pupils' understanding of concepts. In general, over the course of the project, teachers developed greater sensitivity to the role of their own use of language. Investigation of classroom interaction showed a range of ways in which teacher talk, intended to convey ideas, can also confuse or mislead pupils:

- by being too difficult, e.g. use of unfamiliar analogies, too many new lexical items at once, use of multiple clause complexes;
- by being imprecise within turns, e.g. leaving key utterances unfinished, unhelpful repetition;
- by being unstructured at discourse level, e.g. rapid switching of topics (some relevant, some not);
- by not explaining fully enough, or explaining in too much detail;
- by not relating to pupils' previous relevant experience.

Teachers could see these kinds of problems in action in the lesson transcripts, which also provided examples of interaction that was helpful to pupils. By thinking explicitly about their own talk, teachers began consciously to avoid some of these problems.

Language use as language input

Teachers' language use has a role as a key source of exposure to English, particularly for pupils who encounter very little English outside school. Use of transcripts enabled us to find examples of helpful, and less helpful, teacher talk; one teacher's good practice could serve as modelling for other teachers.

If it is to function as a language development opportunity, the project experience would suggest that teacher language use:

- must be attended to by pupils;
- should provide meaningful exposure to new and recycled vocabulary, clause structures and discourse formats, including adequate repetition of new items;

- should provide modelling of language use that can be appropriated by pupils
- should be dynamic, getting more complex as pupils' language and subject content mastery develop.

The two central roles of teacher language use, to convey ideas and to provide input for language development, do not always easily coexist. If the first is to be achieved unproblematically, language is not usually attended to by pupils consciously and is probably used at a level of complexity somewhat below that of current capacity. The project teachers commented on how they felt their own language use had simplified over time, and how they realised that they often did not employ the precise terms of their subject specialism. Teacher talk that serves as useful input for language development does not necessarily facilitate the uptake or development of ideas. Although this potential conflict of interests is in need of further investigation, it raises doubts about a central assumption underlying mainstreaming: that natural, classroom use of language will provide helpful exposure to language.

Increasing pupils' opportunities to use language

It is widely accepted that use of language is required for development (Swain, 1995), and that language development is manifested in increasingly complex, accurate and fluent use of language (Skehan, 1994). However, examination of transcripts showed that pupils very rarely had, or took, the opportunity to *produce* new language used by the teacher, and that group or pair-work tasks sometimes failed to produce talk of any length. Indeed, pupils' utterances in class talk were often limited to single words. It would seem that mainstream secondary classrooms do not naturally provide frequent opportunities for increasingly skilled language use.

An episode from classroom interaction will serve as an a example. The class of Year 10 pupils has been asked for examples of graphs or charts, and have suggested 'bar chart' and 'pie chart'. When one pupil offers 'stick chart' (line 3), the class teacher doesn't know what is meant, and the interaction shows teachers (a class teacher T2 and a special needs teacher ST) and pupil reaching a shared understanding. A potential opportunity for language development occurs through the breakdown in understanding between teacher and pupil.

Extract from classroom discourse: The stick chart

1	P	*pie chart*
	T2	*pie chart*
	P	*stick chart*
	T2	*a wotta?*
5	P	*stick chart* (3.0) *stick chart*
	T2	*stick chart? is that the same as a bar chart?*
	P	*no*
	ST	*don't look at me (.) I don't know*
	T2	*???? explain to me*
10	P	*like (.) a graph (.) make it a graph*
	T2	*a graph is another form of chart isn't it?*
	P	*yea*
	T2	*but the stick chart interests me* (T2, ST and P talk at the same time) *not quite sure what you mean*
	ST	*(to P) so (.) it's a bit like a bar chart only instead of having a block it's just simply a line and a dot*
15	P	*[it's got dots*
	ST	*(.) and a line and a dot so it's*
	T2	*[all right (.) okay (.) yea. I understand that (.) so it's a variation on a bar chart isn't it?*
	P	*yea*

The pupil's use of language in lines 10 and 15 is simple but contains key words *graph* and *dots*. In line 11 and in line 17, which marks the culmination of the episode, the class teacher offers a classification of stick chart to the pupil through a tag question. The pupil has only to acknowledge with *yea* (lines 12 and 18). The Special Needs teacher produces (in line 14) a very clear description/definition of the stick chart, presumably reformulating information from the pupil, since she has previously declared herself ignorant of the concept (line 8). This description is a nice example of potentially very helpful exposure in teacher talk. However, it is heard just once, and is overlapped by the pupil's utterance in line 15, which suggests the pupil does not fully attend to the teacher's utterance. The rest of the interaction in that lesson provided no opportunity for the pupil to *use* the language he had had meaningfully modelled for him. Although the episode shows language in 'contingent employment' (van Lier, 1996, p171), I am doubtful that such instances of co-construction of meaning led to language development, largely because of the very limited role of the pupil in the construction of meaning through English. As a subject lesson, the nature and extent of the pupil's productive role in the construction of meaning may not matter; as provision for EAL development, it was, I suggest, desirable that the pupil should have been more involved in meaning construction through talk.

The issue of pupils' opportunities to produce language became central to the project's concerns and were addressed through task design and attention to questioning techniques. One teacher adopted the strategy of increasing wait time after asking questions, along with explicit discussion with pupils about why she asked questions and her expectations of pupils' answers. Another made clear to pupils that they would be required to respond to questions and adjusted her own practice of passing over pupils who were unwilling to answer, reversing a downwards spiral in which pupil minimal responses led to teacher moving on or answering questions herself.

EXPECTATIONS AND THE DYNAMICS OF SUPPORT

Many other important aspects of classroom action cannot be included in this paper, but I would like to mention two very briefly. The first is the key role of expectations in the construction of classroom action and interaction. The project had a central focus on language. However, once we began examining language in use in classrooms we became aware that what we found happening at the level of actions and operations could also, in sometimes quite subtle ways, be traced back to the expectations that pupils and teachers brought to the events. At a very concrete level, pupils often came to lesson without the necessary equipment or textbooks. Pupils would come to lessons without having done homework set in previous lessons. In both cases, this arose not just from *pupil* action or inaction, but from the *combined* actions of teachers (or school) *and* pupils. The fact that many subject areas did not have enough books for each pupil to use in class, let alone to take home, may have created low expectations on the part of the pupils about books as tools for learning. Teachers often seemed not to expect pupils to do their homework, going through the work in class anyway, and thereby reducing motivation to do homework on another occasion.

We found too that teachers' patterns of interaction often reduced the opportunity for pupils to join in. For example, questions were too complex for pupils to answer in the time given and, rather than struggle, pupils had learnt to wait, and then the teacher would move on and ask someone else. A climate of low expectations of participation in classroom talk was created. Thus, at both the micro-level of turns in classroom interaction and the macro-level of participation, expectations were jointly constructed, often with an insidious downward dynamic. To address this, the school, and teachers in their role as the more powerful participants in interactions, needed to take responsibility for constantly upgrading expectations of performance, participation and achievement, and making these explicit to pupils.

As the project proceeded, the dynamic nature of support for language development across the secondary years became an issue: how to balance the demands of the curriculum with the support given to pupils so that learning continued. It seems that as pupils move through school, the level of support is not always adjusted appropriately, resulting in a net reduction of cognitive or language demands and the closing down of learning opportunities. For example, in one subject area, worksheets that required pupils to tick answers rather than write sentences were used throughout the school; there was no shift in support to lead pupils into free writing at paragraph level, as required at GCSE level. Often reading cards were used rather than books; for reading cards to act as dymanic support, they would need to contain increasingly complex and lengthy texts and serve as a bridge to books at the pupils' age level. Skilled matching of support techniques to language and cognitive development potential is needed, with a continuous process of handover to and appropriation by pupils of language and ideas (Bruner, 1986), followed by new demands at a more complex level.

IMPLICATIONS AND QUESTIONS

Interestingly, neither teachers nor pupils we worked with saw themselves as centrally concerned with EAL development. Pupils saw themselves as language users, rather than as language learners. While teachers were enthusiastic about how the project had opened their eyes to language issues and helped them find strategies to deal with them in classrooms, they were also clear that their prime job remained the teaching of their specialist subject. They commented, for example, on how long it took to plan lessons with language development in mind. That the project teachers felt this after three terms of intensive work, suggests, at the very least, that language-sensitive subject teaching does indeed require expertise. The expert skills and understanding need to be documented and appreciated, so that they can be constructed in initial and in-service teacher education.

The discussion so far suggests that the expertise of language-sensitive mainstream teaching would include:

- sensitivity to the language-related needs of different pupils in a class, at different ages/phases, at different points in development, e.g. beginner/continuing;
- skills to spot and exploit language development opportunities that arise in lessons;
- skills to create language development opportunities when planning lessons and teaching;
- skills to provide different and changing types of support for understanding ideas through language;
- skills to use teacher talk dynamically as useful exposure;
- knowledge to talk about language development issues with pupils;
- skills to design tasks to balance demands and support dynamically, so that each pupil learns, and continues to learn, both content and language;
- explicit knowledge about how English is used to express meanings;
- skills of assessment of language;
- maintaining the highest expectations of pupils.

We can also add the following two areas of expertise to the above list (they have not been discussed here but have emerged as issues in this project):

- awareness of and positive attitudes towards home languages and cultures;
- knowledge about the relation of development of first and additional languages, of spoken and written language.

Reviewing this list, I wonder if it is realistic to expect that, even with an enormous teacher education programme, we could expect to build this level of expertise in all mainstream teachers. As we found, even building the foundations of this expertise took close 1-1 involvement that went into the detail of lessons over a long period of time. Any less focused work would, I contend, have been less effective; it is not so much a matter of finding the right mode of teacher education, but of acknowledging the size of the task. If we require less of mainstream teachers, as seems inevitable, then which skills or knowledge are we going to forsake, and how will this lack of language-sensitive expertise be compensated for in mainstream secondary schools?

I suggest that the need for language development work at secondary/more advanced levels has not been sufficiently documented or recognised. It is likely that different strategies will be applicable from those used at earlier levels; but to assume that once started on EAL development, children will receive all the support they need from mere participation in mainstream classrooms severely underestimates the language demands of public examinations and employment, and may restrict the opportunities of some EAL pupils.

A further assumption increasingly voiced over the last few years, is that, if classroom language is adjusted to be helpful to EAL development, this will be helpful to all pupils. I suggest this sounds dangerously simplistic, and that it should not be assumed, but researched. If teacher use of language is dynamic and sensitive to pupils at different stages in their additional language development, then it is unlikely that a single set of adjustments would improve matters for all first language pupils, who themselves come to the classroom with differing language skills and experiences.

I would argue further that the apparent assumptions of mainstreaming as policy that EAL development does not need to be specifically attended to at later stages, or that skilled language teaching has nothing to offer pupils in the mainstream need to be questioned. The written and spoken English of some bilingual pupils was not of the level we, or they, might expect after more than seven years of EAL development in the mainstream. If mainstreaming is failing to equip pupils with the language skills they need to play a full role in society, then some serious rethinking of this aspect of language education is called for.

ACKNOWLEDGEMENTS

I acknowledge the contribution of my colleagues, Martin Bygate and Jayne Moon, to the development of ideas used in this paper.

REFERENCES

Bourne J (1997) 'The continuing revolution: Teaching as learning in the mainstream multilingual classroom', in C Leung and C Cable, *English as an Additional Language: Changing Perspectives*, NALDIC

Bruner J (1986) *Actual Minds, Possible Worlds*, Cambridge, MA: Harvard University Press

Cameron L J (1997) 'Critical examination of classroom practices to foster teacher growth and increase student learning', *TESOL Journal*, 7, 1, pp25–30

Cameron L J, Moon J P and Bygate M (1996) 'Language development in the mainstream: How do teachers and pupils use language?', *Language and Education*, 10, 2, pp221–236

Clark H (1996) *Using Language*, Cambridge University Press

Clark H (1997) 'Dogmas of understanding', *Discourse Processes*, 23, pp567–598

Rogoff B (1990) *Apprenticeship in Thinking*, Oxford University Press

Skehan P (1994) 'Second language acquisition strategies, interlanguage development and task-based learning', in M Bygate, A Tonkyn and E Williams, *Grammar and the Language Teacher*, Prentice Hall

Swain M (1995) 'Three functions of output in second language learning', in G Cook and B Seidlhofer, *Principle and Practice in Applied Linguistics*, Oxford University Press

van Lier L (1996) *Interaction in the Language Curriculum*, Longman

Wertsch J (1985) *Vygotsky and the Social Formation of Mind*, Cambridge, MA: Harvard University Press

Interactive Storymaking for Contextualised Language Learning

INGE CRAMER, Bradford and Ilkley Community College

This paper explores the opportunity for extended 'output' that oral storymaking offers to young children who are learning in their additional language, English. It uses as an exemplar *The elephant and the king,* a story told by Samadul, an 8-year-old boy whose family is of Bengali origin.

Initially, I suggest that recurring patterns of classroom organisation and discourse combine powerfully to work against opportunities for such extended output by children working in English as an additional language (EAL). By placing the storyteller largely in control, however, oral storymaking may provide a particularly supportive curriculum focus for developing extended output by learners of an additional language. Sections three and four offer evidence of Samadul's narrative skills and the ways in which he monitors and modifies what he says as he speaks. Such metacognitive processes are generally accepted to be important factors in linguistic development.

Sections five and six explore the interaction between Samadul and the researcher. Interactive 'scaffolding' is double-edged; it can be helpful but it may also curtail a child's output. This story is one of 137 collected in a research context, but there are implications for the similar kinds of dialogues that occur in classrooms. The analysis undertaken may offer possible starting points for teachers and intending teachers who wish to explore the effects of their own language practices on their students.

CLASSROOMS AS SUPPORTIVE CONTEXTS FOR LANGUAGE LEARNING

The argument that classrooms offer supportive environments for developing English as an additional language is based on several premises. These include the ideas that the curriculum content offers cognitive challenge whilst simultaneously developing appropriate language uses, that there is more opportunity for collaborative learning, that issues of equal opportunities become a whole-school responsibility, and so on (Levine, 1990).

The successful planning of activities to promote cognitive and linguistic development for EAL learners often requires that the activities are undertaken collaboratively and co-operatively (Hall, 1995; SCAA, 1996). In talking together, learners both practise and receive feedback in appropriate ways of using language. Furthermore, the linguistic resources of the multi-ethnic classroom, in other words, the languages of the children themselves, offer almost the only way in which, currently, bilingual provision is implemented (Blackledge, 1993; Bourne, 1989).

That English classrooms place great value on oracy is perhaps, however, a myth. Large-scale surveys of primary classrooms undertaken in the 1980s indicated that most work was set individually (Mortimore et al, 1988; Tizard, et al, 1988). Since then, the National Oracy Project and the Language in the National Curriculum project have promoted the importance of talking to learn. The English National Curriculum stresses the significance of oracy, yet Galton (1995) estimates that the pattern of individual work persists: only 8% of classroom time is spent in collaborative work. If this is so, how do children get opportunities for much interaction with their peers, let alone extended output?

Much teacher-pupil interaction, with its rapid 'Initiation, Response, Feedback' cycle, tends to confine pupil responses to minimal one and two word answers (Sylva, 1992; Westgate and Hughes, 1997). The focus on individual work leaves teachers with little time for extended interaction and, therefore, cognitively demanding questions. In practice, teacher output is dominant: teachers have the most and the longest turns, and display the greatest variety of functions. Evidence also suggests that teachers often interact less with children of ethnic minority background and in less cognitively demanding ways (Torr, 1993; Biggs and Edwards, 1994; Gillborn and Gipps, 1996). Such practices may be underpinned by beliefs about language learning, the importance of accurate 'output' and therefore of explicit and immediate grammatical correction, and so on (Wagner, 1991). A combination of conditions, practices, beliefs and legal requirements may thus produce classroom environments that are unlikely to meet the optimum conditions for learning, in which children are active problem-solvers in meaningful contexts.

Whilst talking at length is not necessarily of particular benefit (Mercer, 1994), telling stories orally is one way of offering children a task that is cognitively challenging and extensive in terms of output. Simultaneously they are enabled to control the interaction. In addition to other works cited in this paper, extensive research demonstrates the enormous potential of storytelling in education (e.g., Bruner, 1990; Gregory, 1996; Heath, 1983; Hester, 1983; Meek, 1988; Rosen, 1985, 1988; Morrison and Sandhu, 1992). However, oral storymaking remains a relatively rare phenomenon in classrooms. In the following section, I show how Samadul constructs a lengthy and complex plot, and how he pays attention to linguistic features like lexical selection, reference and embedded clauses as he does so. When children are only given the role of responding to teacher initiation, they cannot begin to use language in these manifold ways.

THE NARRATIVE COMPETENCES DISPLAYED IN SAMADUL'S STORY

Just eight years of age, Samadul is already an accomplished storymaker. He produces an entertaining and very complex story, *The elephant and the king,* which has echoes of *Dear Zoo* (Campbell, 1982) and Disney's *Aladdin.* Labov's model (1972) of personal story, with its six elements of abstract, orientation, complicating action, resolution, coda and evaluation, has become accepted as a useful starting point for narrative analysis (Fox, 1993; Mason, 1994). Samadul's story, perhaps because it is fictional, appears to be more complex. The story is structured episodically (de Beaugrande, 1982), with interesting patterns of reversal and more than one complicating action. The outline below offers a sequence of these:

Initial orientation	king wants some animals but does not have any
Complicating action I	servants bring a variety of animals, including elephant
	king rejects them
	tripled pattern: *they got him a … but he didn't want that*
Mini-resolution	servant brings black horse, king satisfied

Complicating action II	elephant jumps on stable, black horse dies king orders servants to shoot elephant arrival of elephant's master elephant and master begin to leave servants shoot
Mini-resolution	elephant's master puts spell on servants, servants die
Complicating action III	king arrives in litter, gets his gun out king tries to shoot the boss of the elephant
Resolution	elephant jumps on litter, servants and king die
Formulaic closure	elephant and master live happily ever after

Unfortunately, the story is too long to be included in its entirety, but I cite sections where appropriate below. It must be emphasised that Samadul can produce such a complex text structure only because he is telling the story. At this point in his development he cannot yet write as much as he can say.

There are 53 T-Units, an approximate device used to analyse utterances into independent clauses and their associated subordinate or embedded clauses (Hunt, 1965). About half the T-Units in this story contain evaluative devices that highlight affect. For example, *but he said he didn't want that elephant* uses:

- three intensifiers: the repetition of a previous clause, the demonstrative adjective *that,* and accompanying phonological stress;
- a negative comparator *didn't;*
- internal evaluation by a character.

Although oral narrative clauses are often simple, Samadul's use of embedded clauses illustrates the linguistic complexity which storytelling can elicit. For example, in the T-Unit *the king when he noticed that he told his servants to kill the elephant,* he uses an adverbial clause of time. The T-Unit simultaneously supplies a motivation for the next episode. Samadul employs both direct and reported speech forms which include, moreover, a range of functions beyond simple actions and descriptions. For instance, the king commands, rejects and evaluates:

(i)   *he said . to his sla . servants . he um . to get him a animal*
(ii)   *he said I didn't want 'em*

(iii)   *but he said he didn't want that elephant . he wants a . erm (2.0)*
        <sighs> (2.0) he wants a (1.0) horse
(iv)   *and the king said um . that's all right*
(v)   *he told his servants to kill the elephant*

Only one construction causes him difficulty. It is unclear in (ii) which form of speech he is using, because he changes tense but not pronominal form. However, the required change is managed perfectly in (iii). The shift back to the present tense in this example may not be an error but a form of emphasis.

Samadul's narrative competences have been elaborated to reaffirm the immense value of oral storytelling. Self-monitoring and reformulation may be seen as manifestations of the teller's effort to communicate. However, stories need audiences. The story, from the teller's point of view, has to be communicated. The communicative processes involved place significant demands both on the teller and on his or her audience.

SELF-MONITORING AND REFORMULATION

Current research with adolescents and undergraduates learning languages suggests that extended 'output' is important because it can promote 'repairs', both 'self-repair' and 'other-repair' (Shonerd, 1994). 'Repairs' are sometimes known as 'garbles', or 'false starts'. Whilst they may represent unimportant changes of mind in the planning process (O'Donnell et al, 1967) they may also be evidence of 'noticing', some kind of metacognitive analysis of language by the learner (Swain and Lapkin, 1995, p386).

Self-monitoring is clearly an important and striking aspect of Samadul's output. A brief inspection of Extract 1 below shows that Samadul's speech is punctuated by fillers like *erm*, which probably indicate a need for planning time. Sometimes he takes longer pauses or 'wait' times (approximate seconds indicated by numbers in brackets).

He also appears to reject certain words as he makes up the story. Some of the changes appear marginal, for example, the choice between *then, first* and *then* (line 3). The repetition of *he wants* a (lines 8–9) may represent thinking time, a hypothesis strengthened by the 'wait' time of five seconds, in total, and the sigh. However, Samadul also pays precise attention to other features. He changes the beginning of *slave* to *servant* (line 4). In replacing the superordinate *man* by *servant* (line 10), maybe Samadul recognises the potential for referential confusion: *man* could refer anaphorically to either *king* or *servant*. In line 11 Samadul again clarifies the subject slot to avoid confusion: he refers back, potentially, to the servant rather than the king as intended.

Extract 1   Transcript of the opening of *The elephant and the king*

1   Samadul   *er . once there was a . erm . elephant and a king .*
2   *the elephant . no the king . wanted um . some animal . animal .*
3   *but he didn't have no animals then . first . and then . um .*
4   *he s . he said . to his sla . servants . he um . to get him a*
5   *animal but th . er they got him animals . but . he didn't want*
6   *them . um . some of 'em got . er snakes . erm . dogs and cats*
7   *. he said I didn't want 'em . then .they got one . erm erm .*
8   *elephant but he said he didn't want that elephant . he wants*
9   *a . erm (2.0) <sighs> (2.0) he wants a (1.0) horse . and then*
10   *erm . the . man . um the servant . er got him a horse . and*
11   *that was a black horse . and then he . and the king said um .*
12   *that's all right . and then um . the . er um elephant . um . the*
13   *. you know . um . the k . like . kings . put horses out . heh*
14 Inge   *out*
15 Samadul   *nn . they don't leave them in their castle . do they (...)*

These examples of self-monitoring and modification are not isolated; more can be found in the rest of this story and many others in my data. The opportunity to tell stories may be a particularly favourable context for their occurrence, because the child can attend to her or his own meanings with less fear of interruption. The rapidity of conversation, and classroom conversation in particular, often deprives children of the thinking time necessary to produce complex thought verbally (Cameron, 1996; Wood, 1992). Although, as we shall see below, there can be competing claims for the floor, the position of storyteller more or less accords control of the speaking turn (Pratt, 1977). When, for example, a 'gap' appears, it is not immediately filled. Samadul therefore has opportunities to exercise self-repair.

THE POSSIBLE EFFECTS OF INTERACTIVE STORYMAKING

Interactive participation may help children to construct fuller stories before they can do so independently (Hausendorf and Quasthoff, 1992; Paley, 1990) or to develop the explicit coherence required of 'autonomous speech' (Wood, 1992, p129). Responses by adults and other children may:

(a)   maintain the flow of the story

There are approximately 14 nasalised backchannels, variations on 'mmm' that punctuate the story, as well as, for example, my echoed repetition of Samadul in Extract 1 at line 14 above. They assure Samadul of my continued attention, just as other non-verbal gestures could, but have a variety of communicative functions. They may indicate that output is clear or uncertain, that an utterance is surprising and so on (Spolsky, 1994). On this occasion Samadul was working individually with me. With larger groups, an adult may sometimes need to model listening and to ensure that another child does not threaten the teller's speaking rights, as happened occasionally even when I was working with just two children.

(b)   help the teller to assess how 'tellable' the story has been

Within the conventions of most cultures, audience reaction indicates a story's effect (Polanyi, 1982) although there are crosscultural issues in the evaluation of a 'good' story and appropriate structures or storytelling stances (Michaels, 1981; Scollon and Scollon, 1982). When the elephant jumps on the stable, I show surprise with a backchannelled *mmm* that rises sharply (see Extract 5 below). Samadul seems to treat this as a question, for he replies *yeah*. Later, my *oof* when the elephant jumps on the litter may be a recognition of the story's resolution. Once again, Samadul affirms it verbally: *yeah that thing*. He also laughs slightly, perhaps acknowledging the force of the ending.

(c)   indicate points where communication is uncertain

As noted above, audience puzzlement may encourage 'other repair'. There are a variety of reasons for communicative uncertainty, amongst them the following:

(c1)   access lexical items in an appropriate language

Extract 1, line 13 shows that Samadul predicts that he does not know the English word for *stable*. He draws particular attention to his compensatory conceptual substitution with the device *you know like* and the tag question *heh* (Kellerman, 1991). My backchannelled repetition of *out* acts as a covert request for further clarification (Extract 1, line 14), to which Samadul responds with an expansion. Extract 2 shows the ensuing conversation:

Extract 2   Transcript of the partial continuation of *The elephant and the king*

16	Inge	*oh they could put them in a stable . or they could put them*
17		*in a field . do you know what a stable is . like a special*
18		*building for the horses (1.0) where they kind of keep them*
19		*with straw . or they can put them into a field*
20	Samadul	*oh I know . ^ and . it's only their heads sticked out*
21	Inge	*right . that's a stable . they put it in a special . little building*
22		*for the horse . yeah*
23	Samadul	*yeah*
24	Inge	*the stable*
25	Samadul	*yeah . them . one of the them . and . um (2.0) that horse was there and . um . you know the . um (1.0) um that . the . the slaves that got the elephant (…)*

Samadul has used two explanations to make himself clear and confirms *stable* rather than *field* (line 20) by imaging it: *and . it's only their heads sticked out*. He needs his audience to understand that he means a stable for the next episode to be clear. An appropriately bilingual listener, of course, could have offered far greater support.

(c2)   reference

The maintenance of clear reference for the 'protagonists' in a story is a highly challenging linguistic demand for children of this age (Karmiloff-Smith, 1985; Berman and Slobin, 1994). Extract 1 shows that Samadul can manage reference very expertly but he does not always achieve it as Extract 3, taken from an earlier story, demonstrates:

Extract 3   Transcription of part of *Jason lives*

Samadul	*yeah . ^ and the thingy couldn't get out . but the key was in the thingy*
Inge	*who couldn't get out*
Samadul	*the two boys*
Inge	*the two boys*
Samadul	*in the jail . but the key was inside the police coat*

When listening to each other, children, like adults, often assume from context what cover words like 'thingy' or 'stuffs' mean (Stubbs, 1983). Questions or backchannels when reference is genuinely unclear, however, may help Samadul to become more precise, and ultimately to be able to tell a story without such interruption. At line 41, Extract 5 below, he independently amplifies *thingy* as *horse.* By the end of the year, he was asking other children what they meant by 'thingmy'.

(c3)   thematic coherence

Whilst 'thematic coherence' may be problematic in presupposing a certain unity in the patterns that can be constructed from a text, we nevertheless behave as though we expect coherence or 'vraisemblance' (Fox, 1993). There seem to be patterns of development in young children's storytelling, although there is no agreement on their analysis (Applebee, 1978; Sutton-Smith et al, 1981). Samadul's story is remarkably well-constructed but others in my data are less so. Interaction may then help to develop them.

One of my two questions during the story queries why the elephant jumped on the stable. It thus signals an expectation that stories are motivated. Samadul does not answer it in the story itself, saying *I don't know,* but does so in later discussion:

he thought if he killed the . erm . horse . then the king will take him for a . pet

Though the main point of the question is not to provide Samadul with the chance to practise embedded clauses of condition, its cognitive challenge enables him to do so.

(c4)   phonological/syntactic confusion

A second question occurs at a later point. My mishearing of *picking* as *kicking* (Extract 4, line 57) is compounded by Samadul's apparent confirmation of *kicking,* leading me to query the relationship between elephant and master. Samadul, realising my mistake, expands *picking* with the adverbial *on his back* (Extract 4, line 62).

Extract 4   Transcript of partial continuation of *The elephant and the king*

55 Samadul   *(…) elephant and . sat on the elephant and the elephant*
56   *was ?kicking him . and the . er . er*
57 Inge   *was kicking the master*
58 Samadul   *yeah*
59 Inge   *didn't he like his master*
60 Samadul   *yeah he did*
61 Inge   *he did . but he was kicking him*
62 Samadul   *no . the elephant was picking him on his . back (…)*

Although this interchange seems to arise from a combination of semantic, syntactic and phonological miscues, it is meaning-focused. The error matters because it makes a difference to an interpretation of the plot, but it simultaneously leads to clarification. In contrast, there is no intervention when Samadul uses syntactic constructions that are not found in the dialect of standard English or that represent his growing approximations of the conventional adult form. Samadul still overgeneralises the weak form of the simple past tense for some, though not all, of his verbs: *falled, sticked;* he uses double negatives and on one occasion says *there bes kings in them.* If teachers are confident in their knowledge of syntactic development, they will recognise that too early an intervention to 'correct' is likely to have little impact on syntactic forms but a very damaging impact on a child's social and linguistic identity and educational positioning (DES, 1988). Unfortunately, teachers may feel under pressure to intervene much earlier and more directly, given the current emphasis of the National Curriculum and the related assessment arrangements.

(d)   encourage through approval

Who listens to the story has an impact on both what is told and how it is told. Ethnicity, gender, class all place constraints even on as simple a measure as length but it is possible for children to tell stories relatively freely. Approving listeners, who accept and encourage what the children say, seem to make a difference (Labov, 1972; Peterson and McCabe, 1983; Sutton-Smith et al, 1981; Romaine, 1985).

THE PROBLEMATICS OF INTERACTION

Whatever our intentions, not all interaction is supportive. I have cited examples of interaction which are intended to support Samadul, who is a confident storyteller. However, there are at least two issues for me to consider:

(a)   maintenance of storyteller's speaking rights

There are four sections of the story where Samadul is not fully in control of his speaking rights, and the interchanges are more conversational. My misapprehension of *picking* (Extract 4) is one example. In another, when we discuss *stable* (Extract 2) I take two long speaking turns with explanations (lines 16–19, 21–22). Even as Samadul reclaims his turn, I still interject with *stable* (line 24). Fortunately he seems to be able to maintain the flow of his story, although his increased pausing (lines 25–26) probably indicates some disturbance. Although I am attempting to be facilitative, I talk too much.

(b)   length of 'wait' time

I have discussed the importance of increasing 'wait' time (section 4). Even if one is convinced of its efficacy, learning to wait is difficult and requires constant checking. In Extract 5 below, had I waited longer rather than intervening after a pause of approximately only one second and a hesitant *um,* it is possible that Samadul might have used *stable* in line 41, instead of line 44.

Extract 5   Transcript of partial continuation of *The elephant and the king*

40 Samadul *(…) yeah . erm or . um . that elephant um . came um where*
41   *that . thingy . horse was . ^ he was inside that (1.0) um*
42 Inge   *stable*
43 Samadul *yeah . and then . the elephant jumped up and . broke the*
44   *stable*
45 Inge   *mmm* <rising intonation>
46 Samadul *yeah (1.0) (…)*

Self-analysis of this kind is time-consuming and may feel threatening to teachers, but is valuable in helping to produce strategies that are more supportive of children's speaking rights. It is therefore very important that teachers analyse their own interactions. Doing so may help one gradually to implement changes in style and pedagogy. An analysis of someone else's transcript may illuminate issues, but may leave it there, as theoretical knowledge and as someone else's problem. Michaels (1981), for example, acknowledges difficulty in changing her own patterns of interaction, despite her perceptive analysis of the cultural match and mismatch of discourse expectations between a teacher and different groups of children.

CONCLUSION: ORAL STORYMAKING AS A STARTING POINT FOR CHANGING PATTERNS OF CLASSROOM DISCOURSE

In this paper I have suggested that it is important for children to be given significant opportunities to be in control of what they say but that in many classrooms little priority is given to this. Oral storymaking offers one such opportunity, for it is cognitively challenging and can reverse the pattern of teacher dominance. Samadul uses story to produce a powerful text that gives him opportunities to manipulate all kinds of meaning relationships through language. By telling it out loud, he modifies his output quite significantly, probably because he largely controls the discourse. However, teachers often feel that they cannot afford to give extensive time to storytelling, given what they 'must' cover. Additionally, younger children telling stories to one another may not always give each other the attention an adult might. Further research, therefore, is needed to see if similar effects are obtained in classroom contexts, and to find ways of providing practical support.

Interaction is part of the classroom process. Interaction can be supportive; equally, it may undermine a child's control. It is therefore important that teachers themselves analyse how their interactions affect children's story-telling, and that they are given time and encouragement to do so. The analytical tools used are based on narrative discourse and critical discourse analysis, informed by research in first and second language acquisition. These forms of investigation into the joint construction of extended discourse are a vital part of teacher education.

ACKNOWLEDGEMENTS

I should like to thank Samadul for his story, his school for encouraging story-making, and Lynne Cameron and Constant Leung for their helpful comments on this paper.

KEY TO TRANSCRIPTS

.	micropause
(2.0)	longer pause in approximate seconds
^	nasalised backchannel
<sighs>	additional, non-verbal information
(...)	omission of prior or later continuation of utterance
?kicking	unclear word

REFERENCES

Applebee A N (1978) *The Child's Concept of Story Ages Two to Seventeen*, Chicago: University of Chicago Press

Berman R A and Slobin D I (in collaboration with others) (1994) *Relating Events in Narrative: A Cross-linguistic Developmental Study*, Hillsdale, NJ: Lawrence Erlbaum Associates

Biggs A P and Edwards V (1994) 'I treat them all the same: Teacher-pupil talk in multiethnic classrooms', in D Graddol, J Maybin and B Stierer (eds) *Researching Language and Literacy in Social Context*, Multilingual Matters

Blackledge A (1993) 'We can't tell our stories in English: Language, story and culture in the primary school', *Language, Culture and Curriculum*, 6, 2, pp129–141

Bourne J (1989) *Moving into the Mainstream: LEA Provision for Bilingual Pupils*, NFER-Nelson

Bruner J S (1990) *Acts of Meaning*, Cambridge, MA: Harvard University Press

Cameron L J (1996) *Appropriate Demands: A Key Element in Language Development in Mainstream Secondary Classrooms?*, NALDIC Occasional Paper 8

Campbell R (1982) *Dear Zoo*, Abelard

de Beaugrande R (1982) 'The story of grammars and the grammar of stories', *Journal of Pragmatics*, 6, pp383–422

Department of Education and Science with the Welsh Office (1988) *English for Ages 5 to 11*, HMSO

Fox C (1993) *At the Very Edge of the Forest: The Influence of Literature on Storytelling by Children*, Cassell .

Galton M (1995) *Crisis in the Primary Classroom*, David Fulton Publishers

Gillborn D and Gipps C (1996) *Recent Research on the Achievements of Ethnic Minority Pupils*, HMSO

Gregory E (1996) *Making Sense of a New World: Learning to Read in a Second Language*, Paul Chapman Publications

Hall D (1995) *Assessing the Needs of Bilingual Pupils: Living in Two Languages*, David Fulton Publishers

Hausendorf H and Quasthoff U M (1992) 'Patterns of adult-child interaction as a mechanism of discourse acquisition', *Journal of Pragmatics*, 17, pp241–259

Heath S B (1983) *Ways with Words: Language, Life and Work in Communities and Classrooms*, Cambridge University Press

Hester H (1983) *Stories in the Multilingual Primary Classroom: Supporting Children's Learning of English as a Second Language*, Centre for Urban Educational Studies

Hunt K W (1965) *Grammatical Structures Written at Three Grade Levels*, NCTE Research Report No.3, Champaign, Illinois: National Council of Teachers of English

Karmiloff-Smith A (1985) 'Language and cognitive processes from a developmental perspective', *Language and Cognitive Processes*, 1, pp61–85

Kellerman E (1991) 'Compensatory strategies in second language research: A critique, a revision and some (non-)implications for the classroom', in R Phillipson, E Kellerman, L Selinker, M Sharwood Smith and M Swain (eds) *Foreign/Second Language Pedagogy Research: A Commemorative Volume for Claus Faerch*, Multilingual Matters

Labov W (1972) *Language in the Inner City: Studies in the Black English Vernacular*, Basil Blackwell

Levine J (1990) 'Responding to linguistic and cultural diversity in the teaching of English as a second language', in J Levine (ed) *Bilingual Learners and the Mainstream Curriculum: Integrated Approaches to Learning and the Teaching and Learning of English as a Second Language in Mainstream Classrooms*, Falmer Press

Mason R (1994) 'The development of narrative skills and the evaluative use of modal verbs in the narratives of young non-native speakers of English', *International Journal of Applied Linguistics*, 4, 1, pp79–99

Meek M (1988) *How Texts Teach What Readers Learn*, Thimble Press

Mercer N (1994) 'Language in educational practice', in J Bourne (ed) *Thinking Through Primary Practice*, Routledge

Michaels S (1981) 'Sharing time: Children's narrative styles and differential access to literacy', *Language in Society*, 10, pp423–442

Morrison M and Sandhu P (1992) 'Towards a multilingual pedagogy', in K Norman (ed) *Thinking Voices: The Work of the National Oracy Project*, Hodder and Stoughton

Mortimore P, Sammons P, Stoll L, Lewis D and Ecob R (1988) *School Matters: The Junior Years*, Open Books Publishers Ltd

O'Donnell R C, Griffin W J and Norris R C (1967) *Syntax of Kindergarten and Elementary School Children: A Transformational Analysis*, Champaign, Illinois: NCTE Research Report No 8

Paley V G (1990) *The Boy Who Would be a Helicopter: The Uses of Storytelling in the Classroom*, Cambridge, MA: Harvard University Press

Peterson C and McCabe A (1983) *Developmental Psycholinguistics: Three Ways of Looking at a Child's Narrative*, New York: Plenum Press

Polanyi L (1982) 'Literary complexity in everyday storytelling', in D Tannen (ed) *Spoken and Written Language: Exploring Orality and Literacy*, Norwood, NJ: Ablex Publishing Company

Pratt M L (1977) *Toward a Speech Act Theory of Literacy Discourse*, Bloomington: Indiana University Press

Romaine S (1985) 'Grammar and style in children's narratives', *Linguistics*, 23, pp83–104

Rosen B (1988) *And None of it Was Nonsense: The Power of Storytelling in School*, Mary Glasgow Publications

Rosen H (1985) *Stories and Meanings*, National Association for the Teaching of English

School Curriculum and Assessment Authority (SCAA) (1996) *Teaching English as an Additional Language: A Framework for Policy*, HMSO

Scollon R and Scollon A B (1984) 'Cooking it up and boiling it down: Abstracts in Athabaskan children's story retellings', in D Tannen (ed) *Coherence in Spoken and Written Discourse*, Norwood, NJ: Ablex Publishing Company

Shonerd H (1994) 'Repair in spontaneous speech: A window on second language development', in V John-Steiner, C P Panofsky and L W Smith (eds) *Sociocultural Approaches to Language and Literacy: An Interactionist Approach*, Cambridge University Press

Spolsky B (1994) 'Comprehension testing, or can understanding be measured?', in G Brown, K Malmkjaer, A Pollitt and J Williams (eds) *Language and Understanding*, Oxford University Press

Stubbs M (983) *Discourse Analysis: The Sociolinguistic Analysis of Natural Language*, Basil Blackwell

Sutton-Smith B (in collaboration with D M Abrams, G J Botvin, M-L Caring, D P Gildesgame, D H Mahony and T R Stevens) (1981) *The Folk Stories of Children*, Philadelphia: University of Pennsylvania Press

Swain M and Lapkin S (1995) 'Problems in output and the cognitive processes they generate: a step towards second language learning', *Applied Linguistics*, 16, 3, pp371–391

Sylva K (1992) 'Conversations in the nursery: how they contribute to aspirations and plans', *Language and Education*, 6, 2,3&4, pp141–148

Tizard B, Blatchford P, Burke J, Farqhar C and Plewis I (1988) *Young Children at School in the Inner City*, Lawrence Erlbaum Associates Ltd

Torr J (1993) 'Classroom discourse: children from English speaking and non-English speaking backgrounds', *Australian Review of Applied Linguistics*, 16, 1, pp37–56

Wagner J (1991) 'Innovation in foreign language teaching', in R Phillipson, E Kellerman, L Selinker, M Sharwood Smith and M Swain (eds) *Foreign/Second Language Pedagogy Research: A Commemorative Volume for Claus Faerch*, Multilingual Matters

Wells G (1985) *Language, Learning and Education,* NFER-Nelson
Westgate D and Hughes M (1997) 'Identifying "quality" in classroom talk: An enduring research task', *Language and Education,* 11, 2, pp125–139
Wood D (1992) 'Culture, language and child development', *Language and Education,* 6, 2, 3&4, pp123–140

Exploring Gendered Talk:
Some Effects of Interactional Style

JEAN BREWSTER, Thames Valley University

THE CURRENT FOCUS ON GENDERED TALK

Recent official publications (HMI, 1993; SCAA, 1997) describe a perceived widening gap between girls' and boys' ability in English, including their differing ability to communicate effectively. They offer a variety of suggestions, one of which exhorts us to 'appreciate girls' perspectives'. This kind of appeal begs several questions, such as whether 'girls' and boys' perspectives' in talk are useful concepts for understanding, teaching and assessing talk in classroom situations.

Following a brief review of studies of gendered talk, this paper proposes that conceptualising interactional styles in relation to four interactional strategies may be a useful way to understand apparent differences in girls' and boys' talk; it elaborates the concept of interactional style, particularly coercive, persuasive, collaborative and compliant interactional styles, in relation to interactional strategies: facilitating, inhibiting, co-operating and controlling.

GENDER MARKED LANGUAGE USE

The early literature on gender and communication began with the development of a concept of gender-marked language use (see, for example, Lakoff, 1975; Edelsky, 1978; Thorne, Kramarae and Henley, 1982). Male speech was characterised by some as competition-oriented or adversarial, while female speech was characterised as collaboration-oriented or affiliative. Research on boys' language use by Miller, Danaher and Forbes (1986), for example, claimed that boys are more 'forceful' in pursuing their own agenda than girls, have more conflict episodes than girls, show greater amounts of controlling speech acts and more negative reciprocity. Goodwin (1990) found that in certain activities, girls mitigated their attempts to control other girls and avoided the appearance of hierarchy, thereby avoiding or limiting self-assertion during competition and conflict.

The kinds of stereotyped behaviour described above have more recently been reinterpreted (see, for example, Cameron, 1990; Coates, 1993; Freed and Greenwood, 1996; Freeman and McElhinney, 1996). Many studies of gendered language rely on a model of linguistic 'dominance' and 'difference'; the former retains a traditional, negative evaluation of women's talk, stressing men's dominance over women, while the latter stresses women's and men's cultural differences as explanations for gendered talk. Maltz and Borker (1982), for example, accord value to women's interactional styles without condemning men's styles. Other representatives of the 'difference' view are Maccoby (1986) and Leaper (1991) whose studies illustrate how girls use language more co-operatively, share turns to speak more often than boys, show more verbal organisation of group behaviour, acknowledge what others have said and express agreement more than boys.

Freeman and McElhinney (1996) claim the choice between dominance or difference is a false opposition; linguists should rather turn to 'much more highly contextualised and localised studies of interaction' (p242) which question the assumption that issues of gender are always the most relevant. Goodwin (1990) argues that activities, rather than cultures, gender groups or individuals should be the basic unit of analysis. As Freeman and McElhinney write, 'A crucial point here is that it is not just talk which varies across context but also the kind of gender identity portrayed by individuals. Talk and gender covary' (p245). Now may be the time to move from a concept of stable and mutually exclusive gendered speech styles to one which incorporates an understanding of interactional styles. Accordingly, a more careful consider-ation of gendered talk must ask, 'when, whether and how men's and women's speech are similar and different. (Freeman and McElhinney, 1996, p245).

Effective talk and assessment

Many studies into 'effective talk' in schools over the last three decades have examined small group interaction (see Barnes, 1975; Barnes and Todd, 1977; Edwards and Mercer, 1987; Wells and Chang-Wells, 1992, to name but a few) There continue to be at least three imperatives for understanding this kind of collaborative talk. First, it underlies the current constructivist model of learning, which requires convincing and generalisable evidence of how learners accommodate to new concepts and give them shape. Secondly, the 'new vocationalism' is a recent imperative since the labour market has firmly established group problem-solving skills as amongst the 'transferable' skills on which employers place emphasis. Thirdly, talk in the classroom has been accorded official status since its inclusion within the statutory orders of the National Curriculum and the assessment apparatus of the GCSE. Teachers in England, Scotland and Wales are required to assess talk, although recent studies have shown that some teachers may be unsystematic in their application of the National Curriculum descriptors when assessing talk (see, for example, Cheshire and Jenkins, 1991; Jenkins and Cheshire, 1990; Ball, 1994; Wareing, 1994; Leung and Teasedale, 1997).

Some research (e.g. Mercer and Fisher, 1992; Fisher, 1993; Mercer, 1995; Wegerif and Mercer, 1996) has provided a useful frame of reference by identifying three kinds of talk used in small groups: 'disputational', 'cumulative' and 'exploratory' talk. In disputational talk, participants disagree with each other and take decisions individually with little constructive criticism. In cumulative talk, speakers build positively but uncritically on what others have said, while in exploratory talk, considered the most effective for learning, participants engage critically but constructively with each others' ideas. This classification, however, may over-emphasise logical problem-solving skills and 'argument' where assertions are developed, justified and tested; meanwhile other kinds of useful interactional skills may be ignored. The research discussed in this paper points toward a four-way, rather than three-way, conceptualisation of 'effective' talk in order to identify ways participants may engage one another.

Boys' and Girls' Interactional Styles

Cheshire and Jenkins (1990, 1991) found that the interactional behaviour of boys and girls was often assessed differently by teachers, and that girls and boys were differentially skilled at co-operative talk. The authors found boys' pronounced use of contributions which closed down the discussion, and this led the authors to conclude that:

> *... this category contained some of the clearest evidence that the girls in this study were, on balance, more sensitive than the boys to the co-operative nature of discussion ... The boys in this study were not such careful listeners as the girls and they were less sensitive to the reciprocal nature of group talk.* (Jenkins, 1990, p284)

Teachers' use of assessment criteria associated with 'collaborativeness', such as encouraging others to participate, was found to apply more to girls than to boys; however, the authors concluded that there were few clear-cut gender differences regarding boys' and girls' contributions, rather that the most important factor in the interactional outcomes of groups was the effect of the conversational styles of individuals.

These findings are supported by Wareing's study (1994) of competition and co-operation in small-group interaction at secondary level. Both girls and boys displayed 'co-operative', 'non-co-operative' and 'competitive' features, although girls in the study displayed certain co-operative features not displayed by the boys. However, overall, stable, polarised gender-associated differences did not emerge in the styles used by girls and boys: 'pupils did not always use one style consistently, but adapted their style depending on their relationship with the addressee' (p285).

Fisher's study of effective educational talk discusses how social roles either realised or acted-out through talk may 'lead to switches in style as well as content' and that social factors like roles and status can affect the discussion (1996, p248).

Despite the work of the National Oracy Project (1987–93) which promoted oracy in classroom contexts, Westgate and Hughes (1997) stress the need for interactional studies to include more convincing and generalisable evidence. This might focus firstly on systematically analysing what is observable, for example, in terms of 'turns' and 'moves', or in terms of inferring or exploring roles, and then to identify patterns in the form or functions of the discourse that emerges. This call for systematicity highlights the contributions which conversational analysis (CA) and discourse analysis (DA) can continue to make to the field. The next section outlines research using these techniques.

RE-THINKING GENDERED TALK

The data presented here are drawn from a fuller analysis of Year 6 boys' and girls' interactional strategies while working in single-sex groups on three different task types (see Brewster, 1987). The data have been re-examined in light of more recent concerns as outlined above to develop a more unified construction or model of interactional strategies and styles that may account for, in this small study at least, what elsewhere is hallmarked as gendered talk. Four types of interactional styles and two continua of interactional strategies are identified. Language functions and other characteristics of two interactional styles, persuasive and collaborative, are illustrated with speech samples taken during the 1987 study.

The original study

Brewster (1987) analysed interactional performances and outcomes of four single-sex groups working on three types of tasks (two of each for six activities total), thus allowing cross-task and cross-group comparisons. Each activity was predicted to require different kinds of interactional skills, specifically those concerned with gaining interactional control and those concerned with maintaining affiliation in group work (see Harlen, Darwin and Murphy, 1977; Smith, 1985). Subjects were six Year 6 boys and six Year 6 girls. Performance by all four groups on one of the tasks (involving 'closed' decision-making) was examined with CA and DA techniques and the interactional strategies deployed by single-sex groups cut across gender boundaries; that is, boys and girls displayed the same kinds of interactional strategies during 'closed' decision-making. These are called interactional styles: collaborative, persuasive, coercive and compliant (Brewster, 1987).

However, distinct gender differences did emerge when comparison was made between the other two task types (expert jigsaw and 'open' decision-making). Moreover, typical, if not stereotypical, gendered talk was observed especially with boys during questioning that was part of an 'expert jigsaw' information exchange task (Extract 6). The limitations of the study must be noted since the findings are drawn from a very small sample (for more details see Brewster, 1987).

Findings

Interactional outcomes during a 'logical' problem-solving task showed varying ability to provide appropriately timed, detailed, evidence and ability to manage conflict; however all speakers seemed to draw upon four main types of interactional style: persuasive, collaborative, coercive and compliant.

Gender-associated differences in talk were observed, particularly with an 'expert jigsaw' task that directed individuals to question one another in turn: boys' talk tended to impede task completion for example by the use of challenges, while girls tended to display facilitating kinds of interactions and challenged each other far less than the boys. Impeding and Facilitating are therefore two interactional strategy types associated with gendered talk.

Brewster's original study thus confirmed an importance of gendered talk particularly in the use of challenges and impeding strategies; however, in cases other than the problem-solving and the jigsaw tasks interactional styles were observed that seemed to transcend gender differences.

Dynamic model of interactional styles and interactional strategies

Reconsideration of the interactional styles observed with all speakers (persuasive, collaborative, coercive and compliant) and the 'gendered talk' polarity of facilitating and impeding led the investigator to construct a model that positions the interactional styles in a framework that also describes 'gendered talk' strategies. Gendered talk strategies are conceptualised as continua of Facilitating and Impeding along one dimension and as Controlling and Co-operating as a second dimension. When the continua are portrayed as a Cartesian model (Figure 1), each of the interactional styles is in a separate area bounded by two strategies and each interactional style is thus depicted as a kind of combination of those two strategies. Conversely, the continua strategies may be expressed through either neighbouring interactional style, so Facilitating or task completion is expressed either by persuasive or by collaborative style discourse and Controlling may be achieved either by coercive or by persuasive discourse.

Gaining interactional control in a facilitative manner is referred to as persuasive style (cf Wegerif and Mercer's 'exploratory talk'); gaining interactional control in an impeding manner is referred to as coercive style and is comparable to 'disputational talk'. Similarly, co-operating strategies are divided into those deployed in a collaborative style (likely to facilitate) or a compliant style (unlikely to facilitate). The latter is similar to Wegerif and Mercer's 'cumulative talk', although there is no separate category in their work for 'collaborative talk' to represent the former.

Figure 1   Types of interactional strategies and styles

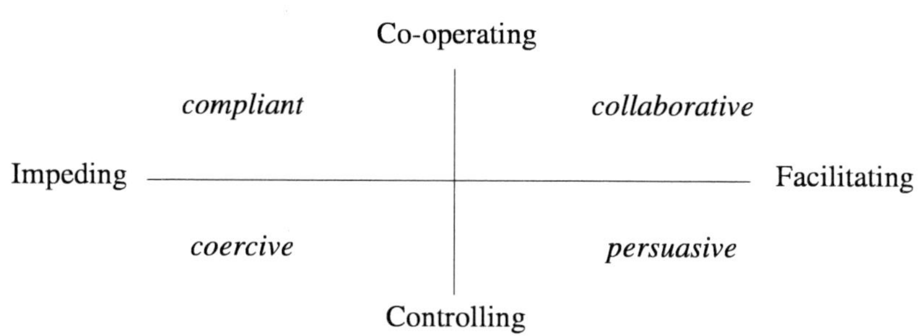

Strategies describe the x- and y-axes, and styles are located in fields bounded by strategies.

Two styles of Enhancing interactional strategies, persuasive and collaborative, are characterised below. Talk samples are from the 1987 study of participants discussing a task called 'Castle Sites'.[1]

Persuasive interactional style

Speakers who display persuasive style listen carefully so that they can follow, build on and challenge others' arguments. They take the initiative in making assertions, providing evidence and making decisions. This is illustrated by speakers making a decision early on in the discussion (often using a 'decision-

---

1   The task called 'Castle Sites' is a decision-making task that required groups to evaluate six possible castle sites in order to recommend the optimal site. Source materials included a map describing the features of each site and an explanatory list of considerations such as the need to ascertain the availability of wood or stone. In a grid completion activity, each of the seven considerations were evaluated using a six point scale (0 = poor, 5 = excellent).

type' opening) which forces other participants to react to this opinion, thus moving the discussion forward quickly. Where other participants disagree or are unsure, they are persuaded through force of argument to revise their opinions or agree. Persuasion is achieved by giving and justifying opinions in a very explicit manner with detailed reference to the source materials, frequently using long turns. Speakers in effective discussions use persuasive strategies to good effect to successfully challenge others' views or provide counter-challenges. The most effective speakers remain sensitive to others' views and are open to revision of their opinions in the light of other speakers' counter-evidence. Topic management and turn-taking characteristics of the persuasive style are summarised in Figure 2.

Figure 2   Characteristics of 'persuasive' style facilitating interactional strategies

---

Topic management
1   adopting a large number of key 'major' discussion roles, i.e. opening topics, providing evidence, responding to questions, challenging, making the final decision;
2   making 'decision-type' topic openings, e.g. 'workers one or two?'
3   justifying opinions and decisions with detailed use of evidence using long turns both before and after being challenged;
4   challenging others by drawing on evidence from the task materials using long turns;
5   being willing to revise decisions after listening to others (where alternative cases are judged to be well-argued).

Turn taking
1   taking a larger proportion of turns than others;
2   making the most long turns, i.e. those containing at least 3 functional categories, usually asserting, providing evidence and awarding a mark;
3   gaining the floor with success most frequently without recourse to upgrading (increased volume/shouting);
4   dealing assertively with others' attempts to take their turn so that their turn is maintained (without recourse to shouting etc).

Functions

(All groups working on the 'Castle Sites' problem-solving activity drew on all or some of the following functions)

–	opening a topic	e.g. site three, water
–	making an assertion	e.g. *it's got water*
–	providing evidence for an assertion	e.g. *it's close to a river*
–	agreeing with an assertion	e.g. *yeah, right next to it*
–	disagreeing/challenging	e.g. but it says 'river is shallow'
–	asking for information	e.g. *is there a village nearby?*
–	supplying a response to a question	e.g. *it says 'near village'*
–	awarding a mark	e.g. *I'll give that three*

Persuasive style functions are described in some detail to illustrate the differences between groups.

Examples of persuasive style functions

Making assertions and providing evidence, two of the functions associated with Persuasive style, include establishing the explicitness of the criteria to be used by the group, providing detail when both giving and justifying assertions, timing justifications to occur before (and not after) decision-making and giving signals of 'reciprocity' such as ratifying topics, supplying evidence to others' assertions. For example, in Extract 1, four girls are discussing suitability of potential castle sites in terms of foundation, defence and water. J's talk shows topic management (line 1 and line 6) as well as providing evidence (lines 6).

Extract 1   Four girls discussing foundations, defence and water

1	J	*it needs to be good for defence*
2	E	*what shall we put for foundations?*
3	M	*four* (pause)
4	J	*yeah*
5	E	*well erm*
6	J	(reads from card) *'good for defence' so so give that four as well*
7		*it can't say say because it doesn't say it's very good*
8		*it's just. or excellent*

Extract 2 shows an extended or long turn of providing evidence (lines 12–15). Providing evidence either draws upon the speaker's general knowledge or makes explicit reference to stimulus materials provided. Detail is generally likely to be contained within long turns, defined as those which contain at least three functions. The most commonly observed were asserting, providing evidence and awarding a mark (rating value).

Extract 2   Four boys discussing workers and food

1	S	*workers*
2	Jo	*well*
3	Ja	*no*
4	S	*no they're not all that*
5	Jo	*[well they're not that far*
6	S	*two*
7	Jo	*three*
8	Ja	*it's about one two it's about three miles*
9	Jo	*no it is quite*
10	S	*two?*
11	Jo	*yeah six miles if you go there*
12	S	*look but you've look. you've got soil the soil for crops so food has gotta be*
13		*five if you've got good soil for crops*
14	Ja	*yeah you've got good soil for crops well fish is good* (reads) *'plenty of*
15		*fish, good soil for crops' that's plenty of food.*

By contrast, extract 3 illustrates coercive style, e.g. giving justifications for an assertion after conflict arose (line 23). R failed to establish the topic (lines 2–5). After conflict and up-grading (lines 15–19), evidence is provided after the decision (line 23).

Extract 3   Four boys discussing foundations and defence

1	R	(reads aloud) *'wet marshy. good for defence'*
2	A	*what we doing?* *site three now?*
3	R	(reads with increased volume) *'on lake island. fish in lake' food water*

4	A	*oy is there good is there good*	*(defence?*
5	R	(reads, raising the volume)	*'good for food close to quarry and near*
6		*village*	
7		*but hard to build on*	*(soft'*
8	S	(reads)	*(marshy land swampy*
9	R	*erm yeah*	
10	S	*so I don't think*	*(it's*
11	R		*(it's a very good defence*
12	S	*found. very*	*(good defence*
13	R		*(five*
14	S	*five. and foundations is I don't think (that good*	
15	R		*(one. none*
16	A	*(one*	
17	R	*(none*	
18	S	*none none. it's a marsh*	
19	R	**ONE** (very loud volume)	3 second pause
20	S	*one or nought?*	
21	A	*one*	
22	S	*one*	
23	R	*it's because it's on an island*	

COLLABORATIVE INTERACTIONAL STYLE

The collaborative style has features of both the Facilitating Interactional Strategy and the Co-operating Interactional Strategy. Collaborative style speakers do not dominate or control the group, and their talk generally helps the group move toward task completion by involving all group members.

Speakers with collaborative interactional style are characterised by skilful listening in order to accommodate to other speakers' topic shifts, maintaining a smooth flow of discussion, encouraging others to participate and providing support for others. Groups using these strategies in the expert jigsaw task 'Ants', negotiated a more equitable share of turns and contributions than others. In this way, decisions were made with recourse to key re-occurring strategies that allowed more equal participation. The use of collaborative style strategies facilitates compromise; however, speakers may be less likely to challenge others' views, thus reducing one possible benefit of group discussion. Nevertheless, collaborative style facilitating interactional strategies identified in Figure 3 generally ensure that each group member has time and encouragement to contribute to the discussion.

Figure 3   Facilitating Interactional Strategies: characteristics of 'collaborative' style

Topic management
1   sharing major discussion roles more evenly between participants, i.e.opening topics, providing evidence, responding to questions, challenging, expressing the final decision;
2   sharing minor discussion roles more evenly between participants, especially agreeing with and providing evidence for others, i.e. making assertions, agreeing, asking for information;
3   sharing the discussion role of challenging between all participants;
4   using 'we' rather than 'I';
5   avoiding conflict.

Turn taking
1   encouraging more equitable turn allocation;
2   avoiding the use of up-grading or other competitive strategies for maintaining turns.

Functions
1   repeating the question
2   allowing thinking time without a countdown (ten,nine, eight etc);
3   encouraging his/her partner to refer to the texts;
4   providing positive feedback/encouragement;
5   providing an explanation;
6   avoiding taunting his/her partner when the answer is not known or incorrect;
7   avoiding asserting that the questioner knows the answer when the partner does not know the answer.

Examples of collaborative style functions

Extract 4 shows J repeating questions (turn 3), allowing thinking time (turn 3), encouraging R to consult texts (turn 3), giving encouragement (turn 3) and giving feedback (turn 5). R is the 'expert' previously provided with written material that was unavailable to J, so J is the non-expert for this part.

Extract 4   Two girls discussing ants

1	J	*how is the queen ant useful in building the first chamber of the ant nest?*
2	R	*how is she useful?*
3	J	*yes* (repeats question)
		3 second pause
		if you're desperate look at your B card or your card (supporting text).
		yes. if you absolutely have to mind. absolutely have to (laughs)
4	R	(reads card again)
		she is the mother of every ant inside the nest (laughs)
5	J	*right*

Extract 5 shows functions of providing an explanation, avoiding taunting, and avoiding asserting that the questioner knows the answer. E and M are both girls.

Extract 5   M is the 'expert' being questioned by E

1	E	*you're not meant to copy it. you're meant to just. just say. you just say a shorter version of it*
2	M	*I know but I can't*
3	E	*well just. you've read about this haven't you? so now just tell us about it*
4	M	*I know but I haven't got a very good memory*
5	E	*I know. I haven't*
6	M	*I'll try to*

Impeding interactional strategies

The following were observed mostly with boys in the expert jigsaw activity. These are considered to be *impeding* interactional strategies because they do not directly contribute to task completion. Additionally, they may contribute to communicative stress which in turn may exacerbate or compound the impeding effect.

Figure 4   Impeding strategies

1   do not repeat the question;
2   do not allow thinking time or alternatively time partners' answers using a countdown;
3   discourage partners from referring to their texts;
4   do not provide positive feedback/encouragement;
5   repeat the answer or asking What? using high rise intonation (taken to express incredulity);
6   demand to know more when the partner has obviously finished;
7   laugh when partners do not know the answer or are hesitant;
8   assert that the questioner knows the answer when the partner does not (even though the questioner has not read the relevant sections);
9   use of name-calling/taunting.

In Extract 6, S is the 'expert' being questioned by J. J uses impeding strategies (turns 2, 4, 6 and 8). Both S and J are boys.

Extract 6   S is the 'expert' questioned by J

1   S   *how is the queen useful? cos she hollows it. erm she*
        (he pauses to think while J clicks his fingers to time him)
2   J   *what? mmm* (laughs) *say that again*
3   S   *cos she erm digs inside and makes it hollow*
4   J   *she what?*
5   S   *how is the queen useful in making the first chamber of the ants'*
        nest? cos she hollows it out so you can get inside
6   J   *you pathetic old runt you are*
7   S   *all right*
8   J   *check your thing dumbo*
Note: the answer S gives is correct.

IMPLICATIONS FOR TEACHING INTERACTION

Edwards (1992) reminds us that 'communicative competence' includes being able to draw upon a repertoire of ways of speaking and that flexibility, sensitivity to context, is an important part of oral competence (p65). Schick-Case (1993) writing about the workplace, refers to the need for speakers to develop wide verbal repertoires, both 'male' traits, i.e. those stereotypically concerned with gaining and maintaining interactional control, and 'female' traits, i.e. those concerned with establishing group solidarity and co-operation.

The notion of interactional style, as comprised of sets of interactional strategies with identifiable characteristics, strategy sets and language functions, explored in this paper may contribute to fuller understanding of interactional features and whether they can or even should be addressed in schools. For example, can speakers learn to recognise their own interactional styles and interactional styles that others use? And can this self-awareness contribute in some way to expanding their repertoires? More specifically, can instructed awareness of these four interactional styles contribute to expansion of repertoires or even modification of preferred interactional style? And if indeed desirable, is interactional flexibility teachable?

Examining how far the notions of interactional style are valid or useful when studied on a much larger scale, how far they are realisable or desirable, what their interactional components might be and whether the insights gained could (or should) be taught in schools, nevertheless promise to make fascinating areas for future research.

REFERENCES

Ball B (1994) *An analysis of what a group of teachers in a mainstream London primary school brought to the assessment of oral proficiency of bilingual pupils*, Unpublished MA thesis, London: Thames Valley University

Barnes D (1975) *From Communication to Curriculum*, New York: Penguin

Barnes D and Todd F (1977) *Communication and Learning in Small Groups*, New York: Routledge & Kegan Paul

Brewster J (1987) *Co-operation and Control: A study of interactional strategies used in task-based collaborative learning*. Unpublished M.Phil thesis, Birmingham: University of Birmingham

Cameron D (1990) *The Feminist Critique of Language: A Reader*, New York: Routledge

Cameron D (1992) *Feminism and Linguistic Theory*, 2nd edition, New York/London: Macmillan

Cheshire J and Jenkins N (1991) 'Gender issues in the GCSE oral examination: part II', *Language and Education,* 5, 1, pp19–37

Coates J (1993) *Women, Men and Language,* 2nd edition, New York/London: Longman

Edelsky C (1977) 'Acquisition of an aspect of communicative competence: learning what it means to talk like a lady', in S Ervin-Tripp and C Mitchell-Kernan (eds) *Child Discourse,* New York: Academic Press, pp225–243

Edwards T (1992) 'Language, power and cultural identity', in K Norman (ed) *Thinking Voices: The Work of the National Oracy Project,* London: Hodder & Stoughton

Edwards D and Mercer N (1987) *Common Knowledge,* Methuen

Fisher E (1996) 'Identifying effective educational talk', *Language and Education,* 10, 4, pp237–255

Freed A and Greenwood A (1996) 'Women, men, and type of talk: What makes the difference?', *Language in Society,* 2,5, pp1–26

Freeman R and McElhinney B (1996) 'Language and gender', in S McKay and N Hornberger, *Sociolinguistics and Language Teaching,* Cambridge: Cambridge University Press

Goodwin M (1980) 'Directive/response speech sequences in girls' and boys' task activities', in S McConnell-Ginet, R Borker and N Furman (eds) *Women and Language in Literature and Society,*New York: Praeger

Goodwin M (1990) *He-said-she-said: Talk as Social Organization among Black Children,* Bloomington: Indiana University Press

Harlen W, Darwin A and Murphy M (1977) *Progress in Learning Science Project: Match and Mismatch,* Oliver & Boyd

HMI (1993) *Boys and English: A Report from the Office of Her Majesty's Chief Inspector of Schools,* London: HMSO

Jenkins N and Cheshire J (1990) 'Gender issues in the GCSE oral examination: part I', *Language and Education,* 4, pp261–292

Lakoff R (1975) *Language and Women's Place,* New York: Harper & Row

Leaper C (1991) 'Influence and involvement: Age, gender and partner effects', *Child Development,* 62, pp797–811

Leung C and Teasedale (1997) 'What do teachers mean by speaking and listening? A contextualised study of assessment in the National Curriculum', in A Huhta et al (eds) *New Contexts, Goals and Alternatives in Language Assessment,* Finland: University of Jyvaskyla

Maccoby E (1986) 'Social groupings in childhood', in D Olweus et al (eds) *Development of Antisocial and Prosocial Behaviour,* USA: Academic Press

Maltz D and Borker R (1982) 'A cultural approach to male-female miscommunication', in J Gumperz (ed) *Language and Social Identity,* Cambridge: Cambridge University Press

Mercer N and Fisher E (1992) 'How do teachers help children to learn?', *Learning and Instruction,* 2, pp339–355

Mercer N (1995) *The Guided Construction of Knowledge: Talk amongst Teachers and Learners,* Multilingual Matters

Miller P et al (1986) 'Sex-related strategies for coping with inter-personal conflicts in children aged five to seven', *Developmental Psychology,* 22, 4, pp543–548

Schick-Case S (1993) 'Wide-verbal-repertoire speech', *Women's Studies International Forum,* 16, 3, pp271–290

School Curriculum Assessment Authority (1997) *Boys and English,* London: SCAA

Smith P (1985) *Language, the Sexes and Society,* Blackwell

Thorne B, Kramarae C and Henley N (1983) *Language, Gender and Society,* Rowley, Mass: Newbury House

Wareing S (1994) *Gender, Speech Styles and the Assessment of Discussion,* Unpublished Ph.D thesis, University of Strathclyde

Wegerif R and Mercer N (1996) 'Computers and learning through talk in the classroom', *Language and Education,* 10, 1, pp47–64

Wells G and Chang-Wells G (1992) *Constructing Knowledge Together,* Heinemann

Westgate D and Hughes M (1997) 'Identifying quality in classroom talk: the enduring research task', *Language and Education,* 11, 2, pp125–139

Wilson J and Haugh B (1995) 'Collaborative modelling and talk in the classroom', *Language and Education,* 9, 4, pp265–281

Teaching and Learning Styles
in Multi-ethnic Classrooms

Viv Edwards, University of Reading

When children start school, they are required to make important adjustments, many of which concern the use of language. They need, for instance, to take turns in large groups; topics of discussion acceptable at home may not be deemed appropriate in school; and teachers may respond very differently from parents. But, while all children need to make adjustments, some experience far greater cultural discontinuity between home and school than others.

This paper reviews recent explorations of differences in discourse strategies and styles in multilingual British classrooms. It identifies a number of important themes which may have an important influence on children's adjustments and perhaps ultimately on their schooling success.

DISCOURSE STRATEGIES AND EDUCATION

A large and growing body of research worldwide draws attention to the very different ways in which speech communities organise discourse and to the implications of this diversity for formal schooling. Sometimes differences result in reluctance on the part of children to speak in class (cf Philips, 1972; Jones, 1987; Zinsser, 1986). On other occasions, divergent discourse norms are perceived by teachers as examples of disruptive or inappropriate behaviour (cf Malcolm, 1979).

When teachers and students share the same cultural and linguistic background, the teacher is able to mediate differences between dominant and minority communities. Erikson et al (1983), for instance, point to the importance of *cariño,* a politeness strategy used by Latino teachers to demonstrate knowledge of students' family life and characterised by close physical behaviour. In a similar vein, Foster (1991) discusses African-American teachers' use of 'connectedness' to underline strong kinship bonds and a sense of mutual obligation with same ethnicity students. In classrooms where teachers and student come from culturally diverse backgrounds, however, the challenge is first to identify differences in discourse style and then to develop ways of building on these differences (see, for instance, Heath, 1983; Vogt et al, 1987; Gregory, 1993).

Much British research in this area consists of largely descriptive work based on speech observed outside the classroom (Edwards, 1986; Hewitt, 1986; Rampton, 1995; Sebba, 1993; Sutcliffe, 1991). In contrast, two studies conducted as part of an Economic and Social Research Council initiative on the 'Educational Needs of a Multiracial Society' (Troyna and Edwards, 1993) focus specifically on discourse norms in multilingual classrooms. In the first of these, Ogilvy et al (1992) worked in eight multi-ethnic nurseries in Strathclyde staffed exclusively by white teachers. A series of 'key' situations allowed researchers to observe and analyse teacher-children interactions using quantitative methods. Although the sex of the child and the ethnic mix of the school were moderating influences, the analysis suggested that children were treated differently according to their ethnicity. In each of the situations observed, teachers assumed a more controlling style with children of South Asian origin than with their white peers.

In the second study, Biggs and Edwards (1992) explored the effects of ethnicity on discourse in four multilingual classrooms in Reading. The children in this study were slightly older, between the ages of five and six, and in their first year of compulsory schooling. The analysis of teacher responses showed that ethnicity was statistically significant in relationships with three separate variables. The total number of interactions initiated by teachers with black pupils was significantly fewer than those initiated with their white pupils. Teachers had fewer extended exchanges with black children than with their white counterparts. They also spent less time with them when discussing the particular task which had been set.

Both the Strathclyde and the Reading studies not only highlight the importance of understanding how subtly the dominant culture affects class-room communication but also they suggest, worryingly, that un-sensitised teaching may cultivate and perpetuate stereotypes, if not more insidious racism. At the very least, these studies draw attention to the need to sensitise teachers to the ways in which they interact in subtly different ways with different groups of pupils and to the implications of these patterns of behaviour for different educational outcomes.

TEACHER–TEACHER RELATIONS

Teacher-student interactions represent just one aspect of the complex realities of multilingual classrooms. Other research has explored implications of differences in discourse style for working relationships between teachers: Callender (1997) studied black teaching styles and Thompson (1991; forthcoming) discussed bilingual support teaching.

Black teaching styles

Callender (1997) in a recent study in one LEA in England put forward the notion of a 'black teaching style' characterised by both communicative behaviours (cf Foster's (1991) notion of 'connectedness') and distinctive strategies for praising and reprimanding children. Five out of six of the black teachers included in the study made liberal use of very public and enthusiastic praise strategies. White teachers were also generous in their praise. However, in the classrooms observed by Callender, white teachers seemed to relate more often to children on a one-to-one basis, whereas black teachers were more likely to use praise as a communal event, reinforcing group values.

Differences in the ways in which teachers reprimanded children were also observed. White teachers tended to take a more indirect approach and, wherever possible, seemed to allow children to save face. In contrast, Callender identifies a range of reprimanding strategies all of which are characterised by their directness. At one end of the continuum lies the use of instructions in situations where white teachers would be more likely to use questions or indirect requests. Mrs Adesanya, for instance, tells 'Bryan' very clearly: 'If you have finished get up and move out'. The use of direct instructions of this kind is often perceived as authoritarian by white observers; however, it can be argued that they follow patterns of discipline familiar from home. Direct instructions also avoid the frustration which white teachers sometimes express when children fail to comply with instructions stated as requests (cf Heath, 1983).

At the other end of the continuum are the 'truth-telling' strategies which draw attention to the individual and are intended to embarrass. These are very much a feature of parent–child relationships in some families and are taken to indicate both care and concern (Hooks, 1993). Mrs Adesanya, for instance, rebukes Jordan, a child who has recently returned from Nigeria (Callender, 1997, p114). Although her method is to humiliate, her aim is to impress on Jordan that if she is to make her way in life, she must take every possible opportunity.

Mrs Adesanya	*Did you go to school when you were in Nigeria?* (Mrs Adesanya's hands are akimbo and she is looking directly at Jordan. She has a stern look on her face)
Jordan	*No miss*
Mrs Adesanya	*Your parents should have sent you to school there then you would know how fortunate you are to have these facilities.*

It is interesting that, while there were no differences in the amount of praise directed at black and white children, black children were reprimanded significantly more often than their white peers.

Callender argues that both praise and blaming strategies need to be interpreted in the context of 'connectedness' between black teachers and pupils. Black teachers saw themselves as working alongside children and parents as an extended family member in the same way as they would have done in Africa or the Caribbean. They regularly behaved as 'significant others' correcting and informing parents of undesirable behaviour. They were also very aware of how much more difficult it is for a black child to succeed in a predominantly white society and how reprimanding strategies can be used to motivate and strengthen black children's resolve.

The notion of a 'black teaching style' is, of course, an oversimplification. We are talking rather of a cluster of language behaviours and attitudes present in varying degrees in black teachers and more commonly associated with black teachers than with their white colleagues. The presence of these attitudes and behaviours, however, poses something of a challenge. White teachers may perceive a black teaching style as unduly harsh and in direct opposition to the expressed philosophy of British schools. White pupils, for their part, may interpret black reprimanding strategies as a personal attack with little understanding of the underlying rationale.

The sensitiveness of this issue is underlined by reactions to the publication of Callender (1997). The teachers who formed the focus for the study were denied permission to comment on its findings by their local education authority. One of the headteachers in whose school the research took place explained this decision by saying, 'Promoting this kind of research can lead to allegations of inverted racism' (Ghouri, 1997, p12).

Bilingual support teachers

Differences in teaching style concern not only African and African-Caribbean teachers, but also the large numbers of teachers from India, Pakistan and Bangladesh working in British classrooms, very often in a support role. The move towards support teaching within the mainstream classroom (cf Bourne, 1989; Edwards and Redfern, 1992) has brought this question into sharp focus. It is sometimes the case that the class or subject teacher is a monolingual English speaker while a bilingual colleague offers second language learners support either through English or through their first language.

The collaboration of bilingual and monolingual teachers very often brings together not only different linguistic backgrounds but also different experiences of learning and teaching. Many bilingual support teachers have been educated in the home country where the culture of learning may be very different. When asked to work in British classrooms, different experiences and expectations can result in confusion if not frustration for all parties.

Amy Thompson (1991; forthcoming) describes an experiment in bilingual support teaching undertaken at a secondary school in Hounslow. One of the problems which emerged during observation over a one year period of the teaching partnership between a maths teacher and a bilingual support teacher was the difference in teaching styles. The subject teacher preferred a 'non-directive' style; the bilingual support teacher favoured a more directive style. Thompson (forthcoming) questions to what extent teachers from different cultural backgrounds can come to a common understanding of teaching and learning. Such a question is central to the development of pedagogies for bilingual support.

PARENT–TEACHER RELATIONS

Differences in cultural norms within the classroom affect relations not only between teachers but also between teachers and parents, a theme which has been pursued in relation to Japanese children by McPake and Powney (1995) and, in relation to Chinese children, by Cortazzi and Jin (1996) and An (forthcoming).

Japanese children in British schools

The Japanese community in Britain is very different from the African Caribbean and South Asian communities discussed above: it is much smaller and more affluent and is generally composed of temporary rather than permanent migrants. McPake and Powney (1995) identify various areas of dissonance in Japanese children's experience of British education, including the role of talk and silence in the classroom.

Different views of the role of talk in classrooms can be very challenging for parents, teachers and children. Influenced by the writings of psychologists such as Piaget, Vygotsky and Bruner, the prevailing UK view is that children are active learners; that speaking and listening play a vital role in the learning process; and that teachers can use children's classroom talk to assess what they have understood. In Japanese education, in contrast, it is believed that the main way in which children learn is by listening to the teacher; children are encouraged to speak only in response to teacher questions and talk between pupils is not tolerated.

These different educational philosophies give rise to dissonant experiences in British classrooms as children struggle to make sense of contradictory notions of how they should behave. At the outset, Japanese children are reluctant to speak, partly because of limited competence in English but also for cultural reasons. Even when they become proficient speakers of English, it is rare for them to make active contributions to classroom discussion. British teachers' frustration at Japanese children's reluctance to take part is fuelled by their belief that much learning is achieved through talk. Japanese parents, for their part, expect their children to be silently respectful. Advice from teachers that parents should encourage children to talk is baffling and culturally unacceptable.

Teacher anxiety would seem to be singularly inappropriate given the high achievements of Japanese children in the British education system. Two possible explanations can be put forward for this apparent paradox: the first is that British confidence in the universal importance of talk for learning may be misplaced; the second is that classroom assessment procedures, ways teachers evaluate student comprehension and participation in learning, may have failed to keep pace with changes in pedagogy.

Another area of dissonance identified by McPake and Powney (op.cit.) concerns educational aspirations. Although the pupil assessment required by the National Curriculum has created a demand for more detailed reporting, British parents have traditionally tended to be satisfied with teacher reassurances about their children's development, particularly in the primary years. There is also an acceptance that relatively few children will achieve the highest levels of academic success.

In contrast, Japanese society believes that all children have the potential for high achievement and expect them to be good 'all-rounders'. Parents expect detailed feedback from teachers on children's performance, partly so that they can make comparisons with age-related standards and partly so that they can help them perform more effectively, through supervised homework, 'crammer' classes or other kinds of private study. When teachers fail to offer evidence for their assessment of children's performance, Japanese parents often opt to send their children to private schools where they believe more emphasis is placed on academic achievement.

The Mainland Chinese

There are clear parallels between the experiences of Japanese children and the Mainland Chinese communities in the UK. Martin Cortazzi and Lixian Jin focused mainly on students in higher education in the People's Republic of China and the UK; An (forthcoming), in contrast, is concerned with the perceptions of British education of Mainland Chinese families temporarily resident in the UK.

Cortazzi and Jin (1996) explore the question of perceived student passivity. In an analysis of essays on the topic of 'Why students don't ask questions', the most common reasons offered included shyness, fear of being laughed at, not wanting to interrupt the lesson and being afraid of making mistakes. Such explanations tend to reinforce Western perceptions of passivity. Other comments, however, suggest that students are active, reflective, independent thinkers who express these qualities in ways which Western teachers often fail to recognise. Chinese students think carefully about the questions that they ask and, mindful of the importance of collectivity, try to sense whether other students share their need to know. They often prefer to ask questions after class, a strategy which avoids the risk of losing face but also means that they do not interrupt the other students. Cortazzi and Jin conclude that, while both Chinese and Western education systems emphasise activity, this activity takes very different forms. In a Western context the emphasis is on the verbal: children demonstrate their interest and level of understanding by asking questions and making contributions. In a Chinese context, the activity is mental: it takes the form of listening and learning from an authoritative teacher, as well as memorising and preparing for classes.

British teachers unfamiliar with the expectations of Chinese families may well advise Chinese parents to encourage their children to make a more active – verbal – contribution to the class. This position not only fails to recognise essential difference between Eastern and Western learning and teaching styles, but is likely to cause confusion and concern.

Chinese children are expected to be good all-rounders; they are also expected to compete fiercely with their peers (Luk, 1991). The apparent lack of competition in British schools is particularly perplexing for Chinese parents who attach considerable importance to children being placed within the first few in the class. Many parents interviewed by An (forthcoming) expressed puzzlement that children's reports did not specify their position. In China there is little time for leisure. Parents remarked that children in Britain have a great deal of free time and some expressed the fear that this might make them lazy. They were also surprised by the fact that many primary age children were not given any homework.

It was against this background that attempts were made to investigate what happens when Chinese parents immersed in one educational tradition and with only a partial understanding of the British system try to negotiate the needs of their children with teachers immersed in a quite different educational tradition who may have a very limited view of the Chinese system. An (forthcoming) interviewed families before they attended a parent-teacher evening in order to establish their expectations and what they hoped to achieve; I carried out parallel interviews with the children's teachers. The parent–teacher meetings were videorecorded. Finally, we conducted post-meeting interviews with parents and their children's teachers to explore the extent to which expectations had been met and to identify and explore any unresolved issues. The interviews with parents and teacher demonstrate several issues which can emerge when children from one educational background are required to participate in another very different tradition. This can be illustrated by looking more closely at the data from one set of teacher and parent interviews.

Before the meeting, the parents expressed general satisfaction with the teacher. They identified as problem areas which they wished to pursue their daughter's ability to write at length in English and her need for more practice in spelling. They were very aware of the limited help which they could offer because they were neither native speakers nor primary teachers. While they felt better placed to help with maths, they expressed frustration that their daughter was not allowed to bring textbooks home from school and that they could not find the books in question at the library or in book shops. They also perceived as a problem the limited amount of homework which their daughter was asked to do. Finally, they noted that the teacher seemed to spend more time praising their daughter than complaining or pointing out her weaknesses.

The teacher, for her part, saw the parent-teacher interview as having two main functions – to celebrate the pupil's achievements and to identify and agree targets for her future learning. The conduct of the interview embodied many of the principles enshrined in current educational philosophy and, in many ways, could be upheld as an excellent example of 'good practice': the teacher showed a genuine respect for the child's achievements, in the belief that this positive approach would enhance her self-confidence and ability to achieve still further. However, her praise in no way demonstrated complacency: she clearly identified targets which would move the pupil's learning forward.

The post-interviews demonstrated that some progress had been made. The mother succeeded for the first time in explaining that she wanted her daughter to bring her maths textbook home so that she could assess what she understood and where she needed further support. She also explained that if the child was asked to do more exercises to reinforce a learning point, they would not expect the teacher to mark her work. The teacher was happy to cooperate.

On other points, however, the parents still expressed reservations. They were surprised that the teacher seemed satisfied with both the child's writing and handwriting. Their perception was very much that British teachers make excuses for children in order to encourage them, whereas Chinese teachers criticise children in an effort to pressure them to improve.

In many ways, it seems as though parents and teacher had been travelling along parallel tracks, seldom making contact. From the teacher's perspective, the emphasis on the child's achievements will help to spur her on. However, she has also introduced targets and been quite specific about what the child should do to make further progress. From the parents' perspective, the teacher has failed to identify the child's weak points and they therefore feel unable to take the necessary steps to help her improve her performance. The apparent failure to 'connect' may well be due to differences in educational philosophy which prevent each side 'hearing' the other. While the parents are listening for 'weak points', the teacher describes 'targets'. Although parents and teachers have the same aims, these are constructed with terminology reflecting different world views which obscures the common aims.

CONCLUSION

Differences in discourse strategies, then, can give rise to a range of misunderstandings in schools which serve multilingual communities. These misunderstandings can influence the interactions of many participants: teachers and children; teachers and teachers; teachers and parents. They also have important implications for equality of educational opportunity and outcomes.

One crucial insight which emerges from the research is the importance of making explicit any differences in discourse strategies and styles which exist. Furthermore without an understanding of the reasons for these differences, there is a serious risk of inappropriate labelling which, in turn, may serve as the basis for self-fulfilling prophecies of future interaction.

The research reviewed here not only highlights the importance of understanding how culture can shape discourse and educational processes, but also it draws attention to the need to sensitise teachers to the ways in which they interact in subtly different ways with different groups of pupils, parents and colleagues.

While an awareness of difference is clearly an important first step in improving communication in schools which serve culturally diverse populations, it is not enough in itself. The challenges are very real. The different discourse strategies and styles associated with different world views can be very difficult to resolve. African-Caribbean teachers often feel that black children 'connect' more readily with the directness associated with parent-child interactions in the home. Yet this approach may be anathema to many white teachers more comfortable with the indirect control strategies and face-saving approaches which they believe enhance self-esteem, an essential ingredient in educational success. In a similar vein, Chinese parents may fail to 'hear' when teachers frame discussions of children's progress in the positive terminology of 'target setting'; instead they continue to seek feedback on children's weaknesses which will help them identify the support which they can offer outside the classroom.

These issues bear on wider assumptions in education. The unquestioning belief that the approach adopted by the school is necessarily more 'knowing' or superior is an important obstacle to equality in education. While it is not at all clear which synergies might be achieved, the need to move away from a pathological interpretation of difference to a more critical stance is becoming increasingly evident. This avenue of inquiry may well unlock a more realistic approach to raising standards than the simplistic attempts to impose a traditional – for which we may read Anglocentric and middle-class – curriculum which have been the hallmark of the 1990s.

REFERENCES

An R (forthcoming) *Mainland Chinese Experiences of Teaching and Learning in the UK.* Unpublished PhD thesis, University of Reading

Biggs A and Edwards V (1992) 'I treat them all the same': Teacher–pupil talk in multi-ethnic classrooms, *Language and Education,* 5, 3, pp161–176

Bourne J (1989) *Moving into the Mainstream: LEA Provision for Bilingual Pupils.* Windsor: NFER/Nelson

Callender C (1997) *Education for Empowerment: The Practice and Philosophies of Black Teachers,* Stoke-on-Trent: Trentham

Cortazzi M and Jin L (1996) 'Culture of learning: Language classrooms in China', in H Coleman (ed) *Society and the Language Classroom,* Cambridge: Cambridge University Press, pp169–206

Edwards V (1986) *Language in a Black Community,* Clevedon: Multilingual Matters

Edwards V and Redfern A (1992) *The World in a Classroom: Language and Education in Britain and Canada,* Clevedon: Multilingual Matters

Erikson F, Cazden C, Carrasco R and Maldonado-Guzman A (1983) *Social and Cultural Organization of Interaction in Classrooms of Bilingual Children.* Final report to the National Institution of Education

Foster M (1991) 'Constancy, connectedness and constraints in the lives of African-American teachers', *NWSA Journal,* 3, 2, pp233–261

Ghouri N (1997) 'Black teaching style a "sensitive issue"', *Times Educational Supplement,* 10 October, p12

Gregory, E (1993) 'Sweet and sour: learning to read in a British and Chinese school', *English Education,* 27, 3, pp53–59

Heath S (1983) *Ways with Words: Language and Life in Communities and Classrooms,* Cambridge: Cambridge University Press

Hewitt R (1986) *White Talk, Black Talk: Inter-racial Friendship and Communication among Adolescents,* Cambridge: Cambridge University Press

Hooks B (1993) *Sisters of the Yam: Black Women and Self-recovery,* London: Turnaround

Jones A (1987) 'Which girls are "learning to lose"?', in S Middleton (ed) *Women and Education in Aotearoa,* Wellington: Allen & Unwin, pp143–152

Luk Hung-kay B (1991) 'Chinese culture in the Hong Kong curriculum: Heritage and colonialism', *Comparative Education Review,* 35, 4, pp650–668

Malcolm I (1979) 'The Western Australian child and classroom interaction: A sociolinguistic approach', *Journal of Pragmatics,* 3, pp305–320

Martin-Jones M and Saxena M (eds) (1998) *Bilingual Support in the Mainstream Classroom,* Clevedon: Multilingual Matters

McPake J and Powney J (1995) *A Mirror to Ourselves? The Educational Experiences of Japanese Children at School in the UK.* Paper presented at the British Educational Research Association Conference, Bath

Ogilvy C, Boath E, Cheyne W, Jahoda G and Schaffer H (1992) 'Staff attitudes and perception in multicultural nursery schools', *Early Childhood Development and Care,* 64, pp1–13

Philips S (1972) 'Participant structures and communicative competence: Warm Springs children in community and classroom', in C Cazden, V John and D Hymes (eds) *Functions of Language in the Classroom,* New York: Teachers College Press (reprinted by Waveland Press, 1985)

Rampton B (1995) *Crossing: Language and Ethnicity among Adolescents,* Harlow: Longman

Sebba M (1993) *London Jamaican,* Harlow: Longman.

Sutcliffe D (1991) *System in Black Language,* Clevedon: Multilingual Matters

Thompson A (1991) *Exploring Bilingual Support in the Secondary School.* A report on the Bilingual Support Project. Hounslow: Hounslow Language Service

Thompson A (forthcoming) *Bilingual Support in a Secondary School.* Unpublished PhD thesis, University of Reading

Troyna B and Edwards V (1993) *The Educational Needs of a Multiracial Society.* Occasional Paper No 9, Warwick: Centre for Research in Ethnic Relations, University of Warwick

Vogt L, Jordan C and Tharp R (1987) 'Explaining school failure, producing school success: Two cases', *Anthropology and Education Quarterly,* 19, pp276–286

Zinsser C (1986) 'For the Bible tells me so: Teaching children in a fundamentalist church', in Schieffelin and P Gilmore (eds) *The Acquisition of Literacy: Ethnographic Perspectives,* Norwood: Ablex

Teachers' Response to Linguistic Diversity

Constant Leung, Thames Valley University

English as a second or additional language (EAL) is a well-recognised phenomenon in the increasingly multi-ethnic and multilingual school population. There is, however, little initial teacher education and only spasmodic in-service training for this area of work (see Cameron, this volume). Furthermore, the current National Curriculum subject specifications do not explicitly embrace EAL as a discipline. Yet all teachers are expected to help promote EAL development as part of their everyday teaching. This paper seeks to explore teachers' representations of EAL development. The discussion will draw on data from a research project on teacher assessment.

Position of EAL in the National Curriculum

Linguistic diversity among the school population is officially acknowledged. Officially 10% of the school population is of ethnic minority background and there are over half a million pupils for whom English is their second or additional language (DfEE, 1997).

Concern for underachievement at school on the part of some ethnic and linguistic minority groups is part of the educational policy discourse (Swann, 1985; Squire, 1996; Morris, 1997). It is widely accepted that there is a linkage between school achievement and competence in English (as an additional language). The special additional funding made available for EAL provision in schools bears witness to this recognition.

Paradoxically, there is no mention of EAL in the English (subject) National Curriculum (DfEE,1995) or indeed in any of the other official subject curricula, although there is now an advisory document on the development of school EAL policies (SCAA, 1996). This document offers some advice on teaching EAL pupils, e.g. 'the teacher paraphrases in English to demonstrate alternative ways of expressing meaning' (op.cit, p14). It is noticeable that EAL development is framed within subject domains of the National Curriculum:

> *English is the area of the curriculum in which pupils have the opportunity to learn language and learn about language in many ways. The programmes of study require focused work on English that allows specific attention to be given to the needs of EAL learners, as well as indicating how teaching about English – its forms, characteristics and range of uses – forms part of the curriculum. The use of English in other subjects extends and deepens pupils' developing competence as speakers, readers and writers.* (op.cit., p8)

There is no suggestion of an alternative or different conceptualisation of EAL as a distinct discipline.[1] Brumfit (1995, p21) observes that 'there is ... a "lingual" role for English in England: that is the claim that English is not so much a particular language, as the source of language development in general'. Brumfit was commenting on the positioning of English in relation to other languages within the National Curriculum. It is easily seen that the same analysis can be applied to EAL.

One of the consequences of insisting on a universal teaching agenda for English is that there are few professional development opportunities[2] and materials for mainstream teachers to familiarise themselves with EAL issues. Another is the absence of a national framework of EAL assessment.[3] All pupils are, under the National Curriculum, assessed and tested with reference to the English Level Descriptions (and Programmes of Study). So, in a sense,

---

1 For an example of an English curriculum framework which admits of an EAL dimension, see the English Curriculum and Standards Framework of Victoria, Australia which has an ESL Companion (Victoria Board of Studies, 1996). For an example of an explicitly EAL-oriented curriculum statement, see ESL Standards for Pre-K-12 Students (1997) produced by US TESOL.

2 The recent GEST 16, 11 and 7 programmes notwithstanding, there is no systematic attempt to provide EAL training at ITE level (Edwards, 1997). It is understood that the 'bilingual pupils' element within the GEST framework will cease to exist from 1998.

3 See Leung (1996) for an account of the current EAL assessment practices at the local education authority level. See OFSTED (1997) for an official view on EAL assessment and see South (1997) for a professional response to the official position.

the EAL pupils are invisible in mandatory Key Stages 1–4 curriculum and assessment frameworks.[4]

TEACHERS' VIEWS ON EAL

The discussion in this section draws on some of the interview data of an on-going study of Teacher Assessment of speaking and listening in English of 7-year-old pupils.[5] Under the current statutory arrangements, at Key Stage 1 (ages 5–7) the assessment of pupils' speaking and listening is carried out by teachers in the context of normal classroom teaching and learning activities. In other words, it is meant to be an integral part of teaching and learning. The National Curriculum Level Descriptions for Speaking and Listening serve as both mapping and calibration instruments (North, 1995) (see Appendix 1 for Level Descriptions). This aspect of the assessment system assumes that teachers interpret and apply the Level Descriptions in ways which are consistent with official curriculum conceptualisation. Teacher Assessment is a key moment in the curriculum activities when teachers' views and beliefs about their pupils' attainment and the nature of language and language development are crystallised in action. (For a more detailed argument on this point, see Leung and Teasdale, 1997a.)

Theoretical considerations

Epistemologically, the use and the value of interview discourse data for this study can be seen from at least two perspectives:

- Eraut (1994) suggests that professional knowledge comprises a number of components, one of which is referred to as *impressions* which are summary

---

4   At the time of going to press, the Qualifications and Curriculum Authority is trialling a set of guidelines for profiling pupils with EAL as well as two pre-National Curriculum Level 1 (English) step descriptors for beginners in EAL.

5   This study was funded by the Centre for Applied Linguistic Research, Thames Valley University. For reports of the earlier phase see Leung and Teasdale (1997a); Leung and Teasdale (1997) and Teasdale and Leung (1997b). This paper reports on one aspect of this study. One of the relevant findings from the earlier phase of this study for this discussion is that there is evidence that primary teachers (in the sample population) operate a 'native-speaker-like' criterion in the more language system-oriented aspects of assessing spoken English in multi-ethnic and multilingual classrooms.

forms of previous knowledge and experience and they inform or influence everyday practice at a self-evident non-analysed level. Members of a profession, through shared experience and culture, are likely to hold some common impressions in so far as they are seen to assist their daily work.[6] The teachers' comments on assessment criteria and on individual children can be regarded as at least partial evidence of some aspects of their collective views on language attainment and development. Furthermore, van Dijk (1993, p257) attributes a more active role to these collective views which he conceptualises as social cognition:

Discourse, communication and (other) forms of action and interaction are monitored by social cognition ... The same is true for our understanding of social events or of social institutions and power relations. Hence social cognitions mediate between micro- and macro-levels of society, between discourse and action ...

- McCallum et al (1995) show that the practice of Teacher Assessment is diverse and, furthermore, it does not manifest itself in easily observed actions or behaviours. Indeed, the data of this study (see footnote 34) and that of McCallum (op.cit.) suggest that for some teachers a great deal of day-to-day assessment of children takes place in fleeting moments of classroom interaction and decisions are held in memory; it does not always occur in clearly bounded assessment events. The study of teachers' accounts of assessment thus represents a possibility of discovering at least some aspects of their views on language attainment and the basis of their decisions.

At a more local level of handling discourse utterances, the task was to find out the teacher informants' representations of assessment criteria in multi-ethnic and multilingual contexts. The notions of frame and schema seemed to offer an analytically helpful way of identifying discourse meaning in relation to specific social and knowledge domains. Gumperz (1992) draws a distinction between frame and schemata.

---

6   For a discussion on the inter-subjective nature of mental representation see Marton (1981), Moscovici (1984), Potter and Wetherall (1987), Säljö (1988). For a discussion on the socially constructed nature of everyday reality, see Berger and Luckmann (1967).

Frames are concerned with the interpersonal relationship between the inter-locutors and schemata are concerned with content meanings. One way of understanding the importance of the notion of frame is to apply it to a real-world activity, say, that of a doctor-patient consultation interview where the two parties, as doctor and patient, interpret each other's utterances as information offering, advice giving, prescription issuing and so on. The content of the patient's health report and the doctor's prescription is not determined by the medical consultation frame. Gumperz (1992, p44) puts it more formally:

When we are talking about sociocultural knowledge entering into discourse via frames, the fact that this knowledge is seen in relational terms limits some of the indeterminacy associated with the view of indexicality as retrieving world knowledge and making it available as an input to interpretation.

The idea that frames delimit the range of possible interpretations of utterances, apart from being intuitively appealing, is supported, albeit indirectly, by work in other areas. For instance, Read (1992), working on the psychological processes of constructing accounts, suggests that when people put together an explanation they try to assess what the audience already knows in order to achieve a better sense of the constraints on the information to be selected. In a discussion on the non-arbitrariness of the semiotic sign in social communication, Kress (1993, p174) argues more decisively that:

... in relation to a particular object or event, 'interest' leads the producer of the sign to focus on a particular characteristic of an object or event (whether an object or an event in the physical or in the social/cultural, semiotic world) to make that the criterial characteristic of the object or event, that is, make it the basis of the production of the signified.

Thus, it may be reasonably argued that there are grounds to treat the teacher informants' utterances as meaningful reflections of social experience and social action.

For the purpose of analysing the discourse data for this study, the notion of frame, adopting Gumperz's conceptualisation, is particularly helpful in that it narrows down the range of possible interpretations of some indexical utterances, utterances which are highly suggestive of specific and implied meaning in context, whose meaning might otherwise be more difficult to decipher (see discussion below).

Data collection

The data collection consisted of two overlapping phases. In phase one approximately 35 hours of video recording of Year 2 and Year 3 classes in two schools were edited into two sets of short clips focused on individual pupils engaged in a variety of normal classroom activities, one set for each of the two schools. The short clips (of individual pupils) were about five minutes in duration. In School A one Year 3 class was videoed (in October) and in School B three Year 2 classes were videoed. In School B the three classes shared a central activity area, but each class had their own quiet area (a room bordering a central area) for whole class teaching and carpet time sessions. The use of a common central activity area made it relatively easy to include most of the children in the footage. An additional advantage of this arrangement was that all three teachers were familiar enough with most of the children in the three classes to be able to discuss them in assessment terms.

In the second phase, all four teachers were interviewed three times. In addition they were asked to keep an audio diary of 'assessment event' related to the Speaking and Listening of particular children during the interviews period which spanned over four weeks. Each of the interviews was of a semi-structured type and focused on a different aspect of Teacher Assessment. Interview 1 (espoused theories) elicited detailed information on teachers' interpretations of the meanings of each of the first four levels of the National Curriculum Level Descriptions for Speaking and Listening. Interview 2 (focus on children) focused on some of the children in each of the teachers' class and the teachers were asked to talk, from memory, through their assessment of each child. In interview 3 (theory in action) the teachers were asked to watch the video clips of the children in their own class (in the case of School B, in a colleague's class as well); at the end of each clip they were invited to comment on what they saw in relation to the assessment of Speaking and Listening. All the interviews were audio-recorded and transcribed. The data were then analysed using the NUD·IST qualitative data analysis software package (QSR, 1996).

Findings

The data reported in this section are drawn from the three phases of interviews; only those comments specifically made about bilingual children learning EAL are shown.[7] Since the main purpose of this discussion is to explore teacher representations of assessment descriptors and not to report frequency or regularity of occurrence, only representative samples are shown (for a more quantitative report, see Leung and Teasdale, 1997b). Following Gumperz, the frame here is a semi-structured interview between a researcher and a classroom practitioner. The explicit purpose is for the researcher to gather information on teachers' criteria for and practice of Teacher Assessment. The social relationship is that of expert (teacher) and information seeker (researcher). The schema is EALness because the data presented here are specifically related to EAL pupils. The indexicals are components of the schema EALness. All the teachers' utterances reported below occurred in the semi-structured interviews. The conversational cues which preceded each of the utterances are also shown. All the names are pseudonyms.

Phase 1 interviews – espoused theories, pupils at a distance

Schema: EALness	Teachers' utterances
Indexical: family	1 Cue: what is important in the NC Level 1 descriptions? *Well, the fact they are talking. I think that's the main thing. And I mean, it's an interesting side line, but I have, I have this theory that there are certain children that, among the bilinguals particularly but I think also among some English children, that aren't encouraged to talk an awful lot at home.*
Indexical: vocabulary and grammar	2 Cue: what are the important features in children's language which you would notice? *Are we getting one word, two words, small sentences, you know, that sort of thing. That's what we're looking at, I think, really. And then when you've got*

---

7   The sample of children included both English as mother tongue speakers as well as EAL learners.

<table>
<tr><td></td><td>sentences, looking for correct sentences rather than, you know, the verbs and everything all round the wrong way and upside down and no pronouns and this sort of thing.</td></tr>
<tr><td>Indexical: different
developmental profiles</td><td>3 Cue: what are the important features in children's language which you would notice?

I think in terms of bilingual children learning English, it's, it's, it's interesting just such as you get involved in their reading development and ... they do the next bit in reading. I think it's nice to see them develop with their language and that interests me so I find it interesting to keep on with the language and see that developing. And I must admit it's not so quite so, so pressing, or important from the English children's point of view because most of our English children are fairly articulate.</td></tr>
<tr><td>Indexical: sequence
of English acquisition</td><td>4 Cue: what are the important features in children's language which you would notice?

And so I'm not sure that we were particularly interested in the curriculum, in the National Curriculum as far as our bilinguals were concerned. But what we are looking for is firstly are they able to communicate in word, two words.</td></tr>
</table>

Phase 2 interviews – focus on children

<table>
<tr><td>Schema: EALness</td><td>Teachers' utterances</td></tr>
<tr><td>Indexical: personality</td><td>5 Cue: would you like to say something about Leela?

The only thing I feel is her level of language, her level of anything is so tied up with her personality. She's this very very strong personality ... it's a real handicap to her in a way because she just cannot contain herself in any way, so often when you ask her questions, she's coming up with the wrong answer, not because she doesn't understand and because</td></tr>
</table>

she's not able to express herself, but because she just can't keep on one track, she's off on the hills somewhere ...

Indexical: family

6   Cue: the teacher interviewer is being asked to account for a particular child's reluctance to respond to others, the interviewer signalled explicitly EAL, personality and language use as possible explanations.

I think it might well be not the language but the customs from the home, and partly because he is the only son ... and he gets a lot of attention and he expects more attention than he's (getting). *I think it could be that* (indistinct speech).

Phase 3 interviews – theory in action (focus on specific children)

Schema: EALness   **Teachers' utterances**

Indexical: personality

7   Cue: having watched a short video clip of a particular child in classroom situations the teacher interviewee was asked to elaborate on the child's reluctance to listen and respond, a feature noticed and mentioned by the interviewee.

Very much personalities, very much tied to her personality sometimes children you can see that they are not understanding because they don't respond when you say something, there's a little boy who'd come up and I said 'but you haven't coloured it in', he's typical of that he listens to a bit but he doesn't have good English and he doesn't always understand the whole task, so he'll keep coming up and you keep sending him back for a little bit more and little bit more, but with Nosheen it's not that she can't understand it's just she won't give herself time to really reflect on what she's been asked to do and I think that's the personality thing.

Indexical: family

8 Cue: having watched a short video clip of a particular child in classroom situations the teacher interviewee was asked to comment on the child.

Sushma's understanding is not bad. Her mother doesn't speak much English, but her father is excellent. He is a leader in the community and his understanding and standard is very good.

Indexical: syntax and grammar

9 Cue: having watched a short video clip of a particular child in classroom situations the teacher interviewee was asked to comment on the child.

Interesting that she, em, said to Sadhna at one point 'Sadhna', and she said this perfect sentence, which obviously she has heard lots, 'Sadhna, can I have ...' something to do with buttercups. And the next sentence the words 'what him had'. So it's interesting again, the variations of awareness of a sentence which has been dependent on, which she has learned and internalised and she's become quite dependent on say, whereas she is wanting to speak more spontaneously and she's getting mixed up, but it is still excellent the fact that she has got that far.

Indexical: different developmental expectations

10 Cue: On seeing a clip of video showing a child trying hard to explain something to her friend, the teacher interviewee commented.

... to me a lot of that just proves the point that a lot of children get to Level 2, it's a very wide range of skills that they've got to acquire and it's before they get to Level 3, which is difficult, and this is a problem we get with most of the Asian children. So they stay at 2 for quite a long time, so we get a big range in that level.

Indexical: sequence of development

11 Cue: on seeing a clip of video the teacher interviewee commented that a particular pupil was able to understand very little until recently. She was invited to elaborate on that point.

Yeah, well she didn't know what was going on, whereas now looking at that tape I could see that she was trying to really interact with the other children. She was trying to join in. She most probably just didn't know what copying mean, when Saeeda said 'don't copy mine' or something and she said like 'yes' or whatever it was. But she most probably doesn't know what copying meant, but she was doing the right things. She knew it was a question and she obviously just wanted to interact.

OBSERVATIONS

1 The discourse data shown above suggest that the teacher informants operated a number of indexicals within the EALness schema: family, vocabulary and syntax, different developmental profiles, sequence of acquisition and personality. Within the three phases of interviews the following distribution was found:

Indexical	Family	Vocabulary & grammar	Different developmental exectations	Sequence of acquisition	Personality
Interview					
Phase 1	✓	✓	✓	✓	✗
Phase 2	✓	✗	✗	✗	✓
Phase 3	✓	✓	✓	✓	✓

✓ = occurred;   ✗ = not occurred

This distribution suggests that in the first interview when the teacher informants were asked to talk about assessment in general terms, they focused on aspects of language knowledge, developmental issues and pupils' background. It was noticeable that personality as a factor was not commented on at that stage. In the second interview when the informants were asked to comment on specific individual pupils from memory, they switched their attention to family background and individual personalities.

In the third interview when they were asked to comment on specific instances of language use on video, all five indexical aspects were commented on.

2 The foci of the three interviews were also reflected in the nature of the information in the teacher informants' responses. In the first interview when the focus was on language assessment in general the informants tended to make general comments covering whole groups of children (see data extracts 1 and 2 above, for example). In the second and the third phases when the focus was more explicitly on individuals, the informants chose to relate their statements to specific knowledge or perception about the individual children (see data extracts 5 and 6, for instance) or to narrativise a specific episode as evidence (see data extract 9, for example).

3 Some of the indexicals cannot be traced back to the National Curriculum English Level Descriptions (Levels 1 to 4, see Appendix 1). Vocabulary is mentioned in Level 2: *In developing and explaining their ideas they speak clearly and use a growing vocabulary.* The sense here is that children already have a working vocabulary and the curriculum expectation is that they show signs of growth; when the teacher informants talked about bilingual children's vocabulary development, they included an ab initio stage. The following teacher description of an English mother tongue child's use of English exemplifies this point well:

Teacher: ... em, excellent. She is very articulate, good vocabulary, got, a second child, very bright brother. I'd say she was a 3, Level 3. She can express herself well, plenty of ideas, likes to very much, is very keen to communicate with her peers and (indistinct speech) *to make observations.* (Phase 2 interview)

Grammar is mentioned in Level 4 but only in conjunction with Standard English, not in terms of grappling with word order and other basic structures. The National Curriculum in general certainly does not mention home and personality considerations; and there is no acknowledgement of different sequences of language development and different developmental expectations.

4 The quote in point 3 above also suggests that family circumstances (*a second child*) and personality (*is very keen to communicate with peers*) as indexicals were not used exclusively with bilingual children. Indeed, in the

data family and home circumstances were often invoked to account for aspects of English language performance for English as mother tongue children. The following is another example:

She's always got her hand up in assembly, always understands the point, always gives the right answer, can always, if I say 'what does this word mean?', can always offer a good explanation, maybe not necessarily completely correct, but she always feels that she knows, a very confident use of language, obviously is spoken to a lot at home, you know, and is used to speaking and listening ... (Phase 2 interview)

This suggests that this aspect of the schema EALness may share certain commonalities with other professional schemata.

5　There is some evidence that the teacher informants used a form of shorthand token to indexicalise family and home circumstances. The following are some examples:

Teacher utterance
- *... it's in contrast between home and school ...*
- *... again, the youngest child I think.*
- *... that's a problem within the family. That's where that's come from.*
- *... partly because he is the only son ...*
- *Her mother doesn't speak much English, but her father is excellent. He is a leader in the community ...*
- *Well I think that's her upbringing.*

These tokens were merely offered but not explained, as if they were self-evident.

6　The language of the teachers' discourse has a quality of everyday ordinariness.[8] For instance, extract 9:

... she ... said to Sadhna at one point 'Sadhna', and she said this perfect sentence, which she has heard lots ...

This narrativised event was expressed in declarative clauses specifying agency; the use of direct speech to report statements suggested the

---

8　The comments here are necessarily interpretative. For a discussion see Fairclough (1989, 1995) among others.

concreteness of the episode; and the past tense was used to recount a specific moment and the use of the present perfect to indicate the perceived truthfulness of the utterance. There is also a noticeable absence of modals; *I think* and *probably* seemed to be the most prevalent devices used to reduce likelihood. Furthermore, there was a total absence of specialist testing or assessment terminology. These textual features, combined together, created the impression of simple truths being uttered.

DISCUSSION

- While it would be unwise to make firm and general statements about the ways the National Curriculum Level Descriptions are being interpreted on the basis of a small database, this study suggests that there was evidence that teacher informants operated on assumptions and beliefs (represented by the indexicals) outside the National Curriculum Level Descriptions; in so far as these may impact on their everyday teaching and assessment there is good reason to doubt the apparently unquestioned assumption made by the central curriculum authorities that the National Curriculum Level Descriptions effectively set the subject domain boundaries (see also footnote 4; see Bourne (1992) for a discussion on teacher construction of pupil achievements and needs).

- The teacher informants seemed to attribute a great deal of English language development to home and family circumstances of the bilingual/EAL; the precise relationship between home circumstances and English language development, however, remains unexplained and unexplored.

- The teacher informants seemed to regard personality as an explanatory factor in children's English language development; discussion on this dimension of learner characteristic is completely absent in the National Curriculum.

- The teacher informants, possibly informed by their professional experience, seemed to operate a different developmental schema for bilingual/EAL children; at present this aspect of teacher perception has not been recognised by the curriculum authorities.

- The use of narrativised accounts by the teacher informants suggests that shared professional beliefs, teaching and assessment are a very closely integrated phenomenon; as such there is a very good and powerful reason to study curriculum specifications and teachers' interpretations and representations of them in any future development in Teacher Assessment.

It would seem then that the data point to the possibility that the current National Curriculum (English and other subjects) may not be an adequate instrument to assist teachers in their work with bilingual pupils who are in the process of learning English. An expanded conceptualisation of the mainstream curriculum content is required to take proper account of the linguistically diverse pupil population.

REFERENCES

Berger P and Luckmann T (1967) *The Social Construction of Reality: A Treatise in the Sociology of Knowledge,* Allen Lane

Bourne J (1992) *Inside a Multilingual Primary Classroom: A Teacher, Children and Theories at Work,* Unpublished PhD thesis, Southampton University

Brumfit C (1995) *Language Education in the National Curriculum,* Blackwell

DfEE (1995) *English in the National Curriculum,* London: HMSO

DfEE (1997) *Excellence in Schools,* Stationery Office

Edwards J (1997) *The Language Education of Newly Qualified Teachers,* National Association for Language Development in the Curriculum, Occasional Paper No10

Eraut M (1994) *Developing Professional Knowledge and Competence,* Falmer Press

Fairclough N (1989) *Language and Power,* Longman

Fairclough N (1995) *Critical Discourse Analysis,* Longman

Goffman E (1986) *Frame Analysis: An Essay on the Organisation of Experience,* Boston, MA: Northeastern University Press

Gumperz J J (1992) 'Contextualization revisited', in P Auer and A di Luzio (eds) *The Contextualization of Language,* Amsterdam: John Benjamins Publishing Company, pp39–53

Kress G (1993) 'Against arbitrariness: The social production of the sign as a foundational issue in critical discourse analysis', *Discourse and Society,* 4, 2, pp169–191

Leung C (1996) 'English as an additional language within the National Curriculum: A study of assessment practices', *Prospect Journal,* 11, 2, pp58–68

Leung C and Teasdale A (1997a) 'What do teachers mean by speaking and listening? A contextualised study of assessment in multilingual classrooms in the English National Curriculum', in A Huhta, V Kohonen, L Kurki-Suono and S Luoma (eds) *New Contexts, Goals and Alternatives in Language Assessment,* Finland: University of Jyvaskyla, pp291–234

Leung C and Teasdale A (1997b) *Raters' understanding of rating scales as abstracted concept and as instruments for decision making,* Annual Language Testing Research Colloquium Conference Paper

Marton F (1981) 'Phenomenography-describing conceptions of the worlds around us', *Instructional Science,* 10, pp177–200

McCallum B, Gripps C, McAlister S and Brown M (1995) 'National Curriculum assessment: emerging models of teacher assessment in the classroom', in H Torrance (ed) *Evaluating Authentic Assessment*, Buckingham: Open University Press, pp57–87

Morris E (1997) 'Equality and the sum of its parts', *Times Educational Supplement*, 26 September, p25

Moscovici S (1984) 'The phenomenon of social representations', in R M Farr and S Moscovici (eds) *Social Representations*, Cambridge University Press, pp3–69

North B (1995) 'The development of a common framework scale of descriptors of language proficiency based on a theory of measurement', *Systems*, 23, 4, pp445–465

Office for Standards in Education (OFSTED) (1997) *The Assessment of the Language Development of Bilingual Pupils* (Reference: 97/97/NS), OFSTED

Potter J and Wetherall M (1987) *Discourse and Social Psychology: beyond Attitudes and Behaviour*, Sage

QSR, (1996) *NUD-IST*, Australia: LaTrobe University

Read S J (1992) 'Constructing accounts: The role of explanatory coherence', in M L McLaughlin, M J Cody and S J Read (eds) *Explaining One's Self to Others: Reason-giving in a Social Context*, Hillsdale, N.J.: Lawrence Erlbaum Associates Publisher, pp3–19

Säljö R (1988) 'Learning in educational settings: Methods of enquiry', in P Ramsden (ed) *Improving Learning: New Perspectives*, Kogan Page, pp32–48

SCAA (1996) *Teaching English as an Additional Language: A Framework for Policy*, SCAA

South H (1997) *OFSTED Report. The Assessment of the Language Development of Bilingual Pupils: A Discussion Paper for NALDIC*, National Association for Language Development in the Curriculum

Squire R (1996) 'Equal opportunities in education', in C Leung and P Barnett (eds) *Managing Equality of Opportunity in Education into the 21st Century*, Commission for Racial Equality and Thames Valley University, pp1–7

Swann Committee of Enquiry (1985) *Education for All*, HMSO

Teasdale A and Leung C (1997) *Teacher Assessment at Key Stage 1: Teacher and Scale Meanings in Speaking and Listening*, British Educational Research Association Conference Paper

TESOL (1997) *ESL Standards for pre-K-12 Students*, Alexandria, VA: TESOL

van Dijk T A (1993) 'Principles of critical discourse analysis', *Discourse and Society*, 4, 2, pp249–283

Victoria Board of Studies (1996) *ESL Companion to the English CSF*, Carlton, Victoria, Australia: Board of Studies

APPENDIX 1
ATTAINMENT TARGET 1: SPEAKING AND LISTENING

Levels for Key Stage 1

* *Level 1*

Pupils talk about matters of immediate interest. They listen to others and usually respond appropriately. They convey simple meaning to a range of listeners, speaking audibly, and begin to extend their ideas or accounts by providing some detail.

* *Level 2*

Pupils begin to show confidence in talking and listening, particularly where the topics interest them. On occasions, they show awareness of the needs of the listener by including relevant detail. In developing and explaining their ideas they speak clearly and use a growing vocabulary. They usually listen carefully and respond with increasing appropriateness to what others say. They are beginning to be aware that in some situations a more formal vocabulary and tone of voice are used.

* *Level 3*

Pupils talk and listen confidently in different contexts, exploring and communicating ideas. In discussion, they show understanding of the main points. Through relevant comments and questions, they show they have listened carefully. They begin to adapt what they say to the needs of the listener, varying the use of vocabulary and the level of detail. They are beginning to be aware of standard English and when it is used.

* *Level 4*

Pupils talk and listen with confidence in an increasing range of contexts. Their talk is adapted to the purpose: developing ideas thoughtfully, describing events and conveying their opinions clearly. In discussion, they listen carefully, make contributions and asking questions that are responsive to others' ideas and views. They use appropriately some of the features of standard English vocabulary and grammar (DFE, 1995, p26).

The Language Education of
Newly Qualified Teachers

JOHN EDWARDS, University of Portsmouth

The language education of pupils within maintained schools in England and Wales has not always proved to be coherent or sufficient during the past twenty years. In particular, the teaching of grammar and syntax together with broader issues relating to knowledge about language have regularly been deemed to be the weakest link in the curriculum provided for pupils in the 5–16 age range. Calls for greater clarity and focus on the teaching of language have been made by Bullock (1975) Kingman (1988) and Cox (1989) and successive Governments have become increasingly interventionist in their approaches to making specific stipulations as to what should be taught in relation to knowledge about language.

Plans are now well advanced to implement a national curriculum for all phases of initial teacher training by September 1999 and the issue of beginning teachers' knowledge about language features as a key concern.

No one involved in the education of beginning teachers would contest that their knowledge about language could and should be enhanced in preparation for working effectively in the complex and demanding language environment of the classroom.

Such knowledge will need to be taught explicitly and incrementally if it is to be effectively acquired and applied. A key issue is where and when in an already crowded training programme, and in the busy world of the newly qualified teacher, such instruction can take place. This is an issue which teacher training partnerships will need to address as a matter of urgency.

Newly qualified teachers enter a professional domain which is more heavily regulated by external agencies than at any time in the past 50 years. The introduction of the Education Reform Act of 1988 and the subsequent development, implementation and revision of the National Curriculum for maintained schools in England and Wales has led to a dwindling of professional autonomy for classroom teachers. Hargreaves (1994, p113) argues that teachers' work is under scrutiny as never before:

> *Driven by concerns for productivity, accountability and control, the administrative tendency is to exert tighter control over teachers' work and teachers' time, to regulate and rationalise it; to break it down into small discrete components with clearly designated objectives assigned to each one.*

This increase in teacher accountability begins with the requirement that student teachers demonstrate a comprehensive range of 'standards' before being granted Qualified Teacher Status (QTS), their licence of professional competence, and continues throughout their careers in the form of appraisal cycles and regular school inspections by the Office for Standards in Education (OFSTED). Nevertheless, despite this scenario, the past decade has witnessed a growing sense of suspicion from the general public that education is in crisis and that it is teachers who are to blame for poor levels of literacy, numeracy and moral bankruptcy among the young. Much of this populist rhetoric, termed by S.J. Ball (1990, pp22–41) a 'discourse of derision,' has been fuelled by politicians seeking easy votes and a popular Press which has always been eager to pillory likely scapegoats for society's ills.

Teachers have borne this cascade of contumely with weary stoicism. They are aware that their professional remit is a demanding one, particularly since the advent of the National Curriculum. Lawton (1989, pp86–87) suggested:

> *The good teacher will no longer be just an efficient instructor, but will have to become an expert classroom manager and organiser of learning experiences ... the teacher has limited 'ownership' of the curriculum and is directly responsible for the detailed planning of lessons within national and LEA guidelines, bearing in mind the specific needs of his or her pupils, as well as the local aspects of the curriculum as planned by the school. To do this effectively, teachers will need to be more than transmitters of their own subject.*

It is possible to see the increased roles and responsibilities of the classroom teacher, instanced by Lawton above, illustrated in the key Principles outlined in *Teaching English as an Additional Language: A Framework for Policy* (1996, p3):

1 *Developing whole-school policies:*
Whole-school policies for teaching EAL should be based on accurate knowledge of pupils' needs and attainments and include ways of monitoring the effectiveness of overall provision.

2 *Using the National Curriculum programmes of study:*
Pupils learning EAL are entitled to the full National Curriculum programmes of study and all their teachers have responsibility for teaching English as well as subject content.

3 *Effective teaching and planning:*
All teachers should structure lessons appropriately and use language in ways that support and stimulate development in English to meet the specific needs of pupils learning EAL. This applies to all staff involved in teaching, instruction or providing support for learning.

4 *Using resources to meet identified needs:*
A school's resources should be organised and used to support teaching EAL, and plans should show how learning targets for pupils are to be achieved and identify the financial commitments.

5 *Assessment: issues and principles:*
A school's assessment policy should link statutory assessments with any additional assessment of pupils' acquisition of English to provide accurate recognition of pupils' attainments, progress and needs.

Implicit in these recommended principles is the notion that teachers will have acquired sufficient knowledge about language through their own educational experiences; will know how to apply this knowledge in relation to all pupils' language needs and will have attained an understanding of the specific needs of pupils learning EAL.

Many teachers have accepted and implemented curriculum change and increased responsibilities during the past decade with considerable energy and insight. They have converted multiple innovations into meaningful learning experiences for their pupils. Nevertheless, it is necessary to recognise that change can lead to a degree of professional de-skilling and lack of confidence and that teachers who are involved in the training and induction of Newly Qualified Teachers (NQTs) may themselves yet be grappling with the updating of their own knowledge and the implementation of new policy and practice. Fullan (1991, p37) suggests that change and innovation are complex:

*Innovation is **multidimensional**. There are at least three components or dimensions at stake in implementing any new program or policy:(1) the possible use of new or revised **materials** (direct instructional resources such as curriculum materials or technologies), (2) the possible use of new **teaching approaches** (ie. new teaching strategies or activities), and (3) the possible alteration of **beliefs** (e.g., pedagogical assumptions and theories underlying particular new policies or programs).*

At its best such elements of change and innovation can produce effective instances of collaborative professional development, with the experienced professional helping the beginning teacher to develop her knowledge and skills and to understand that change is a constant feature of the current educational scene. In less propitious circumstances confusion and partial understanding are the outcomes.

The fact of the matter is that the language education of beginning teachers is in the hands of a number of key players. If we are to be confident that the language education of all pupils and the specific needs of pupils learning EAL are to be met at an adequate level of provision, we need to be clear what are the respective roles of each key player in the training programme and what constraints they operate under which might compromise the possibility of beginning teachers who enter multilingual classrooms being properly prepared for their task.

Government has sought to tighten its grip on all aspects of state education. This has been particularly evident in the way that it has intervened in the preparation of students for teaching. Circulars 9/92, 35/92 and 14/93 required, for instance, that postgraduates following a 36-week course (a typical Postgraduate Certificate in Education Programme) spend 24 of those weeks on a school site. This has recently been strengthened by Circulars 10/97 and 4/98 which set out criteria by which student teachers must be assessed and standards they must meet before they can gain QTS. A notion of partnership is evident yet, as Birch and Ward (1997, p1) suggest:

Although there has been widespread acceptance of this and it is affirmed through higher education institutions' (HEIs) and schools' co-operation, relatively little attention has been given to its predicates and outcomes.

Implicit in these directives is the notion that schools will provide a proper training ground for student teachers where they will be exposed to the practical craft skills of classroom management and curriculum planning, free from the dogma and theory of college-based courses. This might seem a parody of actual reality where, in fact, HEIs and partner schools work extremely hard to produce programmes of initial teacher education which are both coherent and developmental in type and assist student teachers to address the multiple demands made of them in a late twentieth century context.

Teacher educators continue to oppose the notion that their role is to deliver up a series of Gradgrind-like vessels that have been filled with the requisite number of competencies to fit them for classroom use. Foster (1997, p1) suggests that:

*Debates about what is a socially just organisation and conduct of teacher education and about **what** teachers should learn in order to build and operate a socially just education system have tended to slip off the agenda to be replaced by the technical skills of teaching and how or where they should be learned.*

It would seem vital that, at a time when teachers often feel marginalised and ignored, those entering the profession should be offered a type of cognitive apprenticeship which will fit them to be more than competent classroom technicians. They must be able to demonstrate the capacity to make informed ethical choices with regard to pupils' learning and to defend their pedagogic practices in reasoned discourse rather than defensive professional rhetoric. Yet, as Lawton (1989, p84) reflects:

Reforms may be in advance of initial teacher training, so that teachers are rarely completely prepared for the new curriculum in their pre-service professional courses.

The need for sustained collaborative dialogue is particularly vital when addressing the language education of beginning teachers. This should routinely involve the higher education institutions and partnership schools of the initial training phase and the local education authorities and schools to which NQTs are appointed. Each has a role to play in the professional development of the beginning teacher, but it is uncertain whether this role is clearly defined and delineated in respect of the language education of NQTs.

LANGUAGE EDUCATION OF NQTs

Student teachers commencing a programme of Initial Teacher Education face a crowded and complex agenda. For example, current DfEE rubric for a 36-week Postgraduate Certificate of Education states that 'successful completion of a course or programme of ITT, including employment based provision, must require the trainee to achieve *all* the standards for the award of QTS'. The standards are set out under the following headings:

A. Knowledge and Understanding
B. Planning, Teaching and Class Management
C. Monitoring, Assessment, Recording, Reporting and Accountability
D. Other Professional Requirements.

For example, Standard B (v) of Planning, Teaching and Class Management requires:

student-teachers to demonstrate that they plan their teaching to achieve progression in pupils' learning through identifying pupils who:

- *have special needs, including specific learning difficulties*
- *are very able*
- *are not yet fluent in English*

and knowing where to get help in order to give positive and targeted support.

It is claimed that 'the standards have been written to be specific, explicit and assessable' yet it is later stated in the same paragraph that 'there is no intention to impose a methodology on providers for the assessment of trainees against the standards'. This appears to offer a degree of independence to HEIs in determining what type of training is given and how it should be assessed, yet makes it difficult to ensure that *all* student teachers will be offered an equivalent level of provision to address the needs of EAL pupils. The data reported below from a survey undertaken in July 1997 of the language education of NQTs in one local education authority suggests that the amount of language education received both during initial training and subsequently during their NQT year varied to a considerable extent.

The survey

A postal questionnaire was mailed in July 1997 to 150 Newly Qualified Teachers (NQTs) who had been appointed at the start of the 1996–97 academic year to primary and secondary schools in one local education authority (LEA) in Southern England. Seventy-three responses were received. Two-thirds of the NQTs who responded were located in primary schools. Twenty-nine Higher Education Institutions (HEI) were represented, providing a variety of BEd, BA, (with QTS) and PGCE courses identified by respondents. Responses are reported as percentages.

Selected survey results

- 8% of respondents felt very confident in their own knowledge about language on entering the profession;

- 75% received between 5 and 10 hours of input specifically designed to develop their own knowledge about language;

- 2% were confident, on entering the profession, of working effectively with pupils for whom English is an additional language;

- 86% received less than 5 hours of input on their training programme designed to develop their knowledge and skills in working with pupils learning EAL;

- 70% received no INSET on language issues;

- 30% had worked with pupils learning EAL, of that number only 35% (11% of total respondents) were offered classroom support in the pupil's first language.

Some comments

- The survey of NQTs indicates that only 8% of respondents felt very confident in their own knowledge about language on entering the profession.

The reason for this lack of confidence is not difficult to determine. The majority of respondents had received no formal language instruction during their own time in school nor, unless they had taken a first degree in linguistics or a modern foreign language, did they feel that their language skills had been enhanced at college level. Most worrying of all was the claim that, on entering the profession, so few felt confident in their own knowledge about language and, consequently, of working effectively in the classroom.

- Seventy-five per cent of respondents (which included both BEd and PGCE students) claimed to have received between five and ten hours of input specifically designed to develop their own knowledge about language. This would appear a reasonably generous allocation of time within a crowded 36 week PGCE programme, only twelve of which are spent at college. Yet this was clearly seen as insufficient if little or no language work had been pursued formally prior to the training programme.

- More alarming was the claim by 86% of respondents that they had received less than five hours of input on their training programmes designed to develop their knowledge and skills in working with pupils learning EAL. Indeed, it emerged from respondents' comments that much of this provision was not specifically language focused but included elements of multicultural education.

An obvious answer to the apparent lack of confidence in NQTs regarding their own knowledge about language and their ability to work confidently on language matters in classrooms would be to provide more input in the initial phase of training. Plans are already well advanced for the introduction with statutory force from September 1999 of an ITT National Curriculum for Secondary English. In a letter from the Teacher Training Agency, inviting responses to the draft documents for the secondary curriculum, Anthea Millett (1998) suggests that, in the foreword to the Initial Teacher Training National Curriculum consultation document for Secondary English, 'the new curriculum documents represent a step change in the expectations and requirements of new teachers'. Secondary phase trainees must, for example, 'know and understand' the nature and role of standard English and spoken and written language as a system, including lexical, grammatical and textual features.

The question raised by this curriculum requirement is not whether all intending teachers of English should be equipped with this specific level of knowledge about language (or that it should be required of all student teachers); it is rather *how* and *when* this instruction can be provided at an incremental and measured pace so as to make a meaningful addition to the student teachers' confidence in operating and discussing language and in applying such knowledge in classroom contexts. It will be problematic for HEIs to include a substantial additional curriculum input into programmes already heavily timetabled to meet DfEE standards for NQTs. Partnership schools are likely to have neither the time nor the specific expertise in every instance to provide for such specialist training. The proposal that student teachers might develop their knowledge about language through distance learning materials and recommended indicative reading either prior to the start of their training programme, or in non-contact time within the training year, has yet to be tested. In any event, it is unlikely that a thoroughly grounded grasp of knowledge about language and its application to meet the learning needs of all pupils will be achieved within the time-line and crowded agenda of the average training programme. NQTs will need to continue their language education as planned and structured professional development when they take up their first appointment.

The first year of teaching for NQTs is often an exhausting and (possibly) traumatic experience. They are asked to assume the full burden of responsibility for whole class teaching and assessment. They are undertaking administrative tasks in addition to their teaching timetable and they are preparing and assessing work for large numbers of pupils. Nevertheless, they are beginning teachers and their professional development is still in its infancy. They have much yet to learn about planning, teaching and assessment. Their contact with pupils will be continuous throughout the year rather than of the intense but sporadic nature of a block-practice training programme. They will need focused guidance and support to implement, for example, the five key principles for teaching EAL outlined above. Yet if their own confidence and competence in addressing language issues in the classroom is not secure, provision will need to be made for planned and monitored professional development during the first year of teaching.

- Seventy per cent of respondents claimed to have received no specific professional development (INSET) during their first year in post to enhance their awareness of language issues in the classroom. (Those who had received input were positive in their support for the topics which had been covered; these included language and literacy in the primary classroom, assessing reading standards and approaches to working with emergent writing.)

- Relatively few NQTs (30% of the respondents) had worked with pupils learning EAL.

- Of that number only 35% were offered classroom support in the pupils' first language, almost exclusively provided by relevant members of the LEA's Bilingual Learners' Support Service, though the majority claimed to have received additional support from their schools in the form of classroom assistant provision or specialist teachers' advice on key issues.

CONCLUSION

The world of the NQT will never be in a state of equilibrium. Increased statutory demands, the complex social and cultural dynamics of classrooms and the increasing amount of public accountability mean that the beginning teacher must be a robust and resilient individual. She must be confident in her classroom management skills and her curriculum knowledge. She must be certain that her own knowledge about language is secure so that she can engage with and address the language needs of all her pupils. If these foundations of language knowledge are not in place by the time she enters higher education for the first time, or commences a postgraduate training programme, then it is vital that a coherent, incremental and managed programme of knowledge and understanding of language is provided.

Beginning teachers' perceptions of their early classroom experiences are notoriously subjective and their judgements and perceptions are informed by what they believe to have been successful classroom encounters with their first cohort of pupils. Their sense of trepidation and apparent lack of confidence might well be due to diffidence or an overestimation of what is expected of them. Nevertheless, when asked to identify ways in which they would fill ten hours of 'free' INSET on some aspect of knowledge about language they identified:

- further study of grammar;
- further study of children's language development;
- further study in the teaching of reading;
- further study of key elements of differentiation including language work with very able children and with those learning EAL.

They were particularly interested in learning how to work effectively with support staff in the pupils' first language and with developing effective communication and liaison with their families. The findings of this small-scale survey support our professional experience. There is an urgent need to examine the what, the how and the when in the provision of language knowledge for ITT and professional development.

REFERENCES

Ball J (1990) *Politics and Policy-Making in Education: Explorations in Policy Sociology,* London: Routledge

Birch R and Ward T (1997) *A Model for Meaningful Partnership in Initial Teacher Education Courses,* Paper presented at ECER Conference, Frankfurt, Germany

Costello P (1997) *The Teacher as Critical Thinker,* Paper presented at Reforming Teacher Education Conference, Wrexham

DES (1975) *A Language for Life* (Bullock Report), London: HMSO

DES (1988) *Report of the Committee of Inquiry into the Teaching of English Language* (Kingman Report), London: HMSO

DES and the Welsh Office (1989) *English for ages 5 to 16* (Cox Report), London: HMSO

DfE (1992) *Initial Teacher Training (Secondary Phase),* Circulars 9/92 and 35/92, London: HMSO

DfE (1993) *Initial Teacher Training (Primary Phase),* Circular 14/93, London: HMSO

DfEE (1997) *Teaching: High Status, High Standards,* Circular 10/97, London: HMSO

Fullan M (1991) *The New Meaning of Educational Change,* London: Cassell

Foster P (1997) *Models of Social Justice and Teacher Education,* Paper presented at Reforming Teacher Education Conference, Wrexham

Hargreaves A (1994) *Changing Teachers, Changing Times,* London: Cassell

Lawton D (1989) *Education, Culture and the National Curriculum,* London: Hodder and Stoughton

SCAA (1996) *Teaching English as an Additional Language: A Framework for Policy*

TTA (1998) *Initial Teacher Training National Curriculum: Secondary English* (Consultation Document)